PELICAN BOOK

A677

THE CINEMA AS ART

Ralph Stephenson, after working for the British Film Institute for eight years, is now Managing Director of the Paris Pullman cinema. Born in New Zealand, he was formerly in the Colonial Service, in Hong Kong (where he was a Japanese prisoner of war), the Seychelles, Ghana and Sierra Leone. He is the author of a book on *Animation in the Cinema* and five novels, and has lectured and written widely on film subjects.

Jean R. Debrix is currently in charge of the film section at the French Ministry of Cooperation. Before the war he was a journalist, a film-maker and author of the prize-winning novel *Argile*. In a German prison camp he began a book on film aesthetics, *Les Fondements de l'art cinématographique*, published in 1960. Formerly deputy director of IDHEC, the Paris Film School, he has also directed and produced a number of films including *Ombromagie* and *Le Bourgeois Gentilhomme*.

Ralph Stephenson · Jean R. Debrix

THE CINEMA
AS ART

With fifty-four plates

PENGUIN BOOKS

BALTIMORE · MARYLAND

Penguin Books Ltd, Harmondsworth, Middlesex, England
Penguin Books Inc, 3300 Clipper Mill Rd, Baltimore, Md 21211, U.S.A.
Penguin Books Australia Ltd, Ringwood, Victoria, Australia

—

First published 1965
Reprinted 1967, 1968

—

—

Made and printed in Great Britain
by Cox & Wyman Ltd,
London, Reading and Fakenham
Set in Monotype Bembo

Contents

Foreword

FOR the present generation the art of the film is of pressing interest. The cinema is now over sixty years old and has its own discriminating audience, but compared with the other arts it is still little written about or seriously discussed.

The term 'film criticism' is generally applied to a weekly review of new films published in a daily or weekly paper and written by a regular contributor known as the film critic. Although it may refer to questions of aesthetics and may reflect a profound knowledge of the cinema, its main purpose is to give some idea of the story and background of the pictures and to assess them as good, bad, or indifferent entertainment. It is basically a guide to current film-going.

We accept this terminology as a matter of course, but it is not quite what obtains in other fields. In literature, for instance, the equivalent of a film critic writing a weekly review is a book reviewer, and the equivalent of film criticism, as we know it, is book-reviewing. 'Literary criticism' is a different kind of writing, more occasional, less topical, dealing with broad themes, seeking by comparison and analysis to give a fuller knowledge and understanding of literature as an artistic medium and in all its implications.

It is clear that in the literary field, book-reviewing and literary criticism are rather different things, both of value but serving different purposes. It is pertinent, therefore, to turn back to the film world and inquire what there is in this sphere corresponding to literary criticism. No doubt we should look for it in the field of film appreciation, but where are its articles, its books, its exponents? Where indeed? Particularly in English. They are represented only by a few specialized journals such as *Sight and Sound* or *Film Quarterly*, and by a handful of books published over the past forty years.

In any case, the phrase 'film appreciation' is a somewhat under-rated one with, perhaps, rather amateurish connotations. It would be better if the same terminology as is used in literature became current in the film world, if the term 'film reviewing' were reserved for current assessment and 'film criticism' came to imply the broader, thematic approach of literary criticism.

The Cinema as Art can be regarded as a material contribution towards the new concept of film criticism. It discusses in detail and in depth an indispensable preliminary: the language of the film, a language as important as that of the writer, the painter, or the musician, and different from them all. For the film appreciation or film criticism of the future, this, or books like this, will be essential reading.

SIR WILLIAM COLDSTREAM

Acknowledgements

Grateful acknowledgement is made to:

The British Film Institute including the National Film Theatre and the National Film Archive's Information Department, Library, and Stills Collection (for all plates except those separately mentioned);

The Imperial War Museum for plates 10 and 22;

Sebricon Films for plate 25;

A. Conger Goodyear and the Museum of Modern Art for plate 28;

John Gillett for help with the Films Index.

Colleagues for their encouragement and advice.

Introductory Note

THE greater part of this book consists of an analysis of various techniques of the cinema, the ways in which the image they create on the screen differs from reality, and the ways these differences can be turned to account for the purposes of the artist. These chapters are freely illustrated with film examples and make straightforward reading.

Readers may find three chapters more difficult than the rest because they are more abstract in their argument and less susceptible of film illustration. These are: Chapter One, *The Film and Art*, which sets the background for the subsequent discussion; Chapter Five, *Space-Time in the Cinema*, dealing with the cinema's own peculiar combination of space and time; and Chapter Nine, *Reality and Artistic Creation*, discussing the audience's reaction to a film, and how artistic quality is to be assessed.

FILM TITLES

In general French and Italian films are referred to by their original French or Italian title unless they are well known by an English title, e.g. *Bicycle Thieves*. Film titles in other languages are given in English unless, again, they are better-known by the original language title, e.g. *Pather Panchali, Ugetsu Monogatari*. If the original language title has been used in the text, the English title (or an English translation in inverted commas) is given in most cases in the Index of Directors and Films. If a film is known to have been given a different title in the U.S.A., this is also given in the same index and marked A.T.

CHAPTER ONE

Introduction: The Film and Art

WHEN planning a journey one may take out a map, put a finger down on a place marked, and say – 'That is where we are going.' This introduction is just such a preliminary reconnaissance, to give a general idea of the area covered by this book and its relation to the surrounding country. When beginning a book on film aesthetics, it is appropriate to consider the relationship of the art of the film to art in general and to approach the film by regarding it, first, as only one member of a large family. Like most rich concepts, art has been as variously defined as there have been authors to write about it; and this multiplicity of conceptions is welcome, provided we do not take them too rigidly or too exclusively, for each description will illuminate a different aspect of the matter and add to our knowledge.

THE NATURE OF ART

Let us take first the concrete example of a painter who is painting, say, a slum cottage in a poor district. The people of the neighbourhood who know the cottage in ordinary life will probably think to begin with that the painter is crazy to choose such a subject – a dirty old cottage, tumbledown and badly needing a coat of paint. But if they watch his work they may come to realize that, as the painter sees it, with its gentle weather-beaten colours, its outline softened by a weed growing in the brickwork, the cottage is something beautiful. The painting has opened their eyes, and the painter has achieved the first task of the artist. This is how D. W. Griffith, the American film director, saw his work. 'The task I am trying to achieve is to make you see', he wrote. From a slightly different viewpoint, Walter Pater regarded the artist as liberating, or realizing, the potential of his raw materials and quotes Michelangelo in support of his view:[1]

Art does but consist in the removal of surplusage ... the finished work lies somewhere, according to Michelangelo's fancy, hidden in the rough-hewn block of stone.

This is akin to the view that art consists in reproducing or imitating real life; and it is a plausible explanation of the origins of graphic art and sculpture, for instance, to trace them to magical imitations of the real thing – cave-drawn bison for sticking arrows into to ensure the death of the real bison, and little figures of a king's household to go into his tomb to serve him after death. The view that art is imitation has led at times to it being regarded as a second-best. Browning wrote:

> ... that's your Venus, whence we turn
> To yonder girl that fords the burn.

But, even as imitation, art will show us the true essence of things more clearly than we could see it for ourselves. The Venus may enable us to see the girl as we otherwise never would.

In a radio discussion, Aldous Huxley once spoke of art as the imposition of order ('art springs from an urge to order') and this is so in the sense that the artist selects from and arranges the haphazard profusion of nature. As Henry James wrote: 'Life is all inclusion and confusion, while art is all discrimination and selection.' Herbert Read in *The Meaning of Art*[2] expresses a similar idea, but adds another element when he talks of art as 'pattern informed by sensibility' and 'emotion cultivating good form', both leading to 'harmony', which is the satisfaction of our sense of beauty. This idea of selection and arrangement leads to the idea of art as creation. The artist takes his raw

1. Walter Pater, *Appreciations*, Macmillan, London, 1931.
2. See Bibliography for book references not given as footnotes.

materials – clay, colours, musical sounds, photographic images, words, and so on – and, in accordance with his ideas and emotions, fashions from them artistic objects. Art may also be regarded as skill in expression; as the use of the creative imagination (Émile Zola called a work of art 'a corner of nature seen through a temperament'); or as concerned with producing the abstract quality of beauty. Keats equated beauty with truth, and art has also been thought of as a quest for truth. And so it is – provided we qualify the sort of truth we mean. For great art brings us near the true nature of things, particularly of human character and conduct. But both truth and beauty cover a wider field than art; for science, philosophy and religion are concerned with truth – and they also display a kind of beauty (e.g. a brilliant mathematical solution), as does any supreme skill, from football to brain surgery.

Going deeper, to the springs of creation, the American philosopher Dewey considered art to be a kind of experience, and wrote about 'the refined and intensified forms of experience that are works of art'. Joyce Cary in his book *Art and Reality*[1] follows Croce in preferring the word 'intuition' or even 'inspiration'. The word 'inspiration' is unpopular nowadays, because it has been used in the past to give a false picture of the artist as an idle, capriciously favoured person producing art without effort by a divine trick. But provided it is recognized that great art grows out of intense feeling and the hardest possible work, in the sense of utter, devoted absorption, then in some contexts 'inspiration' is a useful word. Cary's first word 'intuition' means something similar to Dewey's 'experience', since he describes it as 'essentially the reaction of a person to the world outside'. Coleridge, thinking along somewhat similar lines, wrote that 'the mystery of genius in the Fine Arts' was 'to make the external internal, the internal external, and make nature thought, and thought nature'.[2] This

1. Cambridge University Press, 1958.
2. *Biographia Literaria*.

quotation neatly sums up the process of artistic creation, and describes the artist absorbing experience and expressing it in the form of art.

Finally, art has been regarded as a form of communication or language. I. A. Richards[1] calls it 'the supreme form of communicative activity'. A number of books on film aesthetics have adopted this viewpoint, elaborate analogies have been drawn between film and written or spoken language, sequences[2] have been compared with paragraphs, shots with sentences, cuts with commas, fades with full-stops, and so on. The camera has often been compared with a pen, the best-known phrase being Astruc's 'Caméra-stylo'.[3] These comparisons are valuable, even though it must be recognized that the cinema is quite unlike written or spoken language, since it does not use abstract terms but, by presenting images, expresses itself in immediately identifiable real terms. As a picture-language it is concrete and objective and, in a sense, non-rational, speaking not through the educated mind, as does the word, but, like painting, sculpture, and music, direct to the native sensibility.

There is one last definition, the modern concept of *anti-art* which amounts, according to Arnold Hauser,[4] to 'a renunciation of art altogether'. Anti-art is a phenomenon of the modern world and connected with such ideologies as communism, for the communist tends to regard art as a means to an end, and seeks to exterminate the aestheticism of bourgeois culture's 'art for art's sake'. The technician, worshipping efficiency, arrives at a similar position by regarding art as a by-product which arises 'in the service of an ideologically conditioned purpose'. A house becomes 'a machine to live in', and the

1. See Bibliography.
2. For the meaning of words connected with films see Appendix: *A Note on Technical Terms*.
3. Alexandre Astruc, 'Le Caméra-stylo', *Écran français*, No. 144, 30 March 1948.
4. *The Social History of Art*, Routledge, 1951.

fastest aeroplane is, by definition, the most beautiful. Modern art's 'relationship to nature is one of violation', and another facet of the same attitude is that modern art is, of set purpose, 'fundamentally "ugly", destroying pictorial values in painting, and melody and tonality in music'. There is a mania for totality and documentary realism, and art is dehumanized. Even the communication aspects of art are in a sense denied – writers invent their own language, musicians their own tonal system, and painters depict a world of their own imagination.

Despite the variety of the descriptions of art which we have given, all of them (even the last – because atheism is the reverse aspect of theology) are recognizable as different aspects of the same thing. We may bring them together, in a rather clumsy omnibus definition, by saying that art is a process in which the artist makes use of his experience, intuition, or inspiration, selecting and arranging it to create beautiful and true artistic objects which to a greater or lesser extent imitate 'reality' (as we define it)[1] . . . and that through these objects he communicates his experience to an audience.

We now turn from describing the qualities of art and try to delimit the territory it covers. All that is attempted here is to give a general idea of where the boundary runs without seeking to draw it too finely or too rigidly. In general, we are concerned with the fine arts, excluding useful or industrial arts, sports, hobbies, science, philosophy, government, social relations. But there are many border-line cases. Ballroom dancing counts as a recreation, but there is a continuous gradation from it to ballet, one of the fine arts. In a film, skilled acting (duelling, gun-play, perfectly timed slapstick) can take on the quality of ballet.[2] But the very similar pleasure given by a great cricketer, squash player, or footballer belongs to the world of sport, not art. There is the same difficulty in distinguishing strictly

1. On page 21.   2. Plate 1.

between fine arts such as poetry, painting, and music (with no function other than to convey experience or feeling), and useful arts such as architecture, pottery, cabinet-making, and dress-designing (which are functional as well as aesthetic). One difficulty in making a clear-cut distinction is that the day-before-yesterday's useful objects become today's *objets d'art* – museum pieces. Another is that fine arts may have secondary 'useful' effects – Dickens's novels helped social reform; Eisenstein's film *Alexander Nevsky* boosted the Russian war effort, just as Leni Riefenstahl's film *The Triumph of the Will* spread the Nazi cult; the music of the *Marseillaise* encouraged the French Revolutionary soldiers; portraits and statues are for commemoration and for stabilizing the social order. Another factor which blurs the distinction is that useful arts (for example, Greek temples, Gothic cathedrals) may convey just as deep a sense of beauty or feeling as fine arts; and, in the film world, a documentary made to persuade or to instruct may be as fine aesthetically as a purely fictional film. Furthermore, if we define the word 'functional' widely enough, the fine arts have a function of their own, ranging from recreation to catharsis, revelation, and ennoblement. Having made these reservations, we are concerned in this book with the film as a fine art rather than as a useful art. A line, however broad, has to be drawn between the two, because the film ranges widely beyond the boundaries of fine art, and there is no field of human activity untouched by the camera: physics, chemistry, mathematics, technology, history, geography, archaeology, logistics, cartography, and many more. There are important applications in medicine, surgery, microscopy, astronomy, the control of machines (motors, propellors, turbines), and the study of high-speed movement by stroboscopic cameras taking 100,000 pictures a second. As we go on, it will be clear where our interest lies and where the line of distinction runs; but it will be a shifting, indeterminate boundary, with exceptions and reservations, and we shall not try to maintain it too rigidly.

THREE STAGES IN ART

Whichever description of the qualities of art or whichever delineation of its boundaries we fix upon, it is important that art should be understood to include the whole process, from the artist's intuition to the spectator's appreciation, and not just the object (film, statue, poem, sonata) produced.

Artistic activity can be divided into three stages:

(a) The artist's experience or intuition;
(b) Expression of this intuition in an artistic medium; and
(c) Enjoyment by, and ideally the kindling of similar experience in, an audience.

This book is mainly concerned with the second of these three stages. At the same time, the process is a continuous and integral whole, and it is debatable how separate the various stages are, or indeed where one ends and the other begins. So far as (a) and (b) are concerned, Croce[1] considered that intuition and expression were the same thing, on the grounds that it was impossible to know what an intuition was until it had been named or expressed in some formal way. This possibly looks at the process of artistic creation too much from the outside. Cary says, and many people can confirm this from their own experience, that for the artist the intuition is quite a different thing from the work of art. Between the two there lies much hard work and possibly the conjunction of various favourable circumstances. Gray's 'mute, inglorious Miltons' really do exist: those who have inspiration but lack the opportunity or the ability to express it. So far as (b) and (c) are concerned, there is no difficulty in distinguishing between expression in a work of art and the audience's appreciation, since in these stages different people are concerned. The danger here is that the opposite might happen: that the two be considered as separate, isolated phenomena, and the doctrine of art for art's sake, combined with an

1. *Aesthetics*, Vision Press, 1953.

ivory-tower outlook, lead to the selfish seclusion of the artist. It is worth stressing that art is a social phenomenon, and the artist's job is to make the world – meaning us – a richer place. The audience may be small and full appreciation may only come after the artist is dead, but art, in one of its aspects, is communication, and only has meaning if there are at least two people concerned. The artist may even serve sometimes as audience for his own work, especially with art-forms which are not fully manifested until they are given expression in a large-scale performance – an orchestral work, an opera, a play, or a film. The finished product is, of course, no more than the physical manifestation of the artist's own dream, but its embodied confirmation may have a very different impact on him, and may affect his subsequent work.

The artist will also be influenced by his audience – or lack of it. For that matter, each of the three stages mentioned will affect the others. It is generally recognized how great an influence the artist's intuition has – how his personality, born of his experience, stamps the finished work. It is not such a commonplace that the second stage, expression in an artistic medium, not only affects the way the intuition comes through, but the type of intuition which can be expressed. A story in a ballet, novel, film, play, or opera will have a different flavour and a different effect on an audience. As a critic says, writing of the book and the film *Lord of the Flies*, 'the written image is so very different from the filmed one'. And though it is rash to set limits to an art, it is hard to imagine Ivy Compton-Burnett's novels, say, being made into films. The spectator also will ultimately have a very powerful effect on the type of intuition and the manner of its expression, and one must understand the term 'spectator' in this context to mean not only the direct audience but also the censor, the critic and, finally, the whole of society.

ART AND REALITY

We have said that this book is mainly concerned with the second stage in the artistic process. As a result, it is frequently concerned with the relation of art to reality – the sort of picture of reality which a work of art gives to the spectator. It may be necessary to make the point that art arises out of reality, though this is evident enough in the case of the cinema. Kracauer bases the whole argument of his recent book, *The Nature of Film*, on the extraordinary facility of the cinema in representing the real world. But even the most abstract art – an abstract painting, a mystical poem, atonal or electronic music – even these arise out of the artist's experience of reality, provided we define this in sufficiently wide terms.

Art has relation to reality at three points at least. First, the artist lives in the real world, and from his living – his experience – draws artistic inspiration or intuition. For this purpose, reality should be widely defined to comprise the whole physical, mental, and emotional world, though naturally things which do not impinge on the artist in any way are irrelevant. Reality, therefore, includes everything in the artist's experience: other works of art; other people; everything he sees, feels, hears, and knows; also his own memory, his own bodily sensations, his own mental states, thoughts, imaginings, and dreams. Thoughts, emotions, and mental states are just as much 'reality' in this context as a table or a chair.

Second, art is related to reality because it has to be expressed in the medium proper to it. At this stage, in the words of Coleridge already quoted, the artist makes 'the internal external', he makes 'thought nature'. We have already said that the artistic medium, the second stage, will affect the type of experience which can be expressed and the way this experience will be manifested. In the first stage, the artist is tied to the reality of his own experience. In the second stage, the artist is fashioning a work of art by combining two things: his own experience, and the physical medium of his art, and so he is further tied at this stage to the reality of the medium.

Finally, in the third stage, the artist – unless he is content to let his work remain unseen or unheard except by himself (in which case it hardly exists) – has to present it to a *real* audience. In some arts, if the artist is out of sympathy with contemporary fashion ('ahead of his time', we say, though the phrase is open to challenge because it assumes that one time is ahead of another), he can execute his work and it may be acclaimed after his death. But in the case of a film the artist cannot pursue his dream in solitary splendour. Film is a group art which involves many quite difficult techniques, and the cost of even a modest film is beyond the means of a single individual.[1] Films, then, are unlikely to be made even by rich patrons unless some sort of immediate audience can be found for them – though this does not mean that films are not sometimes neglected by their contemporaries and better appreciated by posterity, or appreciated for other reasons or other qualities.

This then is a third limiting factor, a third relationship with reality: to be complete, a work of art must – sooner or later – reach out again into the real world from which it has sprung, and touch the feelings of at least someone somewhere.

In this book we are concerned primarily with the second point at which art touches reality, that is, with the influence the film medium will have – the way reality appears through a camera lens, the effect of framing on the image, the effect of different kinds of transitions from shot to shot, and so on – but the two other relationships will be relevant and should be borne in mind.

1. There are occasional exceptions, like Jean-Luc Godard; but even those rich enough to engage in film-making without regard for financial considerations will hardly persist unless they succeed in attracting some audience.

THE METHOD OF INVESTIGATION

It is time we looked more particularly at the cinema itself and examined how this fits into the three-stage process of creation and appreciation which constitutes the complex known as art. But before doing so there is one further general point to make about the method of investigation. We have begun talking about art in the broadest general terms. This has the advantage of presenting, at the start, general principles and broad outlines, so that the particular discussion which follows can be set against a comprehensive background. But this is not the order in which conclusions are built up. All art consists of an endless number of artistic creations; and general conclusions about art – what it is, what it includes, what it should aim at, how it obtains its effects, what is good and bad practice – must in the ultimate analysis depend on what the best individual artists have done. Similarly, the rules of grammar and pronunciation are derived from the practice of good writers and good habits of speech. The definition of 'good' will always present difficulty, but this is a difficulty inherent in the subject and will not be avoided by seeking the guidance of aesthetic 'laws'. The only valid laws are generally those directly based on existing practice. However the findings are ultimately presented, investigation should proceed from the particular to the general and not from the general to the particular. The student or critic should study the material for himself with an open mind, and not start with preconceived notions or follow blindly other people's opinions.

We do not mean that general conclusions should not be aimed at. Many writers on the cinema have either dealt with the subject piecemeal, or have propounded subjective personal views unsupported by objective reasoning. Here we have attempted to make an objective analysis of film aesthetics based on actual films – there are over three hundred film examples quoted in the book – and to develop a coherent system arrived at inductively by examination of individual cases.

Arguing from the particular case has another advantage also: it allows for change and development. Particularly in the case of film, any comprehensive treatment has to allow for the protean nature of the medium. Indeed the great changeability of film may itself be the reason why many writers have not attempted an integral analysis. In its short history the cinema has gone through endless metamorphoses in technical resources and methods of using them, most of which have profoundly affected the finished art form. Silent films, sound films, colour, wide-screen, triple-screen – in three generations the cinema has gone through more mutations than music or painting in three thousand years. We naturally seek not only to write about current films but also to discover principles of general validity throughout these changes. Thus it will be noted that, though the majority of examples are from films made within the last ten years, the examples as a whole range widely and include every country, every period – and every type of film-making.

THE THREE STAGES APPLIED TO FILM

Stage One: Intuition

Let us go back to the three stages in artistic creation and apply them to the cinema. Like any other art, the making of a film can be analysed into intuition, execution, and exhibition. The first stage – the intuition arising out of the artist's experience – is a personal, internal affair, and we find that films usually start from an individual inspiration – a short story, a novel, a play, a scenario, an idea, an experience. Perhaps, because filming is a less individual medium than writing, there may be a tendency for the inspiration of a film to spring from literature or drama: in any case, it frequently does so. But, wherever the film-maker gets his inspiration, he has to translate it into film terms; and this may be as difficult – more difficult – if he starts with another work of art, say, a novel, as if the film grows direct out of an actual experience, situation, or milieu. Some of the strength of Flaherty's films lies in their stemming from a source – Flaherty's excitement about, and sympathy with, a human way of life, through his *direct* contact with it – which is strong and pure, and without literary or dramatic trammels.[1]

Moreover, in most arts, but more particularly in film, the first stage does not usually stop short when execution begins. The intuition goes on growing and developing right through the process of execution until the work is completed. In practice, the two processes of intuition and execution are usually inextricably commingled, one affecting the other, and it is only in theory that we can separate them. There are certain exceptional cases in which the intuition and the execution are clearly separate, when an artist is possessed of an intuition so powerful, so vivid, so complete in his mind, that he can express it without a single correction. This happens occasionally with a great genius and a master of his craft: we read of a long novel, a symphony, or an opera written feverishly in a few weeks, days, or hours, in an explosion of prodigious activity, and achieved *in a perfect form, without revision*. But this is less likely to happen in the case of a film. For although the intuition may be a personal thing, the second stage, the creation of a film, depends on many people. Film production, with its thousands of cinemas all over the world, its film-stock factories, its processing laboratories, its acres of studios, its army of technicians and workers of all kinds, is one of our heavy industries, and the making of a film is normally a group activity.[2]

Artistic creation in a group has certain difficulties, but also certain advantages, and it by no means rules out the possibility of great art. The transfer of the idea to the medium may be more difficult, because for the best results the artistic intuition

1. Plate 2.
2. Plate 3.

has to be shared, other people have to be won over and infused with something of the original inspiration. Because of this, and also because it entails intricate physical apparatus which has to be controlled and complex technical processes, film is a 'tougher' medium than writing or painting. On the other hand an idea may catch fire from the contact of other minds, and an enthusiasm be generated in a group which an individual working alone would lack. Medieval cathedrals, a clear example of group art, are among man's greatest artistic achievements. Nor have the greatest artists been recluses: Shakespeare was at the centre of the activity of the commercial theatre of his day; some of the greatest painting has been produced by 'schools' or 'movements'; music has often run in families – the effect of group environment, as well as of heredity.

If the commercial cinema has produced much bad art, it is not because it is executed by a group – although it has been suggested that group working offers peculiar difficulties in an age of individualism in art – but because of its commercial background. The cathedrals were not built to make money. They were built for worship by people who were sure of themselves and who believed profoundly in what they were doing. All art requires some disinterestedness, some love of art for its own sake, because it is only on this foundation that a strong belief can be built. The weakness of the pure money-maker with only this ulterior motive to sustain him is that in the last resort he is unable to believe in what he is doing in the way an artist can.

It is true that art and morality are not the same thing, and Clive Bell has pointed out[1] that the most exquisite art has been associated with the decadence of the Greek and Roman empires, of Renaissance Italy, of the French Court before the Revolution. But, quite apart from the point that social background is a complex of influences and that any answer to the questions 'What is morality? What is decadence?' may not by any means

1. *Civilization*, Penguin Books, 1938.

be a simple one, it has to be remembered that the rich patron and the artists who produced the things we admire were not the same people. Art and decadence may well concur, because the great wealth and leisure which often result in decadence often also create a demand for artistic products and make it easy for this demand to be fulfilled. And at least the decadent patron is prepared to indulge his senses. In a puritan society there may be the wealth without inclination for leisure or licence to enjoy art. Wealth is then invested in production to create more wealth to be invested in more production and so on *ad infinitum*, with art excluded entirely. No doubt in any society the best patron is the one with the best taste, but a patron may be insensitive, stupid – what you will – without this necessarily affecting the work, provided he gives the artist (who is none of these things) a free hand. But he must be intelligent, or careless, enough to give the artist a free hand. The trouble with the cinema has often been that anxious commercial interests, unsure of themselves, have interfered before, during, and after the making of a film to harm the artist's work, a process clearly shown in Lillian Ross's book *Picture*[1]. It should be noted, too, that film-backers are not patrons commissioning work for their own enjoyment, but businessmen making an investment – and one with a high degree of risk.

Fortunately there are many cases in which the artist is left as free to express himself in film as in many other media, and sometimes, because the technique of film-making is such a comparative mystery, the patron will interfere less. A commercial firm will very likely give a freer hand to a film director making a prestige film for them than to an architect who is designing their board-room or the façade of their new building.

Stage Two: Execution

The second stage, the carrying through of the artist's intuition

1. Gollancz, 1953.

and the resultant work of art, is the most obvious and prominent feature of artistic activity. It is what the world sees. Because of this it may unfortunately be true that of two artists, one with deep inspiration but less facility of expression and another with little to say but a fine technique, the latter is more likely to be successful. The execution is also what clearly distinguishes one art from another. A film is very different from a play or a painting or a symphony; but the emotional inspiration which engenders each and the states of mind which each arouses in its audience, are more alike.

In the case of film this second stage is particularly prominent for one reason because the film medium is tremendously powerful in its impact. A film is such a large piece of work compared with, say, a painting, and it is easy for an audience to accept a film, as one may accept a building, without thinking of the people who made it. Further, it reaches its audience on a scale which is larger than life, and the mere size of its images and volume of its sound can have a stunning effect. It is still more powerful because it is pictorial, and still more so again because it is photographic and brings us face to face with reality, or with something that looks like reality, in a compulsive, actual way. It is far more vivid, and so can be far more shocking, than an abstract art which depends on written or spoken words. Finally, the cinema is a collective form of artistic communication, and only television reaches a wider audience.

Yet, although the film medium is so widely known and so powerful, it arouses less expert discussion than other arts. The main reason is probably this. Most people, when they listen to music, read a novel, or look at a painting, understand the work that lies behind it. They may not understand the growth of the artist's intuition, for this is a mystery of creation in the mind which few of us fully understand. But the process of writing it down on paper, of putting the paint on a surface – these are simple (though not simple to do) hand operations as old as mankind and as uncomplex as an axe chopping wood or a wheelbarrow moving rubbish. By contrast, the processes of the cinema are a mechanical conjuring-trick, new, baffling, complex – like a motor-car, an electronic brain, or a Geiger counter. The *results* are startling in their effect and so simple to understand that they may reach a more ignorant audience than most arts; but the *means* by which they are obtained are another matter entirely.

It is the purpose of this book to investigate this mystery. That is not to say that this is a book about film technique – a practical guide to making films. We are interested in the film as an artistic medium, and propose to examine the factors at work as they contribute to the final aesthetic effect. We do not attempt to describe how to frame a shot, what exposure or what aperture to use, how to cut a sequence and so on. But we shall be concerned with what aesthetic effects can be obtained by framing, by exposure, by different depths of focus and by cutting. And we shall try to deduce if any aesthetic principles lie behind these techniques, and, if so, what they are. There will be such reference to technical processes as is necessary for clarity, but the stress is on film appreciation, not on practical know-how.

The medium of the cinema is little understood for other reasons than those of its mechanical nature, its technical complexity, and its newness. It tends to be a transient medium, although not so transient as television. A book can be read and read again, music can be played on gramophone records, a picture in a gallery can be enjoyed at leisure. But if we miss an effect in a film we cannot turn back and see it again. After a short run, films disappear and may rarely be re-seen. Another difficulty is that the strong impact of films is not helpful to analysis. If the viewer is emotionally absorbed in the film he may very well miss finer points of expression. Even experienced critics may be carried away, and the conscientious ones will try to see an important film more than once. A further consideration is that many technical effects in a film are extremely subtle. It needs fair concentration, for instance, to detect the difference between (a) a very rapid fadeout-and-in, (b) a very rapid mix, (c) a very rapid wipe and (d) a straight cut. No doubt many of the effects of a film, although they occur with great rapidity, will contribute to the total impact, and so will reach the spectator and be unconsciously enjoyed by him even although he may not be fully aware of the reasons for his enjoyment. One is reminded of subliminal advertising which has been the subject of experiments on television. Nobody would suggest that an audience cannot enjoy a film very well without analysing the director's technique. At the same time it is reasonable to suppose that deeper understanding acquired through analysis will increase appreciation, and also that the subtler or more rapid an effect the more likely it is to be lost. At the ultimate extreme of subliminal advertising, it is open to doubt whether even the alert spectator is affected at all. Again, cutting rhythm – the timing of shots, the speed of transition – is of considerable importance in a film, but it is a difficult thing to analyse. It is far more complex than the visual rhythm of a painting – not only is there a time dimension additional to those of space, but there is also the added interrelation of sound and image, and, finally, all these interrelated elements are in constant motion, not static and unchanging.

A further reason for the art of the film not being understood in England and the U.S.A. is that people have not bothered to understand it, because they have not thought of film *as* an art. Dewey referred to things 'the average person does not take to be arts; the movie, jazzed music, the comic strip . . . and newspaper accounts of lovenests and murders'. I. A. Richards lumped together 'bad literature, bad art, the cinema', and said that the latter was 'a medium that lends itself to crude rather than to sensitive handling'. In England, at any rate, few people have written about the cinema, or, if they have, have treated it as a sociological, an economic, or even an anthropological phenomenon, rather than as an aesthetic one. It is significant that the film has been least valued in England and America, countries where the commercial film trade's grip of mass entertainment was for a long time strongest. In these countries for many years cheap, stereotyped, mass-produced films were turned out like sausages, and people of discernment could hardly but be discontented with the standard of taste displayed. It was different on the Continent where the cinema has been a centre for intellectual ferment; where people like Eisenstein, Pudovkin, René Clair, Jean Epstein, Abel Gance, Jean Cocteau, etc., have not only made films but written books and propounded theories – and been accepted as leading thinkers and artists into the bargain. In Britain and America, the people actually in films have either been too successful or not sufficiently articulate to write about film aesthetics. Many books have been written about Hollywood, but they have been memoirs or scandal or satire. The best film critics have often had a wide and important influence for the good, but they have been mostly too busy assessing current films to write generally about aesthetics or history. Over the years there has been a handful of writers on film theory but only one or two are well known: Arnold Hauser, Erwin Panofsky, George Bluestone, Siegfried Kracauer, Roger Manvell, Ernest Lindgren. There have also been intelligent minority groups, but none of them has had very wide influence. It is also true that since the war there has been more intelligent interest in the cinema. In England the documentary school has had its influence. In America there has been a gradual weakening of the monolithic Hollywood empire. But for all this, at the present time many Continental countries remain ahead, and foreign films still have a prestige which recalls that of Continental musicians in Victorian days when British music was at such a low ebb. For all these reasons – because the film depends on complex techniques, because it is new and subject to change, because it is difficult to observe and because it has been underrated – film remains less well understood than other arts, at any rate so far as the aesthetic nature of its realization is concerned.

Stage Three: Presentation

So much for a preliminary survey of the second stage in the artistic process of film-making – realization. The third stage, the viewing of the film by an audience is not the primary concern of this book, although the aesthetic relationship between film and audience is discussed in considering the sort of reality which the cinema shows us. Nevertheless, in the case of film this aspect is again of greater prominence than in the case of most other arts because, just as the cinema is an industrial as well as an artistic phenomenon on its production side, so, on its consumption side, it is not only an artistic but also a social phenomenon. As such, it has been the subject of many sociological studies, designed to analyse mass-viewing psychology and fan-fever and to decide whether films encourage or discourage juvenile delinquency; and of economic studies, mostly attempting to diagnose the so-called decline of the cinema – which artistically has been no decline at all but rather a rebirth.

FILM AND REALITY

In dealing with the aesthetic nature of the film medium, this book will naturally grow out of books which have preceded it – although differing widely from them in its total effect. Special mention should be made of Rudolph Arnheim's *Film as Art*. His approach, consisting of a clearly-developed contrast between the real world of the senses and the world we see on the cinema screen and an analysis of the elements of difference between real and artistic experience, forms the starting point of the main chapters, although the modifications and additions are considerable. It is proper that this contrast between film and reality should occupy a prominent place in discussion of film aesthetics, because the film medium (besides working with the compulsive realism of photography) gives us *more* of physical reality than any other art. The fact that the cinema presents so comparatively complete a picture of the real world is sometimes referred to by describing the cinema as a *total* art, and it has encouraged people to think that the way to artistic perfection lies in approaching nearer and nearer to full physical reality. It will be found that the film does, nevertheless, differ enormously from physical reality, and that it is largely in these differences that its artistic power lies. The truth of this may be illustrated by a *reductio ad absurdum*. Advocates of *cinéma total* consider the cinema imperfect to the extent that it falls short of complete reality; the perfect cinema they say would attain total reality. But if this dream were realized, then the cinema would *be* reality – and would cease to be art.

In the earliest days the attitude that cinema was not an art, which we have described as being common later in England and America, was generally held everywhere. Neither cinema nor photography were at first accepted as forms of art, but were regarded merely as methods of registering the appearance and movement of the real world.[1] Perhaps this was natural, since by the nature of things the first film-makers, like Lumière and Edison, were scientists rather than artists, and quite content to be so. It was only gradually through experiment and improvisation, that the cinema developed into an art by transforming its mechanical means of reproduction into an artistic means of expression. Film-making, as contemporary aesthetics saw it, was a mechanical task which had nothing in common with artistic creation. Film apparatus with its cogs and gears and strips of celluloid was to all appearance far from being artistic, and the shadows jerking on the screen, apart from their scientific interest, were considered good for little more than to provide a few minutes' diversion in a funfair. However, there were visionaries (one of whom was the conjurer Méliès) who saw that this vulgar, showground attraction had hidden powers

1. Plate 4.

of magic. One of the most perceptive writers about the cinema, André Bazin, in an article on its origins, describes it as an 'idealist phenomenon', by which he means that its development was due more to the fantastic imagination and enthusiasm of dreamers like Méliès[1] than to the prosaic research of the scientists. Both were necessary, and it is right to stress the contribution of the artist and the showman as well as that of the inventor. An indication of the explosive energy with which people took up the new invention is shown in the enterprise of a stall-holder in an early French fair who gave his side-show the tremendous title of *Lenti-Électro-Plasti-Chromo-Mimo-Poly-Serpenti-graph*. But even these illusionists, these cinemaniacs, saw the new invention only as a new combination of traditional arts which would enable them to achieve a total spectacle – some grand coalescence of stage and natural effects. Nobody foresaw that there would emerge, quite independent of all the older-established arts and different from all of them, a new autonomous *art of the film*.

The mechanical nature of the cinema was important in another way. Like that of photography, the compelling realism of a film depends on the fact that there is, or seems to be, less human intervention than in other arts. We think that we can rely on a machine to be faithful in reproducing an original in a way that is not possible with human agency alone, and consequently we *believe* in the reality of a machine reproduction. In fact, contrary to common opinion, the cinema with all its technical and scientific resources is quite unable to reproduce reality without imperfection. Although it may appear to be an exact copy, the world we see on the screen is quite different from the world we live in. In particular, neither space nor time have the same characteristics. In the everyday world of our senses, everything exists in a space-time continuum constructed from real space and real time, and forming a continuous framework of reference and identification. The space-time of the

1. Plate 5.

cinema is completely different. Spatially the screen shows us a flat world reduced to a single plane, lacking the basic dimension of depth, and limited by the frame which surrounds it. For much of its history the screen has been without any strong illusion of depth, and without colour. Furthermore, by montage and camera movement the cinema makes all kinds of transformations of space which would be impossible in reality. Time also is constantly subject to contractions, extensions, breaks, and jumps which do not occur in the continuous chronology of the real world. Finally, the cinema was for a long time without sound or speech and when it does make use of these elements it does so in ways which are very different from our experience of them in everyday life.

It is clear, then, that by comparison with our ordinary experience the film world is an entirely artificial one. It is a function of the film-maker to ensure that this film universe, objectively false, should give the spectator, by suspension of disbelief, a feeling of reality like that created by a natural scene. It is in the creation of this false 'seeming', in which the screen world takes on a semblance of nature, that an *art of the film* first makes its appearance. Left to its own mechanical devices, the camera would be incapable of creating anything like so complete an illusion; it needs the intervention of the film-maker with all his technical and artistic skill. The introduction of the human factor brings with it another consequence – the subjectivity of the world represented, and the possibility of a personal cinematic vision. With this all the necessary conditions are present for the emergence of an original art, and for the exercise of artistic creation on the realistic material supplied by the camera and the sound recording apparatus.

In the following chapters we shall consider in much greater detail these basic material differences between film and reality. But between the natural scene and that of the cinema there is a further difference of another kind to be touched on briefly before closing this chapter – not a physical but a psychological difference.

The film world possesses an anthropomorphic quality common to all arts which helps to create a deliberate emotional and mental effect in the spectator simply because, in the making, the film has been charged with this quality by the artist. Scenes which exist in nature are emotionally and dramatically 'neutral', in the sense that they do not seek to move or influence us at the bidding of any exterior will. If an aurora borealis fills us with wonder, or a storm makes us afraid, the emotion comes from within ourselves; nobody has staged them with the express purpose of producing a reaction from an audience. But the images of a film are impregnated with the essence of the film-maker's own feeling and imaginings, and they become mental images as much as physical. They are designed not only to affect the senses but also to seize the imagination, and they even have a dynamic power of arousing the spectator's emotions by subtly following the changing movements of his own inner thought. The natural scene is *there*. It stays detached. It can be enjoyed, but remains aloof, indifferent. But the film as a work of art is deliberately made to attack us, to force its way into our feelings and our beliefs.

CHAPTER TWO

Space in the Cinema: Scale, Shooting-Angle, Depth

WE have already, in Chapter One, mentioned some of the ways in which a film differs from reality. The conditions under which a film is viewed occasion further differences. As soon as we start to analyse the situation of a spectator in the cinema it is apparent that he apprehends the objects on the screen quite differently from those of the world which surrounds him. The most important difference is that the screen is external to the spectator, who is not involved with it as he is with his normal surroundings. At the same time the spectator's normal surroundings (seats, other spectators, etc.) are obliterated by darkness. Secondly, in the cinema we can only see and hear – our visual and auditory sensations are not supplemented by touching, feeling, measuring, or weighing, and as a result we cannot estimate accurately volumes, distances, or densities. Our senses, which in nature operate as a whole, are cut down to sight and sound.

FILM VISION

Let us consider first the sense of sight. The images on the screen show us the external world in a very arbitrary fashion. The camera lens is a crude device compared with the human eye, possessing neither its stereoscopic vision nor its power of continuously refocusing, changing angle, and accommodating itself to light. Because of this, and because of the nature of film projection, the cinema gives us, even visually, only an approximate and incomplete account of the real world. The spectator has to accustom himself physically and mentally to the peculiarities of *film vision*.

Let us take an example. Because the cinema gives a

two-dimensional picture of a three-dimensional world, objects will not necessarily be recognizable on the screen irrespective of how they are photographed. They must be taken from the right angle and with the right lighting, and this involves selection by the cameraman from the many aspects of the objects which exist in reality. This has to be borne in mind even when filming such a simple thing as a cube. In the real world, we can see it from a distance or close to, can walk round it, count its sides, compare it with its surroundings or with ourselves, localize it in space – in short we can identify it completely. It is in the same world as ourselves. In the cinema, the spectator is not only outside the spatial framework of the things he sees in the film; he is also immobile. The camera has to move for him, or the object has to move on the screen. If we film our cube from directly in front, the audience will not recognize it as a cube; it will appear on the screen as a flat surface – a square. To be recognizable the cube has to be suitably lighted, and photographed from an angle which will show three of its sides and so its three dimensions; or else it must be shown turning, or the camera must move round it to show its different faces.[1] It is so easy to misrepresent common objects by using the wrong viewpoint or lighting that such misleading photographs are often used for guessing games.

As another example, let us suppose we want to show an audience either the depth of a valley or the height of a mountain or, generally, the size of any object. To achieve satisfactory results it is not enough to set up the camera anywhere, or film the scene anyhow, even if we get far enough away from the object to include the whole of it in the picture. The spectator outside the screen lacks any system of reference or any scale of dimensions by which to judge its size. The operator must choose a suitable viewpoint or give some other artificial means to help the audience assess the object. In the case of the valley, for instance, a sense of depth will be given by choosing a time

1. This example is taken from Arnheim's *Film as Art*.

of day when the sun casts shadows on the slopes of the hills. In the case of the mountain, the director may arrange to include in the picture a house or a tree or a human figure to give a relative scale of size.[1] This is a rule which even holiday snapshots follow. There is an excellent example in Robert Flaherty's film, *Moana*. In one shot (not a particularly impressive one) he shows waves breaking over rocks and the spray filling the screen. A little later we see exactly the same scene with two Polynesians standing in the shower of spray in the foreground. These two tiny figures at the bottom of the screen show us the true size of the tremendous waves and give the second picture a far greater impact.

From these examples there grows the idea of *lighting*, *shooting-angle* and *scale* as forming the rudiments of an art of the film. Lighting is discussed more fully in a later chapter. Scale and shooting-angle are considered further below.

SCALE

We have seen that a film audience may fail to appreciate the size of large objects. The lack of a scale of reference also works the other way, so that models on a tiny scale, if carefully made and lit, and cut in with shots of live action, are accepted as real. The bombing scenes of the film *The Dam Busters* (director, Michael Anderson), showing the destruction of the Möhne Dam during the war, were photographed from a model no bigger than an ordinary table-top, and the same is true of innumerable film spectacles from the films of Méliès to *The Guns of Navarone*. In the cinema it is as easy to make a mountain out of a molehill as to do the opposite. In John Huston's film *The Night of the Iguana*, lizards are used to set off the credits at the beginning of the film. Actually they are about as large as small dogs but, by shooting in close-up and with no other frame of reference than the letters of the credits, they are made

1. Plate 6.

to look as big as prehistoric monsters. Quite frequently the camera will show us a boat or a train or a house which the director, perhaps by moving the camera, will show to be a toy boat in a pond or a model railway or a doll's house. The scene may then develop in various ways, perhaps moving on to a real boat or train involved in the plot. By making all the rooms, furniture and props. either very small or very large, human beings can be represented on the screen either as giants or as the size of Tom Thumb.[1] In *Third Avenue El* the director, Carson Davidson, wishes to show us the New York elevated railway as a little girl might see it. He films it looking down from a distance so that it looks like a toy railway. In Kon Ichikawa's joyful film, *Alone on the Pacific*, the closeness and crowds of the two cities, Osaka and San Francisco, are contrasted by means of camera technique with the vast spaces and loneliness of the sea between them. In the city scenes the screen is crammed with huge telephoto images of cars and people and buildings; in the seascapes we look down from the sky at the tiny yacht, a distant object in the midst of the ocean. In every film made, the scale of objects is constantly changing, far more often and more violently than in real life. The scale of camera-shots, from long-shot to close-up, is considered later in relation to cutting and camera movement. All we need note here is that scale on the cinema is artificial and unlike our everyday experience.

SHOOTING-ANGLE

The example of the cube shows the importance of shooting-angle for simple identification, but when making a film it is not only a question of recognizing an object and grasping its physical properties. In the case of more complex objects (a building, a statue, a person) shooting-angle may be used to bring out their essential nature.[2] Certain aspects will be more

1. Plate 7.
2. Plates 8 and 9.

typical than others, or will embrace others. Abram Room, in his film *The Ghost that Never Returns* stresses the gross brutality and greed of a thickset detective by filming him at a slight downward angle, from behind his heavy neck and jowl which bulk enormous in the foreground of the picture, as he scoffs his food like an animal. The essential characteristics of a locomotive are its speed and power, and consequently newsreels generally favour upward-angle shots taken as the train rushes past. In Lindsay Anderson's film *This Sporting Life* the mud-covered football players taken from a low angle appear as black brutal giants. In filming a crowd of any size, the only way to show its typical feature (its numbers) is by setting up the camera in a dominating position and shooting at a downward angle.[1] If some aspects are typical others are a-typical, and abnormal camera-angles can be used to give an object or person a misleading character. Seen in a certain way, a frank expression can seem hypocritical, an inoffensive gesture threatening, a dwarf a giant. By filming a ballet dancer from below through a sheet of glass at a vertical angle, René Clair in *Entr'acte* makes her look like a flower. In Jack Clayton's *The Pumpkin Eater*, Jo's father is made into a grotesque figure on his first appearance by photography which gives a distorted perspective of his face. In Joseph Losey's *The Servant*, Dirk Bogarde is made by camera-angles into a dominating, most unservant-like figure.

The way a director shows an object will depend very much on the dramatic action or on the type of film being made or on the audience for which it is intended. An operation will be filmed in one way for an audience of medical students, and in another way for a general audience in an entertainment film. A telephone will be treated differently in a documentary about the G.P.O. and in a feature. Besides its physical properties, every object has other properties – dramatic, psychological, poetic – which in certain circumstances are more important and should be stressed.

1. Plate 10.

In appropriate cases, shooting-angles can be used to express subjectively what things are like as seen through the eyes of a character in the film. In Hitchcock's *Spellbound* and in Jean Delannoy's *Aux yeux du souvenir* the camera shows us the world seen by a sick man coming out of a coma: an upside-down world of people seen from below; a nurse whose silhouette appears on the ceiling lowering a spoon from the skies. A film has been shot from ground-level to show the world as a dog would see it. Gilbert Cohen-Séat, in an experimental film, has tried to show the viewpoint of a new-born baby: furniture taken from below; a worm's-eye view of the bath and the wash-basin; close-ups of carpets. In Carol Reed's *The Fallen Idol* many scenes are shot from the visual angle of a boy of twelve. Unusual angles, abnormal framing and lighting – all suggest with delicate precision a world which is familiar but is not that of grown-ups. A subjective camera-angle is used in Pier Pasolini's film *The Gospel according to St Matthew*, in a sequence showing John the Baptist performing baptisms. As Jesus comes forward to be baptized the camera draws backwards and into the clouds as we hear the words 'This is my beloved Son in whom I am well pleased.' Because the film is restrained and quiet in its general treatment, this larger camera movement is extremely effective.

This question of subjective and objective shots could be developed very much further and it is interesting to compare it to the novelists' technique of switching from the viewpoint of one character, to that of another, to that of the novelist himself. There is an unusual series of shots in a film directed by Stefan Sharff, *Across the River*, in which Brooklyn Bridge plays a prominent part. The chief character is an old rag-and-bone man with his barrow, and we have first an objective upward-angle shot of him going over the bridge high up. Then comes a shot from high up on the bridge and we naturally take this to be a subjective shot from the old man's point of view, looking down on the ant-like people in the street below. However, gradually in the throng below we pick out him and his barrow – what started as a subjective shot from the old man's point of view finishes as an objective shot from the author's view, and with the change of viewpoint there is a subtle change of flavour.

The camera's capacity for misleading us is sometimes used for dramatic or humorous effects. At the beginning of Dupont's *Variety*, the camera tracks in to a fairground where the show-girls are posing outside a booth. At a distance, with the help of soft-focus, they look attractive, but as the camera moves in we see that they are old, ugly harridans. In Duvivier's *Un Carnet de bal*, Louis Jouvet, playing the part of an abortionist doctor, contrives to look handsome at the beginning of the sequence. Then different camera-angles stress the ugly side of his features, and reveal what he has become.

In an early Chaplin film, *The Immigrant*, we see Chaplin bent over the rail of a ship which is pitching violently. From the convulsive movement of his back it is obvious that the poor fellow is sea-sick like the rest of the passengers and we are full of pity for him. But when he turns round we find that in fact he is fishing, and has just landed a monster catch. Another example from a Chaplin film shows Charlie with shaking shoulders, apparently sobbing his heart out because his wife has left him. When the camera moves, it turns out that he is shaking a cock-tail. There is a shot in a film by Pierre Étaix, *Le Soupirant*, in which a dog with long hair looks for a moment like a girl with a Brigitte Bardot haircut seen from the back. There is an effective comic scene in one of Laurel and Hardy's films which shows Hardy apparently strangling Laurel to death. A shot from a different angle shows us that he is only tying Laurel's bow-tie. In all these examples the director has made artistic use of the camera's inability, when placed in a certain position, to give a correct interpretation of a scene. The point of the gags in relation to the present discussion is that the creators of the films have managed to turn a technical defect into an artistic achievement.

PERSPECTIVE

Another peculiarity of the camera which affects the cinema's interpretation of reality, is its rendering of perspective. Film perspective combined[1] with an upward shooting-angle gives some of the cinema's most common effects. Mathematically, the size of objects in nature decreases in proportion to the square of their distance away from us. Thus, *as far as the image on the retina of our eye is concerned*, a man twenty feet away from us appears four times smaller than a man ten feet away, while a man forty feet away appears sixteen times smaller. But, as modern psychologists[2] have demonstrated, we instinctively correct the message we receive from our optic nerve, so that differences in proportion registered on our retina are mentally reduced. If we accept the immediate reaction of our eyes, natural perspective would be much more exaggerated. In practice our mind sees objects in inverse ratio to the distance (not the square of the distance), and we see a man at forty feet as a quarter (not a sixteenth) as big as the man at ten feet, and the man at twenty feet as a half (not a quarter) the size of the

1. Note the word 'combined'. The point should be made here (and borne in mind throughout the book) that to separate one aspect of technique and discuss it in isolation from others (e.g. *scale* separately from *shooting-angle*) is an artificial procedure necessary for purposes of analysis which does not correspond to the conditions of actual viewing. In the actual viewing of a film all the different effects – scale, perspective, lighting, etc. – operate together in combination. It follows that many of the actual examples quoted from films would serve to illustrate more than one point. Generally they are cited as examples of the point for which they make the best illustration, but there will often be other applications which the reader can see for himself.

2. See R. H. Thouless, *General and Social Psychology*, University Tutorial Press, 1945.

man at ten feet. This *mental* correction is the fruit of long experience, acquired from infancy, of the relative size of external objects. We are used to fitting what we see into an intuitive system of reference which makes everything of 'reasonable size', so that our mind 'sees' things differently from our eye. Scientists call this a 'constancy' effect,[1] and it is the same phenomenon which enables the spectator to adjust to the size of the screen in different parts of the cinema.

The camera lens registers perspective in the same proportions as the retina, that is objectively instead of subjectively, so that on the screen the rule of the square of the distance operates. A man photographed with his finger pointing at the camera has a giant hand larger than his head; a skyscraper filmed from a low-flying aeroplane is like a tall pyramid standing on its apex. We see them in this way because, when we are in the cinema watching the screen, we are unable to correct this 'distortion' as we would in the real world, since the cinema presents a special world external to us and outside our ordinary experience.

Once more, film images differ materially from those we experience directly and, as a result, certain shots, certain angles are impossible because they give this unnatural impression – because the difference from our habitual observation is too violent. To bring the camera image into line with our customary way of seeing things, and to give the screen image verisimilitude, the director has to intervene and control the 'automatic' mechanism of the camera. In some cases this is merely a process of control aimed at presenting reality in an acceptable way. But in other cases this very defect of the camera can be deliberately used for artistic effect.

If, instead of filming a building square to the camera and far enough back to approximate normal vision, we go close and shoot from below at an upward angle, then the building will show the violent foreshortening we have described, and will

1. Thouless, *op. cit.*

appear to tower above us, larger than life. A person filmed from the same angle will give an impression of force, power, majesty, even if he is a dwarf. This was a constant device of propaganda films, and has been used again and again to add to the stature of dictators and tyrants. There are innumerable shots of Stalin, Mussolini, and Hitler addressing the faithful as if they were gods looking down from heaven. The same upward shooting-angle is used constantly in feature films to establish predominance, and a downward angle is used to suggest inferiority. An upward angle may also be used more prosaically to increase the height of a short actor.

Some examples of the psychological effect of shooting-angle are worth mentioning briefly. In Jacques Feyder's *Pension Mimosas* a woman (Françoise Rosay), having discovered that her son is stealing from her, bursts into his room to punish him, full of rage and indignation, and is shown in *upward angle*. She goes straight to him and, despite herself, slaps him with all her force (*horizontal angle*); then, realizing that she has been brutal and horribly unjust, she sinks on to a couch and bursts into tears (*downward angle*). The camera-angle very accurately reflects the woman's feeling of moral indignation, of getting even, then of regret at what she has done. In Jean Delannoy's *Baron de l'écluse*, Jean Gabin, playing the part of a man who lives by his wits, is stranded without money in a remote country place. As a last resort, but as usual, full of hope, he rings up the head barman of a fashionable hotel who has lent him money once before. All we see is the 'Baron' in a telephone booth talking (inaudibly) behind the glass. All that happens is the very slightest change in Gabin's expression, and a nearly imperceptible movement of the camera from slight upward angle to slight downward angle. But the slight camera movement is sufficient to make the most pointed comment on the 'Baron's' failure to sponge on the barman for a second time. In Bryan Forbes's *The L-Shaped Room*, the heroine is lying on the grass in a park. The camera looks up to see, obscuring the sun, the towering figure of a policewoman who has come to move the girl on. The shot expresses strongly the overbearing officiousness of authority as it seems to the girl on the grass. In *Days of Wine and Roses*, directed by Blake Edwards, there is a scene in a boarding-house with lodgers on different floors looking up and down and complaining about cockroaches. Extreme camera-angles up and down the stairs are used for humorous effect. The humour of Richard Massingham's short films frequently depends on the use of unusual angles, and on other film techniques such as photographic distortion, dissolves, or jump cuts. In Truffaut's film, *La Peau douce*, the ending of a tenuous love affair is expressed by a long-shot and a downward camera-angle. The man has taken the girl to a half-finished block of flats, where he is planning they should live, and there asks her to marry him. The answer is no; an affair is all right but not marriage. She goes off and leaves him. From the top of the tall building he watches her tiny figure go out into the street, get into a car and drive away. By means of long-shot and downward angle the camera gives an air of finality to her departure and reinforces the mental concept of parting by the physical means of emphasizing the distance between the two.

A further advantage of the camera's unusual vision is that a film can achieve the sort of formalism we find in the work of primitive painters who were ignorant of perspective, or of modern painters, like Picasso and Braque, who reject it. It enables reality to be stylized, and allows a director to express more freely his own personal vision. A good example is Dreyer's *La Passion de Jeanne d'Arc* in which unusual angles are constantly used. With the slight distortion of camera perspective and a non-realistic décor, the whole picture is given a formal, abstract feeling. Stanley Kubrick's *Doctor Strangelove* is another picture with a brilliant style in which an inhuman, unearthly effect is obtained by extreme angles, violent lighting contrasts and unusual aspects (for instance, of cloudscapes). In

Richard Lester's *A Hard Day's Night* camera-angles and sudden variations in scale and pace are used for humorous effect in a ballet sequence of the four Beatles on a playing field – a ballet which is created not by the actors but by the camera. In *Woman of the Dunes* by Hiroshi Teshigahara, strange patterns of sand, extraordinary angles, double-exposure, huge-scale close-ups, unusual lighting – all combine to give this film also a completely individual style.

TRANSFER OF DIMENSIONS

Another phenomenon, connected with perspective, stems from the fact that, in the absence of stereoscopic vision, distances away from the spectator are conveyed entirely by differences in size. In the case of tracking-shots this sometimes leads to an optical illusion. Instead of seeing objects come nearer or go farther away, we get the impression that they are staying in the same place but increasing or decreasing in size. The basis of this phenomenon is that the third dimension of depth is interchangeable with the other two dimensions. What is really a change in depth is 'transferred' and appears as a change in length and breadth. Also because of exaggerated camera perspective, the increase or decrease will itself be exaggerated. With very fast tracking-shots, and especially with the use of a zoom lens, the effect may be so strong as to make the audience feel dizzy. In van der Horst's film, *Praise the Sea*, there is continual violent use of these shots and we 'zoom' up to windmills and buildings with an effect which is sometimes unpleasant.

An early example of transferred dimensions is Méliès's film *The Indiarubber Head* made in 1901. In it a man's head is apparently blown up with a pump. It swells and swells, talking and grimacing to prove it is a real live head, and finally bursts. In fact the man, the rest of his body concealed, is slowly getting nearer and nearer to the camera. Transferred dimensions are also strongly present in shots with long-focus and telephoto lenses which, in addition, tend to destroy relief by flattening the image. It is thus common in newsreels (horse races or cricket matches) and in nature films (close-ups of wild animals). The effect is similar whether the camera itself moves or whether an animal or human being moves in relation to the camera, although transfer of dimensions is less likely in the latter case, since the rest of the scene, which stands still, gives a standard of reference and prevents ambiguity. However, this reference is often absent in telephoto shots because the moving being occupies the whole screen.

This phenomenon is, on the one hand, a defect which needs to be controlled by the film-maker – for instance by choosing an appropriate lens, or by arranging that movement shall be transverse or at a reduced speed or, in extreme cases, avoided altogether. But, on the other hand, it can have striking artistic or dramatic uses. The effect, on an audience already aroused by suspense and vague forebodings, of a threatening figure suddenly increasing to giant proportions is a tool in the hands of a film-maker far more powerful than any exact reproduction of reality. We see this particular effect in thrillers, gangster pictures, Western, and horror films. The opposite effect – the exaggerated rate of diminution caused by a figure going directly away from the camera or by the camera itself tracking back – can express powerful emotional feelings of farewell, of hopeless parting, of final ending or even (if combined with a deep, plunging viewpoint) of a sort of resigned, philosophical *Weltanschauung*. Such shots are typical of hundreds of film endings but, in good hands, they can still be extremely effective; for instance, there are the endings of Stroheim's *Greed* (the two tragic figures in the desert),[1] of Clair's *À nous la liberté* (the couple going down the long tree-lined road), of Renoir's *Le Crime de Monsieur Lange* (the hero and heroine crossing the wet sand and turning to wave at the camera), of Antonioni's *La*

1. In this case, however, the effect is achieved by cutting and not by camera movement.

notte (the camera going away from husband and wife lying in the grass), and of many others.

CONTRASTS IN PERSPECTIVE

So far, we have been considering the camera's peculiar perspective in relation to single objects. But it plays just as important a part in the relationship between two objects. It means that in shots taken in any depth the contrast in size between the foreground and background is very much exaggerated.[1] In the hands of a beginner this peculiarity can give ridiculous results, but properly used it can be another artistic resource. For example, the ending of Antonioni's *Il grido* has, in the foreground of the picture, the man about to commit suicide; he is on the top of a tall tower looking down on the tiny figure of the woman he cannot forget who gazes up from the ground below, and the shot achieves its effect partly by this contrast. The ending of Eisenstein's *Ivan the Terrible*, with a huge close-up of Ivan's profile in the foreground juxtaposed against an endless winding queue of tiny figures in the distance, is not only pictorially effective but makes the point which Eisenstein wants to bring out – the paternal relationship between the Tsar and his flock, the Russian people. This point is made symbolically – the Tsar huge and alone, the people myriad and tiny – but at the same time with the strongest realism. There is another good example of this technique in Pudovkin's *The End of St Petersburg*, in the sequence where two peasants, fleeing from the famine conditions of the country, come to the town to look for a livelihood. One shot shows us in the foreground the huge mass of an equestrian statue of the Tsar, a black metallic silhouette with the horse's and rider's limbs outstretched, and, far off in the background, the two peasants, in minute scale, tramping across the empty square.

Although the basic method is the same in each, the last two scenes have quite different effects. In *Ivan the Terrible* the bond

1. Plate 11.

between the elements is emphasized, while in Pudovkin's film it is the antagonism between them which comes out. This difference partly depends on context and meaning; but in the Pudovkin film both the statue's qualities – the lack of modelling, the deep-black grotesque outline, the hard texture – and also something in the attitude of the peasants, stress the city's might and hostility, and the peasants' miserable helplessness. If the distance between the men and the statue could be assessed by the eye, as in real life, the effect would not be the same. Even when watching the film, we know mentally that the men are not really *so* much smaller than the statue, but the transformation from reality to the cinema throws our usual sense of adjustment out of action, and the men are accepted emotionally as insects crawling at the feet of a colossus which could crush them with its power. In this scene, too, the meaning is expressed through a striking visual symbolism, the sort of symbolism used by Egyptian artists who made their victorious emperors huge figures while the enemies they defeated were shown as tiny beings. But the film, unlike Egyptian art, completely retains the realistic character of the scene. Pudovkin arranges the authentic elements of the real world in a visual relationship which will bring out most strongly the meaning of the scene.

To set against these two Russian examples, there is a striking shot in a modern British film. *A Taste of Honey*, directed by Tony Richardson. The heroine, a slum girl neglected by her mother, has just said good-bye to the handsome Negro sailor with whom she has been having an affair. They part at a swing-bridge across a ship-canal and, with conflicting emotions, she watches him going across to the other side. At this point there is a close-up of her face, and behind it is shown, in the middle-ground, a ship going down the canal – a complicated pattern of machinery, masts, stays, etc., full of life, with the crew working round the hatches and a group on the bridge. Besides being most striking visually, the shot is more deeply expressive, as though the ship symbolized both the vitality of the girl and the confusion of her thoughts. In another film, *The Servant*,[1] which depicts a servant corrupting, dominating, and finally destroying his weak-minded master, this particular technique is used with striking effect to reinforce the impact of the whole film. At the beginning of the picture, the servant (Dirk Bogarde) always appears in the background, an insignificant, subservient figure. Gradually as the film goes on he is brought more and more into the foreground, and he grows in stature and power while the master steadily becomes by contrast smaller and more ineffectual.

The importance of one plane as opposed to another will depend very much on the context. One example from Alventosa's *The Inheritance* is quoted in the chapter on Time (page 105). In another scene in the same film there is a shot in depth, which shows the office telephone-girl bulking large in the foreground, conducting a loud conversation with a boy-friend. All this has nothing to do with the plot and our attention is concentrated on a quarrel which appears on a much smaller scale in the background between two men. The quarrel is entirely silent except for light 'squabbling' music, but from the previous action we know it vitally concerns the plot. We *know* it is important and the very fact that it is small-scale increases its effect, for the same reason that meiosis, litotes, or other forms of deliberate understatement are effective in literature. The technique is strikingly similar in a Swedish film by Bo Widerberg, *Raven's End*. In this case the loud-mouthed, drunken father and his son are shown large-scale in the foreground, listening with great excitement to a noisy sports programme on the radio. But the important action takes place in silence in the background when the son's girl-friend comes in at the back, stands mutely until he becomes aware of her presence and slips away to her; we then see them through the open door of the next room silently talking to each other, and we know she is telling him that she

1. Director, Joseph Losey.

is expecting his baby. One could quote many other examples from modern films. Some of Stanley Spenser's paintings have a similar emphasized contrast between foreground and background and one wonders whether, consciously or unconsciously, he was not influenced by the cinema.

In passing it should be mentioned that the way in which the camera reproduces perspective will vary with the lens used. As we have seen (page 48), a long-focus or a telephoto lens covers a small visual angle, destroys relief by flattening the image, causes foreshortening which can verge on the grotesque, and tends to transference of dimensions. On the contrary, a wide-angle lens of short-focus covers a wide visual angle and can give a greater depth of field, although this advantage may be lost if it is used with a wide stop. A wide-angle lens will not cause such great foreshortening but may give an appearance of longitudinal stretching in the structure of the picture. If a wide stop (or aperture) is used in a setting in depth it will lead to a blurring of the image (soft-focus) in part of the picture. Soft-focus is another camera defect which has its artistic uses and is discussed in Chapter Six.

DEPTH IN THE FILM IMAGE

Finally, we come to perspective as it affects the whole scene. From a technical viewpoint the flatness of the image has always been considered one of the greatest disadvantages of the screen spectacle, and inventors have been trying since the beginning of the century to overcome it by mechanical means. Spencer and Waley in their book *The Cinema Today*[1] mention all the systems which have been in use and some which are still only ideas on the drawing-board: Anaglyphs (used by Lumière and the modern 3-D); polarization systems; vectographs; lenticular screens; panoramograms; parallax systems (using wires). About 1950, when the film industry was looking for any

1. Oxford University Press, 1939.

novelty to retain its mass audience, it seemed as if 3-D might be the answer, and the 1951 Festival of Britain included a Telekinema for showing stereoscopic films (the building later became the National Film Theatre). But somehow none of the systems caught on, and the film image remains as flat as ever. It can, however, very successfully give the illusion of a third dimension. Unlike systems of painting which are flat and completely formalized, a photograph is more like those works of art which use chiaroscuro or perspective to suggest the third dimension, and a photograph naturally gives an effect of depth. This is partly because it so strongly recalls the real world, partly because the shading of a photograph gives strong relief to the picture. Starting from this norm the film-maker can either increase the depth of the image or reduce it by various means: for example, by using different camera lenses and different apertures; by lighting (side lighting intensifies modelling, front lighting flattens it); by camera angles (oblique angles will stress depth); by emphasizing or avoiding contrast of scale; and by using either flat settings or settings in depth. Depth can also be brought out by movement of the actors or of the camera itself in the line of its axis; by movement of the camera *round* a person or thing either horizontally or vertically; by camera movement combining panning and tracking; and finally, by the use of montage to give different view-points of the same object.

Historically, the rendering of depth by film-makers has developed in an interesting way. Space in the theatre and the cinema are very different from one another. The cinema has the advantage that the camera is free to look out from its central point to the limits of the horizon or beyond; it can look out, over a narrow or a broad field, for millions of miles – up to the stars, and down from the clouds to the earth. When Kracauer says that the film enables us to 'penetrate reality' he is talking in a wider, partly metaphorical sense; but this is just as true in purely physical terms. We look out through a window into the whole of the world. Compared with this the theatre is completely circumscribed and contained – we are not looking *out* but *in* – into a box which holds the actors and the action. But the theatre has the advantage that, within this box, the space is real, solid, three-dimensional stuff, not the cinema's moving shadows. Marcel Martin, in *Le Langage cinématographique*, writes: 'In the theatre we sweep the scene, looking for a centre of interest. In the cinema the camera thrusts into the depth of things.'

If the cinema and the theatre are different – one asks – why compare them? For one reason because, in the cinema's early beginnings, film directors thought of their work as similar to that of theatrical producers and one can look on the treatment of depth, historically, as a process of emancipation from theatrical influence. In the beginning films were often handled so as to stress their disadvantages compared with the theatre; gradually film-makers learned to minimize the cinema's disadvantage and to make the most of its very real advantage. In the earliest silent films, treatment was completely static, with no movement of the camera and no attempt to build up a composite scene by cutting. The lack of relief was simply accepted or compensated for as far as possible by *trompe-l'oeil* scenery and theatre lighting. Cinematographic space was circumscribed to coincide with theatrical space, for, in the eyes of producers and audience, the one was a reproduction of the other.

But this was all changed when the camera freed itself (and the spectator with it) from the 'orchestral stalls viewpoint', and became mobile, either changing place between shots by cutting, or by moving during the filming of a single shot by panning or tracking. A new phenomenon had arisen: the combination camera-spectator, which had been outside looking on at the scene, now stepped inside the circle of dramatic action and moved about within it as in a real space. A new concept of *cinematographic* space developed which was different from natural space, but was just as different from that of the theatre stage. The way was clear to develop to the limit depth-of-field effects, and the subsequent development of the film spectacle has been along these lines.

The problem of bringing in the third dimension was partly (but only partly) a technical one. It was also very largely a question of deciding that depth was the thing to go for, and determining the best means of achieving it. In fact, almost the first film made by Lumière, *Arrivée d'un train en gare*, uses depth of setting, movement (of the train) in the axis of the camera, and oblique shooting-angle to achieve a strong three-dimensional effect. Nevertheless, technical progress did affect style. The earliest lenses, such as Lumière's, could be used only with a narrow aperture, so that depth was a natural feature of the image, unless it was limited (as it often was) by a flat theatrical setting. Then, with better lenses, directors used wide apertures more and more, as this enabled them to film under less favourable conditions of lighting, and this led to an era of short depth of field and the popularity of soft-focus effects. It also encouraged directors to operate by brief shots, with frequent changes of camera set-up, and to move between foreground and background by cutting rather than by letting the action proceed naturally within a setting in depth. The German expressionist school compensated for the flatter settings by careful composition of the image and by using strong chiaroscuro,[1] and there is great solidity about, for instance, Fritz Lang's early films, despite shallow-focus and a comparatively static camera.

Then, in the thirties, faster film-stock and stronger studio lighting made the use of small apertures possible under the most difficult conditions, and enabled all parts of the scene at

[1]. Some of the very effective chiaroscuro effects of the time, for example, the use of masks, and circular shading round the picture, have gone out of fashion, although there is an impressive example in Ted Zarpas's recent film of a stage performance of Sophocles' *Electra* and also examples in some French new-wave films.

whatever distance from the camera to be kept in sharp-focus. Although in earlier films we find occasional examples of setting in depth, such as the opening of Renoir's *La Chienne* (a shot through a serving-hatch into the room beyond), or the shot of the statue and peasants from *The End of St Petersburg* already mentioned, it was not until Renoir's *La Règle du jeu*, Orson Welles's *The Magnificent Ambersons*, and William Wyler's *The Best Years of Our Lives* that the style was fully developed.

In *Citizen Kane*, a film typical of this style, scene after scene uses a setting in depth[1] with contrasts in dramatic action between background and foreground: there is the death-bed scene, Kane lying enthroned in bed, the nurse at the door in the background; there is the reporter's first interview with Kane's second wife, Mary Alexander, the reporter in the telephone booth, the drunk woman at a table in the background; there is the shot with Kane's parents in their house and the boy outside in the snow; a counter-shot from outside, the reverse of the previous one; there is the *Chronicle* party taken from behind Bernstein's shoulder; the shot over the shoulders of the *Chronicle* staff looking out of the window at Kane and his fiancée in a cab, just back from Europe; there is the political meeting, Geddes looking down from the gallery at Kane on the platform; opera scenes with Mary Alexander singing; the much-quoted scene of her attempted suicide, with the poison bottle on a bedside table in the foreground; Mary and Kane talking across the vast hall of Xanadu; the scene where she walks through door after door to leave him; and there are many others.

In Tati's *Jour de fête* there is a scene where contrast between background and foreground is deliberately used for humorous effect. We see a reaper in a field on a hill waving his arms about frantically to ward off a wasp, while the postman on the road below is cycling peacefully along. Then the reaper, in the foreground, calms down while the postman on his bicycle, in the

1. Plate 12.

background, starts waving his arms. And so it goes on, the invisible (and improbable) wasp attacking each of them in turn. The effect is irresistibly comic. Again, in Hiroshi Inagaki's *The Rickshaw Man*, the hero abandons his rickshaw and his passenger (in the background) and runs to play with a little boy he is fond of (in the foreground). The passenger becomes impatient, and executes a mime of calling the rickshaw man back, dancing round the rickshaw and finally becoming hopelessly entangled with it. The relegation of all this to a distant view makes it much funnier. The passenger becomes an angry little puppet and his rage instead of being fearful has the delightful ridiculousness of a clown's impotent anger. In the foreground the rickshaw man and the boy bulk large and their very size makes them seem as serene and indifferent as gods.

CAMERA MOVEMENT AND DEPTH

Camera movements are discussed in the next chapter, but should be briefly noted here as a means of giving a scene solidity. Almost the earliest known use of a moving camera was to achieve this result. The story is that Pastrone had had huge pyramids, palaces, and statues constructed for *Cabiria* (1914), but found with dismay that, when they were filmed from in front with a static camera, they looked quite unimpressive, the relief being so flattened on the screen that they resembled the painted backcloths of a cheap film serial. Then he had the idea of mounting the camera on a cart and wheeling it about the set while filming. The result was a complete success and the sets came alive with startling realism. But, no doubt because of the difficulty of moving heavy apparatus with precision, it was not until much later that camera movements became universal. *Citizen Kane* uses camera movements as freely as setting in depth. It opens with a series of forward tracking-shots, each dissolving into the other and penetrating layer after layer of Kane's physical environment. This physical penetration of space in a way epitomizes the whole film, which is a psychological penetration of Kane's character and private life. Nowadays the camera is so mobile that it can walk round or under or over objects at will. In Colpi's film *Une Aussi Longue Absence* there is an effective 360-degree turn round the protagonists as they waltz together alone in the bistro. However, in *Judgment at Nuremberg*, the movement seems to be overdone, and the camera is constantly prowling round the witnesses until we are giddy. The device can become a cliché but (like Doctor Johnson's banging his hand on the table) it can almost *prove* the solidity of the setting.

MONTAGE AND DEPTH

Montage is discussed more fully later, but requires brief mention here in relation to depth. It can be regarded as doing the same thing as a moving camera, but episodically rather than continuously. We look from different *angles* at a scene: we look round a thing through a number of different *shots*. In its way this is equally effective, and we take away just as solid an impression of the space occupied by the Odessa Steps, which are composed from various shots in *Battleship Potemkin*, as we do of Stanley Kramer's Nuremberg court room. There is an interesting shot in a recent Polish film, *Knife in the Water* by Roman Polanski, who made *Two Men and a Wardrobe*. One of the characters on a yacht holds his finger up and, by a jump cut, the director imitates the effect we get when we look at our finger first through one eye then the other. When we do this we are seeing *consecutively* what we see *concurrently* in stereoscopic vision, and it is interesting that the cinema can imitate this. One wonders whether, by intercutting every few frames shots of a scene taken alternately from the right-eye and left-eye position, it might not be possible to convey subliminally a three-dimensional image! However this may be, cutting can very well suggest solid reality.

The fundamental difference between former montage techniques and the recent ones of setting in depth and using mobile camera work, is not so much that the newer techniques make space more solid, but that they allow longer shots, longer periods of continuous action, and thus avoid the extreme chopping up of space and time which is the result of concentrated cutting. In doing this they bring the spectator closer to reality by allowing freedom of choice in the focus of his attention; they reintroduce the possibility of ambiguity. With a montage style the viewer's attention is much more firmly directed by the film-maker. Another difference can be illustrated by an example. When a revolver is lying on a table, and someone comes into the room without seeing it, instead of playing on the tension created by the distance between the person and the object, it may be found more convenient in a montage style to show first the person, then the revolver, in separate shots. If the story gains in clarity however, the drama loses in force. The danger is that directors and audience lose the 'sense of the interplay of objects in space' as well as the dramatic values of their physical relationships. The single shots may be made up of very fine pictures but they are often only 'abstract extracts from reality, whereas the architectural view of the world is founded on perception of volumes, constituting, according to *Gestalt* psychologists, unanalysable wholes'.[1] Because of the extreme fragmentation due to montage, certain sequences of Eisenstein's *Strike*, as we see them today, are downright incomprehensible. Also montage can lend itself to faking which may be convincing up to a point, but becomes suspect in the end. For instance, in Sucksdorff's *The Flute and the Arrow*, we see the leopard stalking and chasing the man in an accelerated rhythm of cutting, but we never see them in the same shot together. André Bazin makes the same objection to the crocodile chase in Flaherty's *Louisiana Story*.

1. From a lecture given by Louis Raitière, at the Institut des Hautes Études Cinématographiques, Paris (1945–8).

Most writers seem to have assumed the desirability of using all means to suggest depth. It has the virtue of using to the fullest the cinema's power to make us kings of infinite space. This is one reason for the success of Westerns, for they allow the eye to travel with more freedom than most films. But it would be wrong to think that depth cannot be created in filming a drawing-room or a prison-cell. Much depends on contrast, and the contrast between one foot and ten feet can be as striking as that between half a mile and two miles. Although styles with depth of field are at present predominant this does not rule out other possibilities. In a Polish film, *Birth Certificate*, directed by Stanislas Rosewicz, there are interesting frieze-like effects in shots of military vehicles in convoy, and also in shots of Nazi troops investigating and looting houses in the middle distance. The whole action occurs away from the camera and there is no contrasting foreground. In Truffaut's *Jules et Jim*, in some of the Paris bar scenes the camera moves sideways as if it were telling the tale in a long tapestry. There are flat procession scenes in Orson Welles's *Othello*. In any sideways tracking-shot following a person or a train, the lateral dimension rather than the depth is emphasized. It is conceivable, especially with the encouragement of the cinemascope screen, that one day a director may come up with a completely new, flatter style.

With regard to all the characteristics of the cinema considered in this chapter – scale, perspective, and depth – we have seen that the technical means fall short again and again in reproducing reality. But these shortcomings are the kind of beneficial restraint in which Paul Valéry, when talking of poetry, saw a source of creation. Pierre Leprohon in a recent history of the cinema says:

Above all, the art of the film is to be looked for in the cinema's imperfections.

The distortions of perspective, the ambiguities of scale, the lack of a third dimension, are deplored only by uninspired artists. For film-makers with real talent the spatial alterations, distortions and limitations inherent in cinema vision have been, as they are in painting, an opportunity to interpret reality in terms of a personal vision[1] and thereby the more fully to express the artist's emotional experience.

1. Plate 13.

CHAPTER THREE

Space in the Cinema: Cutting, Camera Movement, Framing

IN everyday life we are able to focus our whole vision on an object by concentrating our attention on it. This is something we can do consciously at will, but also, just as a matter of everyday habit, we tend to see only what interests us. It is partly the result of moving the head and eyes unconsciously, to direct them and focus them, partly the result of ignoring mentally what is not at the centre of our attention. Our optical system is controlled by the mind, and in the real world the isolation of the object of our attention is achieved subjectively. Part of an artist's training is to unlearn this habitual visual accommodation and educate himself to see the whole scene objectively as the camera does. For camera vision is unlike ordinary human vision in that the camera reproduces the whole of a scene without discrimination and the cinema can imitate the selective capacity of human vision only in a very inferior and clumsy fashion.

In filming, the principal method of isolating a particular object is to set up the camera close to it, so that it fills the whole frame and to take a 'close-up' view. Another common method is gradually to move the camera towards an object so as to draw attention to it. Less common methods are to use masks, or to focus sharply on the important part of a scene and leave the rest in soft-focus. Finally, in a film our attention may be caught by a moving figure in an otherwise still landscape, or may be riveted on a particular character or object in the scene because of the significance it possesses in the development of the plot.

The last two instances are similar to selection in the real world, that is selection exercised by the spectator. The others are dependent on the mechanics of filming and projection, and the first two, cutting and camera movement, have become the central techniques of the cinema. The presentation of changing viewpoints, which began as an expedient to enable film vision to give the same effect as ordinary vision, has become in the course of years the cinema's major means of artistic expression. One could even go further and say it is what makes the film an art. For it was when the film developed from a fixed continuous spectacle into a series of points of view that film-makers were forced to choose their material and arrange it – two fundamental requirements of all artistic creation.

CUTTING

The technique of cutting determines the nature of cinematographic space and differentiates it from space as we know it in the real world. In the real world, space and the things it contains present themselves to us as an unlimited continuity. We isolate different parts of space by an effort of attention, but the adjoining parts are present peripherally. Our total field of vision is of course limited and changes as we walk, or drive, or move round a corner or into another room. But the change is continuous, its nature is predictable both as regards what appears and what disappears. We know by experience that space and objects in the real world exist before we see them and continue to exist after we have lost sight of them.

In the cinema, by means of shot-change, we are continually jumping from one view to another. We are transported in a flash from the house to the street, from the town to the country, and from the present to the past. Different parts of space appear before our eyes discontinuously, and objects on the screen appear and disappear without any predetermined spatial relationship. In the cinema we accept this as a matter of course. It is an artistic convention to which we are so accustomed that we are hardly conscious of it. But it is quite unknown in the real world and it may prevent unsophisticated spectators understanding a film at all. Bela Balazs's *Theory of the Film* quotes the case of a well-educated girl visiting Moscow from Siberia who thought the first film she had seen in her life (a comedy) was horrible, because 'human beings were torn to pieces, the heads thrown one way and the bodies the other'. And when Griffith showed the first close-ups in a Hollywood cinema, and a huge severed head smiled at the audience, there was a panic in the auditorium.

In changing scenes by cutting, the method most commonly used is a straight cut, that is, a shot of one scene is joined directly to a shot of another and when projected the film simply flicks from one scene to the other. For most of the time the spectators watching a film are not consciously aware of these switches, particularly as the director normally takes care to make his cuts unobtrusive. He may do this by 'cutting on movement', that is, waiting until an actor moves before switching the scene. Or cuts may be to an adjacent part of the same set or to another character and following, or motivated by, the action or the dialogue. Even if they are to an entirely different scene the audience will not notice them if there is a sufficiently strong motivation in the story. This is what André Bazin calls 'invisible cutting' and it is the normal practice within a single sequence or scene of a film.

Transitions

However, when the film-maker wishes to change the action, to carry the plot a stage further or to move to a different place, he will normally wish to stress the change more, so as to give the audience time to adjust themselves and enable them to follow the structure of the story more easily. It is like the break a writer makes by starting a new paragraph, a new section or a new chapter. In this case the director will frequently use, not a straight cut, but a slower transition such as a fade, a dissolve[1], or

1. See Appendix: *Note on Technical Terms.*

a wipe, or he may use various other means of emphasizing the change.

In the case of a fade the old image gradually fades out and there may be a brief period of darkness on the screen. Then the new scene will gradually become visible. A slow fade is particularly suited to indicate the passing of a night or a longer period, or to show a change to another place, perhaps by a journey.

In a dissolve, also called a mix, the new image appears on the screen before the old image fades away and for a moment the two images appear together. A dissolve is a special case of double-exposure and is further discussed under the section on double-exposure in Chapter Six. It is mostly used for transitions from the present to the past or the past to the present, to introduce a memory sequence, to connect two characters who may be physically separated but emotionally linked together or to introduce the thought of a deceased character or a ghost.

Again there are devices, such as wipe, iris-out and iris-in, and turn-over[1], which are more obtrusive and have been criticized for this reason. At one time wipes became a wearisome cliché and lines moved over the screen in every possible direction, wiping out the old image and establishing the new. They can, however, if well handled, be effective, as they are in a short film directed by René Clair on Montmartre during the thirties – *Village dans Paris*. Iris-out and iris-in, with its shadow invading from the edges of the screen, is allied to the masking of the German impressionist school of the twenties. It was used by them and also earlier in sentimental silent films but is hardly seen nowadays. It has been used by 'new wave' directors, for example by Truffaut in *Tirez sur le pianiste*, but, if not as a parody, at least with the self-consciousness of a 'literary reference'.[2] Turn-overs in which the whole screen seems to turn

1. See Appendix: *Note on Technical Terms*.
2. This use of 'film allusions' as a method of rendering homage ironically to earlier film-makers is very common among young French

are another artificial form of transition. They are used in Tony Richardson's *Tom Jones*, together with wipes, to make the violent transitions from one sequence to another which suit the hectic pace and jocular tone of the film. Again they were used in the lively credits of Carol Reed's *Bank Holiday*, and, in a recent compilation af Harold Lloyd's comedies, *The Funny Side of Life*, to join sequences from different films.

The transition from one sequence to another may be emphasized not by any cinematic means but by a variety of other methods. There may be for instance a recurrent leitmotiv – visual or musical.

In Griffith's *Intolerance* there is a recurrent shot of a woman (Lillian Gish), rocking a cradle, a symbol of time, of eternity, of rebirth, taken from a poem by Walt Whitman ('out the cradle endlessly rocking') – this shot is used as a link between the different episodes of the film. In Max Ophuls's *La Ronde* there is a hurdy-gurdy tune which connects episode to episode. In *The Rickshaw Man* by Hiroshi Inagaki there is a constantly recurring motif consisting of the turning wheels of a rickshaw, single or multiple, shown in single- or double-exposure, and from different angles. This motif separates different sequences and also, by changes in colour and tempo, evokes different moods.

In a short Polish film, *Dom*, directed by Lenica and Borowczyk, which depicts the fears and imaginings of a young girl alone in a house, the episodes are connected by a close-up of the girl looking at the camera then lowering her head for another think. In Jean-Luc Godard's *Vivre sa vie*, each episode is introduced by fully-worded, numbered chapter headings written as subtitles on the film.

A transition from sequence to sequence may be stressed by a sort of visual or sound pun – in Hitchcock's *The Thirty-Nine Steps* we switch from a woman shrieking to a train whistling.

directors, who even parody their own films, and it has spread to England and America.

In Karel Reisz's *Saturday Night and Sunday Morning* one sequence ends with Albert Finney banging down the dustbin lid because his girl-friend's mother has sent him off home; the noise then changes to the clang of the factory where he works, and introduces us to the next sequence. In a Swedish film, *The Time of Desire* (directed by Egil Holmsen), there is a sequence of a man spying on two girls bathing in the nude in a forest pool. The camera moves in to a big close-up of his goggling eye which changes to a billiard ball. The camera then pulls back from the billiard ball and discloses a billiard saloon where the man is telling his pals what he has seen. In *Raven's End*, directed by Bo Widerberg, there is a series of transitions depending on football jerseys. First we see them taken off the line, then ironed by the hero's mother, then in the dressing-room, then on the football field: the camera follows the jerseys.

Similarity of shape also helps to stress transition – as when the picture changes from the angular limbs of a cricket to those of a reaping machine in Eisenstein's *The General Line*, or from the circle of a face to the circle of a base-ball arena. In Losey's *King and Country* there is a grim transition, by similarity of shape, from a corpse huddled in the mud to the doomed hero, Hamp, lying asleep in the mud of his dug-out prison. In Bert Haanstra's film, *The Human Dutch*, there is a sequence in which he shows live-action shots of streets in Amsterdam completely still and deserted during the ten minutes' silence of Armistice Day; in each case these dissolve into a photo of exactly the same street this time with civilian prisoners being marched away or with Nazis ill-treating the inhabitants. As he has chosen exactly the same places with the same outlines of houses one shot dissolves exactly into the other and forms a most effective bridge connecting the present to the past.

There may also be a connexion through identity of shooting-angle. In Torre Nilsson's *Homage at Siesta Time* there is a sequence in a helicopter, followed by a sequence of people sitting round a table having a meal. To connect the two there is a shot of the people sitting at the table inside a house, but it is taken looking vertically down on them as if it were filmed from the helicopter. The camera may move quickly through one or more intermediate shots. In *Devi* (The Goddess), an Indian film directed by Satyajit Ray, one sequence ends with a young wife thinking of her husband who is away studying at a university. Her face dissolves into a shot of water, the camera pans upwards over the water to a lovely shot of a sailing boat in the distance, then there is a cut to a shot of the husband sitting in the boat coming to visit his wife.

Finally, a transition from one scene or sequence to another may be effected by a straight cut. In this case the director may wish to call attention to the change by making his cut startling rather than unobtrusive. It is normal practice to use a close-up only after the audience is already used to a scene or a character from seeing them in medium- or long-shot, but in certain cases a director may cut directly to a close-up of a new object or character; for a second or two the audience is unable even to identify it – then the camera pulls back and the significance of the new scene becomes apparent. In a novel Italian film, Bertolucci's *La commare secca*, there is a modification of this technique; straight cuts are used between the sequences, but the story is cast in the form of a police inquiry and each part of the film is connected with a particular witness and is introduced by a close-up of the person concerned.

Uses of Cutting

Having discussed the different means of cutting from one scene to another, we consider now the purposes for which cutting can be used by the film-maker. In the first place it enables him to change the scene as the story requires, to further the action and to provide variety. It corresponds more or less to changes of setting or scenery in the theatre although in the cinema the changes can be far more frequent. This is the most important and obvious use of cutting.

The second function of cutting is to eliminate unwanted space. Most of the story or action is simply never filmed. The director takes the highlights, the significant parts of space (and time) which he or the script-writer select. Most often a little more is filmed than will eventually be required and the exact length is determined when the film is being edited. For this reason, and also because a shot may be taken several times and the best of the 'takes' selected, much more film is shot than appears in the final version. The ratio, called 'cutting ratio', will vary widely with the circumstances and the director, and it is impossible to say what this should or should not be. One director will expose five or six – or more – times the amount of film finally projected, another only two or three times as much, and both may produce equally good results. This sort of trial and error is common to all the arts. Cecil Beaton is said to take many photographs of a subject, Cartier-Bresson only a few. One painter will do dozens of sketches for a painting, another will paint it without a single draft. Robert Louis Stevenson was said to have written almost without correction, Honoré de Balzac wrote draft after draft, each a mass of alterations. It is the final result which matters. In the case of the cinema, there should be enough left in the final montage to guide the spectator and enable him to fill in the intervening space and time with his imagination. Omission of irrelevant matter is similar in the case of a novel (but in a film it is the representation of physical space and time which is left in – and left out), and in that of a play (although, in a play, space and time can only be left out between the acts or between the scenes). A play will generally include far less space than a film but by means of its dialogue it can cram far more action into the space at its disposal: it makes its space work harder. Looking forward to the next chapter, one can reason in a similar way in the case of time. A film will normally be shorter than a play, but by means of its visual range will get more action into a given time: it makes its time work harder.

Thirdly, cutting can be used to build up a picture of an object, an action, or a person, by taking them from different aspects. By doing this it can give a very full picture with great economy, perhaps bringing out various traits which can be contrasted, or combined, with emphasis on particular features. Because of cutting, for instance, the cinema can normally show actors' faces (turn and turnabout) large enough to let us see their expression in every detail.[1] This is the cross-cutting, the shot and counter-shot, of conversation. Moreover, cutting enables the camera to follow a glance or a gesture and reveal its meaning; or it may be used to follow a person moving. Thus, like camera movement, it allows action over a wider field to be shown in the closest detail.

Cutting may make space seem larger. Half-a-dozen shots of a prison-cell from half-a-dozen different points of view, seen in succession, will give a mental impression of much greater amplitude than looking round the actual cell from inside it. The camera can give a powerful impression of a crowded party, of a jostling crowd, of packed traffic through cutting together shots which by themselves would be unimpressive.

Again, cutting can create space affinities which do not really exist. We see the hero of a film struggling in a river that is racing faster and faster, then we cut to a shot of a huge waterfall with a body going over the falls. The racing stream and the waterfall may be entirely different rivers, the shots may be taken at entirely different times and the body going over the falls may be a dummy – but the audience accepts absolutely without question the relationships of place and time which the director has suggested by cutting them together. When we see two men struggling on a parapet and then a shot looking fifty storeys down to the street, we are *unable to doubt* that the two men are on top of the building. There is an example in an Argentine film shown at the 1962 London Film Festival (*The Sad Young Men*, directed by Rodolfo Kuhn) of space affinity

1. Plate 14.

used for anticlimax which shows how strongly expectations can be aroused. Three young men are driving from the town to join three girls who are waiting for them in their seaside bungalow. We see shots of the young men in a car, then a shot of the girls in the bungalow expecting them. Then at the bungalow there comes a knock and the girls crowd to the door. The caller turns out to be a strange young man, one of a rival trio (not the ones we have been led to expect by the previous cutting), and the anticlimactic effect, which is remarkably strong, indicates how powerful an association the previous juxtaposition of shots has built up. One remembers a parody once made of the Western in which, in the middle of the usual parallel cutting between the heroine tied to the railway line and the hero rushing to help her, there appears, instead of the hero we have been expecting, a tough-looking guy in a city suit with a gun, who comes up to the bound girl: 'Who are you?' she asks. 'I'm a G-man from the F.B.I., and I've got into the wrong film,' he replies, and he walks out of the frame leaving the girl tied to the rails and is never seen again. Another surrealistic juxtaposition to set beside this – although it is achieved by framing not cutting – is from a film by Adolfas Mekas, *Hallelujah the Hills*. In one scene a bear completely unrelated to the rest of the picture appears in a frame within a frame.

One reason why the juxtapositions made by cutting are so readily accepted by the viewer, and so strongly believed, is that, as we have already said, most cutting is invisible. The director makes the transition in the smoothest possible way so that the spectator is not conscious of the change from shot to shot. The camera follows a glance, a word; there is an underlying musical theme; sight follows sound; a letter sent in one shot is received in the next; and so on. Although the scene-changes of the cinema are many times more numerous than those of the theatre they are not so obtrusive – mostly we are quite unaware of them.

It should be noted that, in the real world, vision is controlled by attention, but in the cinema it is the other way round: attention is controlled by vision. In everyday life we see what we attend to; in the cinema we attend to what we see – that is, what the film director chooses to show us. In fact in a dozen different ways (not only by cutting, but by camera movement, by setting, by lighting, by movement of actors, by composition, by colour, and so on) it is part of the film-maker's art to determine what the viewer will see. This is the difference between art and reality, mentioned at the end of Chapter One: that art sets out to influence its audience. This is not to say that the spectator is merely passive: the spectator's considerable contribution in artistic communication is discussed later. But montage, with the close-up as its full fortissimo, is a tremendously powerful means of expression and can exercise an almost hypnotic power over an audience. We cannot escape the insistent close-ups[1] of the cinema: the hands of Lillian Gish in *Intolerance*; the shattered glasses and face streaming with blood of the woman in the Odessa steps sequence of *Battleship Potemkin*; the ragged feet of the prisoners-of-war in Lean's *The Bridge on the River Kwai*; the fingers of the dying Harry Lime in *The Third Man* as they gradually slip from the grating of the sewer.

CAMERA MOVEMENT

Russian directors in the great era of montage avoided camera movements because, it was said, they tended to remind the spectator of the presence of the camera. It must be supposed that they did so largely because camera movements were something out of the ordinary. Nowadays when they are used so freely in almost every film, the audience takes them for granted and is more likely to get an artificial impression from films like Ozu's *Early Autumn* or *Tokyo Story*, in which camera movements are entirely avoided. From an objective point of view, cutting

[1]. Plate 46.

is just as artificial as camera movement, and in some ways camera movement is closer to our experience of real space than constant cutting from one shot to another. Certainly camera movement can give an emotional effect very different from shot-change. When the camera at the end of *Black Orpheus* (directed by Marcel Camus) pans upward from the sad mortality of the lovers, dead upon the rocks, to finish on the eternal loveliness of Rio's hills and sky and seas – when, in the first part of Antonioni's *L'avventura*, the camera lifts from the scurrying human ants searching the island for the missing girl to brood on the majesty of the approaching storm – when, at the end of *L'avventura*, we lift our eyes from the unfaithful lover and the betrayed girl, from the contemplation of human limitation and weakness to the massive strength of a distant, snow-covered mountain – in each of these three cases it would not have been possible to get exactly the same effect by cutting from one image to the other. Because it is continuous, the panning is able to say: here is this, there is that – so different, yet they belong to the same world.

It is the same with a tracking-shot, which starts off with a general scene and steadily moves so as to concentrate on a particular person or thing of dramatic importance. While cutting to a close-up works suddenly and dramatically surprises us, the tracking-shot takes us by the hand and leads us to the heart of the drama. There is a gradual selective process, progressive elimination of unnecessary elements, until finally only the pure centre remains. Cutting may be regarded as the spatial equivalent of a sudden leap of thought or feeling: tracking as the spatial expression of a gradual growth of ideas or emotion. Tracking can work up to a focus of attention and slowly and fully emphasize the key point of a drama. In *The General Line* when the moujiks are gathered round the separator, Eisenstein uses a slow forward tracking-shot to express their wonder at the magic of the thing, its gradual invasion of their consciousness, a physical projection of their curiosity and expectation.

But camera movement, although it is more natural than cutting, is still very far from reality. When we turn our head there is not the same finality, not the same evenness of pace, as when we turn the camera. In nature our attention bounds, stops, goes on, goes back – it is more flexible, more spontaneous, above all, it is unconscious. Also, in reality both what is to come and what has just been left are *there* simultaneously; there is no edge to our attention. In a panning-shot what is to come is unknown, what is left behind is decisively gone. As with cutting, so with camera movements – in the cinema there is constant 'material creation and annihilation of space and what it contains'.

Again, camera movement gives rise to transference effects. We have already discussed these in connexion with tracking-shots. They can be present just as strongly in panning-shots. To someone watching a vertical panning-shot of a building from the ground floor to the roof, it may seem as if the building is sinking into the earth, while a lateral panning-shot may make it seem as if the landscape for some mysterious reason is moving in the opposite direction. In everyday life when we turn our head so that the landscape moves, the muscular and the visual sensations form a habitual total experience to which we are accustomed, and we know by experience what is happening. In the cinema we miss the feeling of muscular movement – we know we have *not* turned our head and, therefore, the movement must be elsewhere. By going repeatedly to the cinema, viewers become accustomed to making an automatic distinction between the space world which the characters of the film inhabit (the screen) and the space world they are sitting in (the auditorium), but an unsophisticated spectator has the feeling that he is in the same world as that which appears on the screen.

To illustrate the strength of visual habits it is worth mentioning a fairground illusion called 'The Crazy Cottage' which depends on transference. It consists of a small lightly-constructed room, fixed to revolve round a pole which runs horizontally through it. There is a bench fixed along the pole on which a dozen people can sit. To all appearances the room is furnished normally but everything (carpet, table, vase, flowers, plates, cup, books, pictures, etc.) is invisibly fastened or stuck down. When the people have been seated on the bench and, to complete the illusion, strapped in, the box of a room is rocked by machinery. For the people on the bench, habituated all their life to the stability of the rooms they live in, there is complete transference of movement. It is they on the bench who seem to move, and they lean this way and that to maintain an imaginary balance, cling to the bench and to each other, and scream with fear and excitement. In the climax the room is turned completely upside down, and the people feel as if they are hanging, heads down, from the ceiling.

In the cinema, transference can occur, even for those used to watching films, when the movement of the camera is an unusual one. In the early part of *The Ghost that Never Returns*, made by the Russian director, Abram Room, we see repeated shots of a block of prison cells photographed quite normally from in front. Then, when a riot occurs in the prison, we are shown the same block beginning to tilt sideways several times, and nearly falling over. We know that it is really the camera which is being moved, but it looks as if the building is being pushed over and upset, as it were, by the riot inside. The same effect is obtained by a swirling movement of the camera to express fainting or vertigo. In Michael Cacoyannis's *Electra*, there is a particularly effective shot of Irene Pappas who, in a great wave of grief, falls on the grave of her father, Agamemnon. At the same time she utters a great moaning cry, the camera makes a sweeping movement, and the whole earth seems to reel. Again, we have instances of a defect in the cinema's rendering of reality being turned to artistic advantage.

Another departure from reality is that in tracking-shots, especially forward tracking-shots, which are often elevated above the ground, there is a strange sense of dream-like power. The camera can be moved in ways which are denied us in real life. There are vertical tracking-shots up the face of a building (in Renoir's *La Chienne*), or cliff. There is the opening of Wilder's *The Lost Weekend*, when the camera moves smoothly over the skyscrapers of New York to finish at the window of a flat where a flask of whisky is hanging. One of the earliest and most celebrated of tracking-shots is at the beginning of Murnau's *The Last Laugh* (1924). The shot begins in the street, moves in at the spacious hotel entrance past the lordly doorman (Emil Jannings) and finishes in the manager's office. Another is in Renoir's *La Grande Illusion* where the camera moves round von Rauffenstein's room picking out the objects which typify his Prussian, aristocratic background (the part is played by von Stroheim) – riding-whip, gloves, perfume, and so on. The result in the one case is quite unlike someone walking into a hotel, and in the other case unlike someone going into a room and examining the objects in it – but both are undeniably effective.

When watching a film, we are not intended, necessarily, to take camera movements as realistic. Panning-shots, for instance used in conversation as an alternative to cross-cutting (shot and counter-shot), have something of the function of inverted commas. The camera follows the conversation like a tennis rally and animates the scene. Moreover, by showing speakers in turn either while speaking or – more effective still – while listening, it adds immeasurably to the dramatic effect of the words. Panning may act as a conjunction between elements as in the examples from *Black Orpheus* and *L'avventura* already quoted. In *La Marie du port*, Marcel Carné starts with a close-up of a cake, which two hands take to put on the table. The camera follows the movement panning, and ends by framing the guests at the table who are introduced differently, and with more stress on the symbol of the festive cake, than they would have been by cutting. The optical liaison created by panning works in time as well as in space. The camera leaves a scene, pans up to the sky and comes down again to another time and place – or to the same place after a lapse of time. Panning movements may have an entirely subjective effect. In Christian-Jaque's *Boule de suif* (1946), there are a great many panning-shots when the villagers are discussing the imminent arrival of the Germans. The camera swings continually, catching in its movement replies, expressions, and attitudes, and expressing in visual terms the confusion of the people, and the wildness of their decisions.

A striking example of a subjective tracking-shot is in de Sica's *Umberto D*, where the old man, almost at the end of his tether, looks out of the window. With a sudden forward movement – a zoom-shot[1] – of the camera, the stones of the pavement rush up at us. We get a vivid expression of the old man's thought – merely a thought – of suicide. In Bertolucci's *Prima della rivoluzione* there is striking use of a backward zoom-shot. A woman (Adriana Asti) has had a deep, passionate affair with her good-looking nephew, broken it off, and come back to find him engaged to a rich, aristocratic girl. From the stalls of the grand opera house her eyes search for him in one of the boxes with his fiancée. The pulling back of the lens when they see each other is quite violent, and expresses strongly the surge of emotion that is felt. In *Brief Encounter* (director, David Lean), when the heroine nearly commits suicide and leans towards the rails as the express train comes in, there is a light spiral movement of the camera which expresses her feeling of giddiness. Then, like slaps on her cheek, we see the lighted windows of the train flicker across her face while the draught of the train blows her hair, cuts her breath, and brings her back to reason. In Sternberg's *The Blue Angel*, Emil Jannings,

1. See Appendix: *A Note on Technical Terms* for the relation of zoom- and tracking-shots.

dismissed and disgraced, sits in despair in his empty class-room gazing on nothing. The camera draws back foot by foot as if following his gaze, as if measuring the void he sees before him. In Cocteau's *Les Parents terribles* when Sophie, feeling she has lost her son, is stealing out of the drawing-room where her husband, her sister, and her son, Mic, are gathered round Mic's resplendent young fiancée, the camera backs away with her, expressing her withdrawal from a world she feels has rejected her. In this case the lighting (light and gay on the group, sombre and tragic on Sophie) reinforces the effect.[1]

Subjectivity may go further. Following the camera, the spectator may move like a sick man, or a runner, or he may trip, fall, be jostled, trodden on; he may become a rolling stone, a flying arrow, a diving aeroplane, a striking axe, a bird, a top, a projectile. Edgar Anstey in *Granton Trawler* used shots in which the camera had fallen over with its mechanism still running and recorded nightmare gyrations of deck, masts, and flying clouds, to convey the intensity of a violent storm. In *Napoléon*, Abel Gance had his cameras thrown as snowballs, fired as cannon-balls, dropped from a cliff into the sea, fixed to the saddle of a cantering horse, and mounted on a swinging platform during a scene of a stormy meeting of the Convention during the French Revolution, to give the scene the movement of a raging sea. Pudovkin used a mobile camera in the fight scenes of *Storm over Asia*. Gustav Machaty in *Extase* fixed a camera to the pick of a peasant tilling the fields. As Balazs says, the film can show not only a drunk man reeling along the street but the distorted reeling houses he sees with his drunken eye. And his subjective vision is reproduced by the film with objective reality.

FRAMING

The fragmentation of space in the cinema is accentuated by the limitation of the cinema screen with its sharply-defined 'frame'.

1. Plate 15.

The picture in the cinema is a fixed rectangle which shows us only a section of reality. This limitation has in the past been regarded as a disadvantage and attempts have been made to overcome it by using larger and larger screens, the ideal being an unlimited screen whose vast expanse would give the spectator the sensation of being immersed in reality itself. In 1900 Grimoin-Samson tried to do this with his cineo-rama; in 1959 the American circarama, and later the Russian circlorama,[1] by using a screen which curved round behind the audience, succeeded in giving a stronger illusion of reality.

But it is not fundamentally a question of size. Reality exists all round us; above, below, in front, behind. There is *no edge* to our vision. As soon as we try to concentrate on, say, the left limit of what we can see, our eyes and our head move involuntarily, and the limit moves with them; the same happens on the right, or above, or below. Any screen must have some edge, if not at the sides, then at the top or the bottom.

In any case, the frame of the cinema has important artistic advantages. First, it allows film-makers to choose, to isolate, to limit the subject, to show only what is mentally and emotionally significant. Unnecessary or irrelevant material can be eliminated and the camera concentrated on what is essential.

Secondly, the frame forms a basis for the composition of shots[2] by giving them an architecture, an equilibrium, a meaning. The rectangle of the screen constitutes a frame of reference from which to organize and orientate the contents of the picture. Like the proscenium of the theatre, it provides an area of plastic composition as well as a centre of dramatic action. With unlimited space the spectator's gaze would become lost in a disorganized mass of persons and things. A chapter could be written about the composition of the film image in relation to the frame. Here there is space for no more than a few words.

1. Introduced to Piccadilly Circus in 1963 as *Russian Roundabout*.
2. Plate 16.

One notes the constant use of stairways in the cinema to provide diagonal lines of movement contrasting with the rectangular of the frame. In many films the camera has stressed the dominating vertical structure of the modern city overpowering its inhabitants. In Martin Ritt's film *Hud*, the horizontal frame of the cinemascope screen is used to reflect the vast stretches of the prairie and underline young Hud's wild car journeys. A speaker on the B.B.C. Third Programme not long ago said that '. . . the horizontability of the Po marshes is brilliantly used in *Paisà*.'

Thirdly, any picture isolated by strongly marked boundaries has the property of attracting attention. The main function of a telescope's tube is to hold the magnifying lenses – but if we look through a tube with no lenses, we can still see the tiny field it covers much more clearly than with the naked eye. Furthermore, the very act of *framing* by itself can begin to create a work of art. The frame does more than isolate a picture; it pushes it together and gives it a unity it would not otherwise have. By isolating part of a landscape and transferring it from its natural setting to another setting – a house or museum – a painter presents this section of reality under new conditions of vision which bring out artistic values that its natural surroundings would hide or neutralize. The spectator sees it with new eyes. I. A. Richards saw a like effect in poetry:

Through its very appearance of artificiality metre produces ... the 'frame' effect, isolating the poetic experience from the accidents and irrelevancies of everyday existence.

Similarly, by extracting a fragment of reality from the chaos of nature and projecting it on to the screen, the cinema enables us to see beauty and meaning in it which otherwise would be hidden by utilitarian commonplace.[1] There are innumerable examples of unexpected delights of this kind in the cinema: the play of light on water in a filthy gutter, washing drying on the

1. Plate 17.

line, a smoking chimney, the pattern on a dilapidated wall, a hand occupied in some skilled task, the curve of a cheek. . . . Without being isolated, set in a frame and magnified in size, such mundane, such sordid objects would never attract us. In fact they are not beautiful in themselves. It is the way in which, first the artist and then, through his eyes, the spectators, look at them, that makes them beautiful. Once again we come back to the fact that art is unlike nature, and also that it exists only in terms of human interpretation.

Dramatic Use of Framing

The splitting up and delimitation of space not only enables the artist to choose the essential, and to concentrate the spectator's attention; it can be used to obtain powerful dramatic effects, of contrast and surprise.

An interesting example of framing used to bring together dramatically contrasting elements is to be found in Cocteau's *Les Parents terribles*. In a burst of joy, Mic – the son – tells his mother, Sophie, that he has met the girl of his dreams. Mic is behind his mother, his arms round her, his chin on top of her head. At the beginning of the conversation the camera frames the two faces alternately, then at the crucial moment the camera is placed so that it frames the lower part of Mic's face with its radiant smile and the upper part of his mother's face, her eyes filling with bitter suffering and jealousy. The dramatic force of the scene is enormously increased by the framing.

Framing is normally designed so that the centre of attention is within the frame. There are many examples in which, to create suspense and dramatic tension, a framing is used which deliberately excludes the central action.[1] It is effective because it is unusual, because it arouses the spectator's curiosity, and because suggestion can be more powerful than direct statement. Frequently in fight sequences the protagonists are lost on the

1. Plate 18.

ground, behind a pillar or a building. There is a famous scene in Wyler's *The Little Foxes* in which Herbert Marshall, as the husband, dies of a heart-attack which his wife (Bette Davis) had deliberately engineered. The camera, instead of following him as he staggers to the stairs to get the medicine she has refused to fetch, remains fixed on her as she sits motionless in the centre of the scene. The effect is to express very powerfully her strong indifference, as if neither the camera nor the heroine even 'turned their head'.

In Griffith's *Birth of a Nation*, the bloody, heroic sequence of the battle of Atlanta opens with a shot of a peaceful, rural scene, with young women and children sitting picnicking on a hillside. Then the frame moves, following their gaze, and down in the valley we see armed men, troops, moving up. The battle sequence begins, far more dramatically effective for the contrast with the peaceful shot which opens it. This sort of dramatic surprise is common in Westerns. From a shot of the villain on horseback making off with the unwilling heroine, the camera suddenly swings, and we see the sheriff and his posse coming up at a gallop on another road.

In Jean-Pierre Melville's film, *Léon Morin, prêtre*, there are two interesting examples. The setting of the film is a French town occupied by German troops. In one scene the heroine is cycling along a road with her little girl. Suddenly she seems agitated, stops and gets off the bicycle, hurries the little girl off the road and, pushing the bike, starts to go through the fields. We wonder what it is all about. Then the camera swings and shows us in long shot a German road-block with troops lounging about. The dramatic effect depends on the fact that at the beginning of the shot the German troops were shut out by the framing. In another scene the heroine has just walked near a level-crossing and turns off on a rough track by the railway line. Suddenly a shout from outside the frame of the picture startles her. She turns and is overshadowed by a German soldier, a menacing figure, who threatens her and points to a notice forbidding civilians to go near the railway. The treatment is different in the two scenes but in both its effect is dependent on framing. In the first the director arouses our curiosity. Something is up, but we cannot tell what, because we are shut in the frame of the picture and cannot see what the heroine sees. Then the camera pans, and the suspense is resolved. (A cruder example of this is when, for example, in a horror film, the 'Thing' from outer space is out of frame, and all we can see is the horror on the faces of the actors.) In the second example, because we are shut in the frame of the picture, we share the shock of the heroine at the sudden voice off. In the first case the heroine knows, we do not; in the second case neither of us knows. (There is a third type of suspense, when we know and the hero or heroine does not – see Chapter Four.) Near the end of *The Red Shoes*, directed by Powell and Pressburger, occurs another good example of dramatic framing. Lermontov, disappointed in his love for Victoria, is leaving Monte Carlo. We see him in a medium long-shot, on the platform wearing dark glasses. He turns towards the camera then stands still in surprise. What is it? The camera tracks back, widening the field of vision, and in close-up in the bottom of the frame the back of a woman's head with a shock of red hair comes into view. It is the red-headed young dancer in love with Lermontov, who cannot let him go without saying good-bye.

A voice off is used in the theatre, and actors can make a dramatic entry from the wings, surprising those on stage at a psychological moment. The difference in the case of the cinema is the flexibility and subtlety of the effects which can be obtained; and as a consequence the fact that the film can flow on, using them far more frequently. It is something like the difference between cutting in the cinema and scene-changing in the theatre. It is as if the whole proscenium arch of the theatre could be moved at will. The cinema too, can combine these dramatic effects with a realism – because it seems to be reproducing the real world – which does not exist in the theatre.

Oblique Framing

Oblique framing is another example of what could, in certain circumstances, be a defect, used for artistic effect. The camera is held at an angle which is transferred to the image when it appears on the screen. In Duvivier's *Un Carnet de bal* the whole sequence of the abortionist doctor in the last stages of disease and degradation is shot at an angle. This oblique framing adds to the sordid horror of the scene, but it is interesting to note that some contemporary audiences thought it was a technical error. There is another example, in Clouzot's *Le Corbeau*: the nurse's flight through the village pursued by the cries of the crowd. Oblique framing transforms the streets into ramps which seem to slow her down and to join in the general hostility by which she feels surrounded.

In Hitchcock's *Notorious*, a series of shots obliquely framed suggest the hangover felt by the heroine (Ingrid Bergman) after a night out. Then she becomes conscious of a policeman waiting at her door, drinks a pick-me-up to sober herself – and the camera regains its correct position. Another example of oblique framing is in Abel Gance's *Cyrano et d'Artagnan*. In the sword-maker's shop, Cyrano has helped himself to a sword being made for Athos, one of the Three Musketeers. The whole scene, shot in oblique framing, indicates the discord between the two men which leads to a duel and a large scale clash with Richelieu's troops. The oblique framing is also arranged to show Athos, a giant of a man, above and leaning over Cyrano, who by this composition is shown as having tremendous odds against him, a forecast of later developments in the film.

Early examples of oblique framing are found in *October*, directed by Eisenstein and Alexandrov in 1928, where they are used to make crowd movements more dynamic. There is one shot depicting Bolshevik civilians, who have just collected their arms, as a human mass leaning forward, seeming to stream downhill and giving an impression of an irresistible river-like force.[1] Other shots, such as that of Lenin addressing a crowd, use the same means to give an urgent feeling of unbalance. Oblique framing is of course a further example of a transference effect. The people are upright and the camera is held askew – and on the screen it looks as if the actors are askew.

Framing and Pictorial Space

A special application of framing occurs in the case of films on art. In the first documentaries on painting, the pictures were presented as we would look at them in a gallery, on the wall, frame and all, as exterior objects. The camera might move in to stress some detail – like a visitor going up to a canvas – but one never forgot the general set-up – a picture of fixed dimension, limited in space and hence an isolated object. But, in about 1947–8, certain documentary film-makers (Luciano Emmer, Enrico Gras, Henri Storck, Alain Resnais, and Gabriel Pommerand) developed a new technique in such films as *Il drammo di Cristo*, *The World of Paul Delvaux*, *Van Gogh*, and *Légende cruelle*. The camera from the start is set right inside the world of the painting, as if it were a real world. It never goes outside the canvas and we never see the frame of the painting. The painting – or paintings – is cut into fragments, which, by rearrangement, contrast, linkage and visual synthesis are built up into a new total effect. Further (a point developed below in the chapters on Time), the spatial relationships of the painting become, in film, relationships in time. The film-maker dissects the painter's work, organized in spatial immobility, and transforms it into a moving temporal unity formed by cutting, montage, and camera movement.

The result of the camera never going outside the painting is that it appears as unbounded in space. This is due to a curious psychological effect. Instead of the spectator's vision being limited by the frame of the painting which he knows is real, it is limited only by a boundary which he regards as conventional

1. Plate 19.

– the edge of the screen. By substituting its own frame for that of the painting, the cinema substitutes *film space* for pictorial space; and by this trick it assimilates pictorial space into the unbounded space of nature which the camera usually shows us. This illustrates the quite arbitrary nature of our concept of space in the cinema.

The problem of the graphic composition of the film image is more than a question of merely framing the picture, but is connected with it, and we may appropriately consider it – very briefly – at this point. In a general way, composition in the cinema will follow similar rules to those of painting or photography, with this difference – that graphic composition in the cinema is basically mobile. Both the movement within each shot, and the movement created by changes from shot to shot, introduce dynamic considerations unknown in a static composition. Thus, ideally, the director should not only achieve proportion and equilibrium in his composition of each shot, but should also ensure the composition which will best suit the relationship between the shots as they follow one another. It is clear in the extreme case of camera movement, that there would be little meaning in trying to compose, or to analyse a camera movement in terms of static composition, since there is an infinite series of framings and reframings, an infinite and everchanging series of compositions. There is always some danger in laying down rigid rules for artistic composition, and here, such is the complexity of the factors (vertical, horizontal, oblique, curved, and straight lines; masses; light and shade; depth; and all these in movement), it would be particularly difficult. It is best to point to the best examples, to the greatest directors (Eisenstein, Renoir, Satyajit Ray, Antonioni), whose films present not merely individual compositions of formal beauty but a flow of images interrelated in terms of composition. Watching their films, we are conscious of a visual rhythm, something apart from the meaning, the drama, the emotional content, the music, and the dialogue – although, because the art of the film is so heavily laden, often submerged by them – which, if we can train ourselves to see it amid the confusion, can give us an aesthetic satisfaction as deep and pure as a great painting or a fine piece of sculpture.

To come back to the main point, it seems as clear from our discussion of cutting, camera movement, framing, as from our discussion of other elements, that the interesting thing about the cinema is not, as is generally thought, the similarity between the image on the screen and the real world; but, on the contrary, the differences between the two. Thanks to these differences the director can freely choose and compose his scene. He can emphasize features which would be lost in nature; he can alter the scale by enlargement or reduction of details so as to enhance their value as visual symbols; he can establish visual relationships which by their novelty will stimulate the audience to see things anew and with deeper meaning – in short, his work can be one of personal interpretation and re-creation. Like any art the cinema is man-made. But unlike most other arts, it combines a high degree of artificiality with a compelling realism. Like other arts, again, it builds on a basis of its techniques, and transforms optical properties into artistic means of expression. As Balazs says: 'The film's inspiration is to be found in its technical possibilities; the muse of the cinema is its apparatus.'

So far as space is concerned, it is clear that film space has a structure and properties which distinguish it radically from physical, sculptural, pictorial, theatrical, or any other kind of space. Film space forms a wholly conventional world of its own. The director completely re-creates the natural world and the spectator regards it as real only by accepting certain conventions. Film space lacks such characteristics of physical space as tangibility, density, weight, expanse, depth, and continuous existence. But on the other hand it affords possibilities which real space does not. The camera can move at any speed in any direction. It can multiply objects, as in the example in Plate 21. It can divide objects and give significance and unity to a small, chosen section of reality. It can analyse space by fragmenting it, then re-forming it into a new whole.[1] The camera can abolish distances, can make objects as large or as small as it likes. It can accentuate, abolish or distort perspective.[2] Finally the camera can control (by setting, by lighting, by camera-angle) forms, volumes, and appearances.

Thus space in the cinema is not an intractable, solid thing, but something almost like a fluid substance, capable of all sorts of changes; something which can be handled on the screen with the same omnipotence as we manipulate physical space in thought, imagination, or in a dream. It displays the features and properties of abstract space and yet at the same time identifies this abstract space with the reality of the world of our senses. This peculiarity of the cinema has certainly had its influence on the other arts – particularly on painting and visual arts. It also coincides with the new ideas about space which contemporary science and its relativity theories have brought into our concept of the universe, and may very well have helped to spread acceptance of these views. The cinema is capable of demonstrating visually what science has proved empirically: that the experience of space we obtain through our senses in everyday life has only an illusory tangibility. This is a point which can be dealt with more fully when we come, in Chapter Five, to deal with space-time in the cinema.

1. This applies particularly to films on art, films on architecture, or to single sequences, built up by montage – a man chopping wood, a crowd, a meeting.

2. An interesting example of distortion is in the war scenes of Truffaut's *Jules et Jim* (1962), in which documentary film taken on the battlefield forty-five years ago is stretched out to CinemaScope width. The figures are dehumanized, the terrain becomes unearthly and, with the grainy texture of the old film, this sequence gives us a unique combination of abstraction and realism, a grim and very telling picture of war.

CHAPTER FOUR

Time in the Cinema: Physical, Psychological, Dramatic

ON the Continent the cinema is sometimes called the seventh art. Canudo, an Italian writing in the twenties,[1] regarded it as a fusion of three arts of space – painting, architecture, and dance – and of three arts of time – music, theatre, and literature. Canudo's proposition has been used to show that film is not an art in its own right; but the argument is not convincing. The cinema is not just the sum of these six arts, but something new and different from them all. Nevertheless the list is useful in illustrating the complexity of the film, and as a brief catalogue of the elements which compose it. Here it is interesting to note that time ranks equally with space in the analysis. Our discussion would be incomplete without considering the different aspects of time in the cinema, the way in which a film modifies the time of the real world, and the importance of time in its dramatic and rhythmical structure.

Here we look at time in the cinema from three aspects: physical, psychological, and dramatic. For the purpose of our analysis we can define them as follows: *Physical time* is the time taken by an action as it is being filmed and as it is being projected on to the screen; *psychological time* is the subjective, emotional impression of duration which the spectator experiences when watching the film; *dramatic time* is the compression of the actual time taken by the events depicted, which occurs when they are made into a film. This division into physical, psychological and dramatic time, suggested by Bela Balazs, is useful and logical. But, as in the case of space, it should be pointed out that the different kinds of time merge into one another and, in the films we see, they all form part of the total

1. Ricciotto Canudo, *L'Usine aux images*, Chiron, Paris, 1927.

effect and operate as a whole. Consequently although it is necessary for analysis, there is a certain artificiality about dividing the concept of time in this way. It follows that, as in the case of space, some of the examples given are suitable as illustrations for more than one point of the argument.[1]

PHYSICAL TIME

A film to all appearances perfectly reproduces the movement of the physical world in its temporal aspect. We see a man walking, a tree waving in the breeze, or a horse jumping, at exactly the same speed on the screen as we would in real life. But the two phenomena are very different. In the cinema a series of still photographs is projected on the screen each of them visible for one forty-eighth of a second. While one photograph is being changed for another the screen is dark for a forty-eighth of a second. Thus, at the normal projection speed of twenty-four frames a second, there are pictures on the screen for half the time and for the other half the screen is dark. Due to the fact that visual impressions on our optic nerve persist for a fraction of a second, we are conscious of the next picture before the impression of the last one has had time to fade.

The illusion of the cinema depends on the imperfection of our senses. Just as our sense of touch cannot distinguish between a grain of powder and a molecule, and our sense of hearing cannot distinguish the individual vibrations of a sound, so our sense of sight cannot discriminate between still photographs following each other at a certain speed, and continuous movement. The reproduction of movement is therefore quite artificial and time can be stood still (by repeating the same still photograph), reversed (by showing the still photographs in the reverse of the natural order), slowed down, or speeded up.

The artificiality of the reproduction of movement in the cinema is illustrated also by the fact that its effect is different on

1. See page 44.

different sizes of screen. For instance large movements will flicker across a very big screen in quite an unreal manner. We may note in passing that the size of the screen has a general psychological effect on the viewer. We cannot get the feeling of being absorbed in the spectacle with too small a screen, even if we sit relatively close to it, and it may quite spoil a film. On the other hand, too large a screen destroys the illusion, because movements have to cover such a great distance in the same time.

Although we now take it for granted, the cinema's reproduction of movement is a remarkable mechanical achievement. At the same time, the important thing about the cinema is not its ability to reproduce movement in time. Many pre-cinematic devices succeeded in doing this. It is rather to have inscribed and fixed time on such a flexible material as film, one which can be technically manipulated so freely, on which different time values can be recorded, and different moments of time isolated and reassembled to form new wholes.

Time Variation within the Shot

Fast or slow motion in a film is as new a phenomenon as the microscope or telescope, and demonstrates in the most forceful way the relativity of time. A speeded-up documentary on plant growth[1] may introduce us to a universe whose rate of movement is fifty thousand times faster than the one we know, a temporal universe as incommensurable with solar time as ultra-microscopic worlds are incommensurable with visible space.

This order of variation is so great as to be of scientific rather than of artistic interest, although it has been used with poetic effect in, for instance, Georges Rouquier's *Farrebique*. But less violent variations in speed can be extremely effective artistically, and it is curious that they are not more often used. The

1. The work of Percy Smith, begun in 1908, on plants and the flight of birds is worth noting.

scale of the image on the screen from long-shot to close-up is constantly varied in every film we see. Why is speed of movement, which is comparable in the dimension of time to scale in the dimension of space, not varied in the same way?

This suggestion was in fact made by Pudovkin (in *Film Technique*) before 1928 in a passage which was quoted by Ernest Lindgren in *The Art of the Film*; Pudovkin describes a sequence of a man scything grass – which he proposed to make for experimental purposes – in which almost every shot reproduced motion at a different speed. Pudovkin goes on to say that the idea proved sound in practice, and in fact he and Dovzhenko use variable motion in several films – *Storm over Asia, Zvenigora, Earth*. But, whatever the reason, both accelerated and slow motion have remained comparatively little used by directors. As a compensation, the fact that they are infrequent at least adds to their impact when they do occur.

Accelerated Motion

Accelerated motion has been occasionally used, from the very earliest films onwards, for comic effect. There are examples in the farces of Mack Sennett, Max Linder, Buster Keaton, Charlie Chaplin, and in the funeral scene of René Clair's *Entr'acte*. We know how often it is used in cartoons. In *Les Casse-Pieds*, a film made in 1949 by Jean Dreville, there is an endless promenade by a bore and his victim with starting, stopping, waiting, mimic explanations, scenes, and invective. Thanks to accelerated motion it becomes a sort of mechanized and comic ballet. This technique is used in a Polish film directed by Andrzej Munk, *Bad Luck*, to make fun of a parade of boy-scouts. Other recent examples are found in Richardson's *Tom Jones*, in a chase scene in Richard Lester's *A Hard Day's Night* and in Louis Malle's *Zazie dans le métro*. Not only is the effect funny in itself but, since accelerated motion is obtained by filming at slower than the normal rate *while the actors move at their normal speed*, the split-second timing on which so much slapstick depends, seems to be achieved at a much faster pace than is really the case. It lends a brilliance to the action which could not be obtained by any other means, or in any other medium.

Accelerated motion is also effective in adventure and action films, to make the action more exciting: the wild, galloping pursuits of cowboys, the tremendous fist fights on the edge of a cliff, the breathtaking chase of the stagecoach by a band of Indians, the thunderous get-away of the gangsters in their car. Some speeded-up sequences of battle charges, or gun or sword-play – Douglas Fairbanks was a master in this vein – have the quality of a ballet. Even in the most serious films, accelerated motion may be used imperceptibly to underline some effect: the movement of a crowd, a battle-charge, or an expression of anger, fear, enthusiasm, or rapture. In Cassavetes's *Shadows*, where the boy suddenly becomes aware of the girl's colour, the whole film suddenly leaps – and the tone changes completely. In *Farrebique*, as well as showing plants growing and blossoming, Rouquier uses the speeded-up shadows of a cart to express the sequence of dawn, noon, and sunset. Arne Sucksdorff, in *The Open Road*, uses close-ups of opening flowers to inter-cut and give poetic tone to shots of gipsy dances. In *Le Tempestaire*, Jean Epstein uses accelerated motion for the movement of clouds at a magician's bidding. Nicole Védrès used it in *Life Begins Tomorrow* to give concrete expression of the quickened pace of time and history in the world of the future.

Slow Motion

Slow motion has been used for dreams, fantasy, and tragedy. Its first dramatic use is said to have been in Claude Autant-Lara's *Faits divers* in 1923. In Dovzhenko's *Zvenigora* there is a beautiful shot of a group of riders cantering lazily on a hot day. In Leni Riefenstahl's *Olympic Games* it is used to give poetry to athletic movement. In *Storm over Asia*, slow motion, as they lift their rifles, conveys the reluctance of a firing-squad to execute a prisoner. In *Finis Terrae*, Jean Epstein wishes to show a man meditating as he sits by the sea eating a crust of bread. An imperceptible slow motion, a slower rhythm in the man's chewing, gives the impression of deep rumination, effective both dramatically and emotionally. In *Le Tempestaire* slow motion is used to exalt the characters and also to stress the tremendous force of waves and storm. Epstein wondered that slow motion was not more used to express tragedy. One can imagine that an abnormally slow movement, merely the opening or shutting of a door, could intensify the grief of a situation. Armand Cauliez writes:

Accelerated motion is comic because the pace overwhelms us, our only recourse is to laugh. Slow motion is tragic because slowing down time makes it interminable, unbearable. The tragic is the absence of any issue: slow motion removes issues, accelerated motion multiplies them.[1]

Slow motion is often used for dream states. In Buñuel's *Los Olvidados* there is a touching sequence of a young boy's dream, in which his mother is kind to him and feeds him as she never has in his waking life. In Cocteau's *Orphée*, when the poet accompanied by the chauffeur, Heurtebise, is going to his rendezvous with death, the grace and slowness of his movements remind us of some ghostly under-water diver. There is the famous dormitory sequence in Vigo's *Zéro de conduite*, with boys in their white nightshirts and the air full of feathers from a pillow fight. They look like angels floating in a heavenly snowstorm.[2] In Jacques Demy's *Lola* there is a charming scene in which a good-natured American sailor takes a little French girl for a ride on a merry-go-round. As they get off, a shot in slow motion perfectly expresses the little girl's mood of dreamy delight. In this case, because of the context, the slow motion has a lyrical rather than a tragic effect. In René Clair's *Un*

1. 'La Clé des films', *Manifeste du cinéisme* (bulletin of the club Cinéisme), 1956.
2. Plate 20.

Chapeau de paille d' Italie a bridegroom at a wedding is worried by a threat that all the furniture in his flat will be thrown out and smashed. We then see furniture coming out of the flat window in slow motion and other furniture being carted away by men in top-hats. The whole sequence is fantasy, but it is the slow motion which most takes the edge off reality and marks the scene as imaginary.

Reverse motion is comparatively rare[1] and too eccentric an effect to be very often appropriate. In the early days it was used plainly, without any pretext, as a magic or comic effect (broken china mending itself, a wall rising out of the dust, a diver springing back out of the water). Eisenstein used it in *October* to show symbolically the restoration of the *ancien régime* – a statue of the Tsar previously smashed to pieces is miraculously restored. In Cocteau's *La Belle et la Bête* it is used on several occasions – when pearls and precious stones come to fill the hands of the Beast; when Beauty passes through the wall of her room using a magic glove; and at the end, when the lovers are drawn up to a fairy paradise. Chaplin uses it as a trick in *Pay Day* to make it seem as though he is catching bricks in impossible positions. It has been used to fake knife-throwing scenes, the knife being pulled out of the wall with an invisible thread, and the shot reversed. A most striking example, in which the whole film is in reverse motion, is Walerian Borow-czyk's *Renaissance*. From chaos and darkness a group of broken objects – a stuffed owl, a euphonium, a hamper, books, a doll, a plate – slowly, slowly reconstitute themselves to the sound of trumpet music. Suddenly at the climax there is a great explosion and chaos again. It is the reverse motion which gives this film its strange, unearthly atmosphere.

1. Currently it is becoming more common for comic effects, for example, in Richard Lester's *The Knack* (1965), in which an egg broken into the pan climbs into its shell again to the dismay of the straw-hatted cook.

Stopped Motion

Stopped motion[1] is again an artificial device and not very frequently used for artistic purposes.[2] However, films often use still photographs for practical purposes: for historical reconstructions (e.g. of Victoriana), and where authenticity is important, staging impossible, and movie material not available (e.g. photographs of the victims for films about concentration camps). Moreover, some films have been deliberately made entirely from still photographs, because they give the finished production a special quality quite different from a moving image: the work of Ray and Charles Eames (*House*, *Parade*, *Death Day*, *Toccata for Toy Trains*) is perhaps the best known. There is an effective comment in still photos on the modern American scene in *Very Nice*, *Very Nice*, directed by Arthur Lipsett for the Canadian National Film Board. A more important example of the technique is in Chris Marker's film *La Jetée*, in which stopped motion grows naturally out of the subject. The film is science fiction and the characters are survivors of an atomic war who try by telepathy to establish contact with the past, to capture 'images' of a lost era, 'moments of time' from a dead world. Consequently, the use of stills, animated only by music and commentary, is both appropriate and telling. In *King and Country* Losey uses stills with grisly effect to show corpses and death.

A distinction must be drawn between the use of still

1. 'Stopped motion' is used here by analogy with accelerated, slow, and reverse motion as a general term to cover the 'freezing' of the action of a moving sequence as well as the use of still photographs. The terms 'stopped motion' or 'stopped-action photography' are used more particularly to refer to a technique of faking in which the camera is stopped to enable a 'magic' transformation to take place; also for animation in puppet films, and for 'pixillated' photographic effects.

2. Since this was written, stopped motion seems to have become more and more common, especially in short films, and is even in danger of becoming a cliché.

photographs, and stopping the action of an otherwise moving sequence by repeating the same frame when editing the film, for the effect of the two is quite different. In a Japanese film, *The Key* or *Odd Obsessions*, Kon Ichikawa introduces his characters very neatly by holding them still for a moment on their first appearance. In Jack Clayton's *The Pumpkin Eater* the freezing of the action is used as a bridge to switch from the past back to the present. There can be a sort of awkwardness about frozen motion which, in the right context, lends itself to comic effects, especially if an actor is held in an unnatural or ridiculous position. There is a striking use of stopped motion for this purpose in a Czechoslovakian film, *Peter and Pavla*, directed by Milos Forman. One character, the father of one of the young people who form the subject of the film, tries to play the heavy parent but his pontificating is frequently spoiled by his complete inability to express himself. A friend who has come to visit his son says, on going, that he has enjoyed himself because 'it's so interesting here'. The father is indignant at this remark – 'It isn't interesting,' he says, 'it's . . .' Then as he tries to think of the right word there is a long frozen motion shot of him with his mouth open. Here the film ends and leaves him trying to think of the right word for the rest of time.

Stopped motion is strikingly used in Marcel Carné's *Les Visiteurs du soir*. Two emissaries from Hell (Gilles and Dominique), whose mission is to part the lovers (Anne and Renaud), watch the couple dancing at a ball to celebrate their engagement. Using their infernal power they make time stand still. The music dies away, the dancers are transfixed in fortuitous attitudes, time and space are frozen. In this interregnum in time, Gilles and Dominique alone continue to act. Each takes their victim by the hand, animates them with a dream life and drags them into the shadows of the park to sow the seeds of estrangement between them. After a time the two couples return to the ballroom, and life starts again, music breaks the silence, space and time unfreeze. The whole thing has happened in the twinkling of an eye.

The sequence gives a concrete manifestation of the poly-valence of time and shows visually its relative, subjective nature. It could be reconciled with the argument of J. W. Dunne's *Experiment with Time*,[1] that there is a series of different times, more than one of which can be experienced if the concentration of our attention on the present is blocked off by sleep. From another point of view, the sequence expresses the intangible – the realm of pure spirit – in a dimension of time. Just as the cinema can express time in terms of space – as we see later – so here the intangible, spiritual world is expressed by means of duration. There is also a suggestion in the sequence that the outer physical world of the senses is an empty, automatic world – the dancers are stopped and restarted like mechanical toys – and it is the inner life which is real.

Montage and Physical Time

With the exceptions we have mentioned (slow, fast, stopped, and reversed motion), the temporal structure of each individual shot is entirely realistic. But it is a very different matter when we come to what André Bazin has called 'the abstract, intellectual imaginary time of montage'. *Within* the shot, time on the screen is, with the exceptions we have discussed, as fixed and unchanging physically as in nature; but from shot to shot, time is completely free. The relationship of one shot to another may be *from* any tense (past, present, or future) *to* any tense (future, present or past). The change may be to another dimension or another universe of time, to the time of a nightmare, a day-dream or a vision, or – as in the example from Carné's film – to the time of Heaven and Hell, to the time of eternity. Or the relationship may not be a time one at all : time may have nothing to do with it. In a sequence showing different aspects of a room, or a woman sewing, or a crowd in the street, or the architecture of a church, it does not matter which shots were taken later and which earlier. And on the screen they

1. Faber, 1939.

are not shown in the same temporal order or arranged on the same temporal pattern; quite other structural considerations – rhythm, contrast, the building up of a pictorial climax, etc. – are the determining ones. When, as in Fritz Lang's *Fury*, we see women gossiping and then hens cackling, the temporal relationship is not significant; the hens are inserted as a metaphor, a symbol. When, in a film on the bombing of London, we see shot after shot of burning buildings, the juxtaposition is for the purpose of repetition, emphasis, crescendo, and time does not come into it. Again, cutting from one shot to another may merely be ellipsis – the leaving out of the unimportant – an essential feature of any art.

The film has often been compared with literature – by Cocteau,[1] by Bresson[2] and by many others; the camera likened, by Astruc, to a pen; and the structure of a film compared with the grammar of writing. The main difference between the two – the fact that literature uses abstract symbols while film consists of concrete images – is discussed in Chapter Nine. Here we are interested in comparing attitudes to time.

Both film and literature, in narration, can deal very freely with time, more freely for instance than the theatre. Both have forms (essay/documentary; text-book/technical film) in which time is largely irrelevant. In story-telling, as Malraux points out in his 'Esquisse d'une psychologie du cinéma,'[3] the cinema started out divided into continuous parts more like the theatre, but developed the flexibility of the novel with the development of cutting. But there is a permanent difference, in that writing has more exact, readier means of pin-pointing, of describing time relationships. '*Before* he came into the room . . . *Since* I have been here . . . *Then*, as a last resort, he went to the police . . .' Film has no words like these; film has no tenses –

1. *Cocteau on the Film*, Dobson, 1954.
2. Quoted in *L'Art du cinéma*, Seghers, Paris, 1960.
3. 'Esquisse d'une psychologie du cinéma', *Éditions de la Nouvelle Revue Française*, Paris, 1945.

past, present, or future. When we watch a film, it is just something that is happening – *now*. We may know that it is the sinking of the *Lusitania* in 1915, but those people struggling in the water, clutching at the hull as the doomed ship sinks, are in a sense drowning before our very eyes.[1] The immediacy of what a film shows us consequently surpasses anything in other arts, and it can have a terseness and a pace that literature cannot match. But there is a real problem of communication. In general, the cinema is enabled to tell a story because there is a convention that – unless there is some indication to the contrary – the order of shots on the screen is the order of events in the story. The same convention may appear to exist in the written word, for example: 'I came, I saw, I conquered'; but this can be regarded as an ellipsis (which, incidentally, enhances the vividness of the writing), with the word 'then' suppressed.

The Flash-Back

'Unless there is some indication to the contrary...': such indications are used to introduce a flash-back and may take many forms. There may be explicit reference in the dialogue: 'Remember darling ...' (in Carné's *Le Jour se lève*) – and we know that the next shot is a reminiscence, not the next event in the story. The dress fashions may indicate an earlier period, as in a flash-back in Bergman's *Wild Strawberries*; we may see a grown-up actor as a boy, as in James Blue's *Les Oliviers de la justice*, or a calendar with a past year. There may merely be a fade-out and -in or a dissolve, instead of the usual straight cut; a momentary soft-focus, distortion effect or swirling camera movement. The sound track may become blurred or use electronic music, or there may be a tune which recalls the past.

Jack Clayton's *The Pumpkin Eater* is a film with almost continuous flash-backs presented with originality and imagination. The film opens to show Jo (Anne Bancroft), looking haggard

1. Plate 22.

and careworn, wandering like a ghost in her fine drawing-room. Then, when she is on the extreme left of the screen, everything gradually fades to dead white except her figure. She turns her head to the blank part of the screen and, as it were, looks back at her past which then gradually materializes on the screen – we see a younger Jo, laughing and attractive, romping with her children. On another occasion, when she is in the present moping and alone, she stops and listens as voices come on the sound track. She is listening to the past which then gradually materializes visually. We have already mentioned the switch in this film from past to present by sudden stopped action. On another occasion, when she is in the present, her husband's hand comes to clasp hers out of the past – for an instant the camera holds the two hands, clasping, one present, one past, and then turns to the past. In another sequence double-exposure is used very effectively for a transition from the past to the present.

The exact structure of a flash-back may not be apparent until it is over. In *Variety*, a convict, aged and bent with long years in prison, comes before the governor for discharge. Then we cut to the story of the film, ending in the climax when the deceived lover (Emil Jannings) kills the unfaithful woman. We then return to the first scene – the convict turns to show us the face of Emil Jannings, grown old and worn, and only then do we realize that the whole film has been a flash-back from the opening sequence. There is a confusing flash-back in two stages in Duvivier's *L'Affaire Mauritzius* in which we cut from an attorney reading a dossier to the interrogation of the accused (Leonard) and then further *back* still to a shot – his explanation in the interrogation – of how he met the victim and gained her sympathy. In a recent Italian film, *L'assassino* by Elio Petri, a young man detained by the police without knowing exactly what he is accused of, goes through a series of 'agonies' represented by flash-backs. These show shady incidents in his life, which he thinks the police may have found out about, and which may be the reason for his detention. We cut straight into these flash-backs without preamble, and in most cases (especially when the pattern is established) the context is enough to make the meaning plain; but there are some confusing, some ambiguous, moments. In an otherwise charming film from Finland, *Darling*, directed by Maunu Kurkvaara, the time arrangement is complex and so little indication of the flash-backs is given that it is difficult to follow the sequence of the story.

We see that, unless they are carefully handled, flash-backs may cause confusion in the audience. There may be similar difficulty in the case of flash-forwards. In a recent film, a young engaged couple are shown window-shopping and the girl sees a wedding dress in a window. Without any preliminary, we cut straight to a shot of the girl in the wedding-dress coming out of church on the arm of her fiancé, who in a fraction of a second has become her husband. This particular shot comes off perfectly with a modern audience but would hardly have been understood twenty years ago.

Marcel Martin in *Le Langage cinématographique* describes a flash-forward in *Le Château de verre*, directed by René Clément. It is of a real, not an imagined event, which takes place *after the end of the film*. The hero and heroine, Rémy and Evelyn, are shown in an hotel room, worried because Evelyn is late for her train. Then comes a shot (a flash-forward) of Evelyn in her coffin after an accident, and another of Rémy hearing the fatal news. The film then comes back to the couple trying vainly to get in time from the hotel to the railway station, and in the end saying good-bye (temporarily, they suppose) at the aerodrome where Evelyn is taking an aeroplane. The flash-forward shot had the effect of turning a happy ending into a tragic one. But its significance for our present discussion is that the meaning was not grasped by the audience, and in the final version of the film the flash-forward shots had to be put in normal time order at the end.

Laslo Benedek's *Death of a Salesman* and Alf Sjöberg's *Miss Julie* are two films in which past, present and future are freely mixed. In the first film, in an atmosphere of hallucination and subjective mental states, Willy Loman is playing cards with his neighbour Charley. Looking at a portrait of his dead brother Ben brings back the past, and Ben appears and interrupts Willy's conversation with Charley without Charley being aware of it. When Charley leaves, Willy joins Ben in the past.

In another sequence Willy Loman is talking to his wife in the kitchen of their house, and asks her a question. She laughs but we hear a louder, more vulgar laugh, and through the door of the kitchen – now open – we see a woman in a hotel bedroom getting dressed. It is this woman who answers his question as Willy walks into the room and – in the past – takes her in his arms. After a brief love scene, he returns to the kitchen and to the present, and we hear his wife answer the question he asked an instant before. The present and the past are shown in the same shot and with the same realism.

In *Miss Julie* the heroine becomes the mistress of her father's valet, Jean. During the night they exchange reminiscences about their childhood. There is a shot of the little boy Jean being chased for stealing apples (past), then the camera pans to grown-up Jean and Julie walking together in the same orchard (present). We see little Jean being whipped (past), then the same shot pans to the assembled servants and ends with a close-up of grown-up Julie's face (present). When Julie drinks to forget the shame of her liaison, and recalls *her* past, we see the little girl Julie and her dead mother (past) in the same shot, and alongside, the grown-up Jean and Julie.[1] Towards morning, when Julie has decided to run away with Jean, and is taking money from a desk, she hears her father come back, and imagines the scandal. We see her in the foreground, while her voice (off) relates what is enacted in the same shot in the background – her father finding the theft, calling the police, and so on. . . .

1. Plate 23.

Here the present appears in the same shot as the future, and a purely imaginary future at that, since she commits suicide to escape her anticipated disgrace.

Because of the subjective atmosphere, the sequences in *Death of a Salesman* are easier to follow and accept. In the case of *Miss Julie* the objective, realistic treatment is perfectly acceptable and clear on second viewing – but there is no doubt that early audiences seeing this film for the first time and without warning, were confused.

There are some sequences in a film, *The Inheritance*, by an Argentine director, Ricardo Alventosa, which illustrate well the cinema's ability to cover different periods of time (and space) with remarkable economy. A respectable middle-class family is dominated by a strong-minded aunt who is very rich and is expected to leave them her money. After her death, three of the characters, on their way to the lawyers to find out about the will, are waiting on the pavement outside a shuttered window when one of them asks how she made her money. Another starts to explain and, as he does so, his lips go dumb, the shutter of the window behind is open, and we see a young woman undressing. As she takes off her last garment an elderly man comes forward and closes the window. The words of the group outside the window (who have never stopped talking) again become audible and we hear, 'Fancy her being able to make so much.' The sequence brings the past vividly into the midst of the present, and visual illustration is substituted for verbal explanation. In the same film, an unromantic little husband comes home and realizes, when he tries the bedroom door, that there is another man with his wife. Because he is impotent, and because by the terms of the will they can only collect the inheritance if his wife has a child, he accepts the situation with patient resignation, goes out and wanders round the town. All the same, he is jealous and, as he is looking into the window of a gunsmith's shop at a display of duelling pistols, we cut suddenly to a shot of his wife's bedroom with his wife and her lover elaborately dressed in eighteenth-century costume, tenderly embracing. Almost immediately they stagger and fall, shot by an unseen hand. In this case we have moved to the time and place of pure imagination and it is in his mind only that the husband has revenged his honour.

The treatment of time in Alain Resnais's films is very striking. In *Hiroshima mon amour* the main story is a brief love-affair between a film star and a Japanese architect; but there is the freest interchange between this and the same girl's experiences – or her memory of them – during the war, when she had a love affair with a German and suffered terribly, as a result, at the hands of her French compatriots. There is so much interchange between past and present that the two are at times almost fused. The script-writer, Marguerite Duras, and the director together succeed in creating in terms of film the philosophical and emotional world of such writers as Marcel Proust or Rainer Maria Rilke.

In *L'Année dernière à Marienbad* time values are intentionally left completely vague. Robbe-Grillet, the scenario-writer, suggests that the cinema is 'the pre-ordained means of expression for a story of this kind'. He sees Alain Resnais's work as an attempt to get away from the linear plots of old-fashioned cinema which are content to reproduce the continuous sequence of real events. In opposition to such conventional films Resnais aims to construct a purely mental time and space and to follow the mind which goes faster, or slower, than reality – dodges, skips, doubles back, lingers, repeats, and creates imaginary scenes, parallels and possibilities. It is only necessary to think of *Marienbad* to appreciate how exactly this applies.

One would agree that reproduction of every detail of ordinary actions would be intolerably dull, and all films modify reality to some extent. The question is: how far can modification be taken? *L'Année dernière à Marienbad* goes further and succeeds better in enabling the spectator 'to come to terms directly with subjectivities', than anybody might have thought possible before it was made. One might also say this film constructs a poetic as well as a mental time and space, and is virtually the first film conceived as a poem, that is, in which the traditional dramatic construction is replaced by non-narrative construction.

The total effect of *Marienbad* is probably more acceptable than, for instance, the shot discussed above in René Clément's *Le Château de verre* for the reason that a single daring experiment, set in a film otherwise in an established idiom, is more likely to be misunderstood than if the whole film is strikingly, fundamentally, continuously, and totally revolutionary in its style. As E. H. Gombrich writes in *Art and Illusion*: 'A style sets up a horizon of expectation, a mental set, which registers deviation and modification with exaggerated intensity.' Robbe-Grillet himself says about *Marienbad* that what most puzzled audiences – the man's claim to have met the girl before – was intended partly as an excuse to strike up acquaintance. 'I feel sure we've met before somewhere' is almost a standard approach to a pretty girl. There is also the suggestion that they are soul-mates, and also the intimation that the meeting has already taken place, merely in the sense of being pre-ordained. If this feature of the film is understood, the rest is not so difficult. The action moves steadily towards the crisis of the woman's surrender to her wooer, and ends when she goes away with him.

Resnais's films correspond with a view of time suggested in these chapters, and constitute a vindication of the cinema's natural freedom in temporal construction. It is apparent that the lack of time prepositions and conjunctions, tenses and other indications may be an advantage as well as a drawback and can leave the film free to reach the spectator with an immediacy which literature is unable to match. It can also make for speed and economy in a narrative. We see too that the problem of communication between the artist and his audience is not a simple one: it depends on what is to be communicated. Difficulty in communication, demanding an effort to follow on the part of the audience may not be due to any fault or perversity on the part of the film-maker, but rather to the fact that he is trying to communicate something deeper and more profound. Referring to another medium. Browning wrote of 'Feelings that broke through language and escaped.'

We have said (on page 70) that cutting may be an ellipsis leaving out the unimportant. What is left out may be time as well as space. When we cut from a shot of a woman dressing to go out to a shot of her dancing with a young man at a ball, a good deal of time as well as space has been eliminated compared with the physical reality – although not necessarily compared with subjective reality. Camera movement also, though not quite in the same way, may be thought of as abbreviating time and space. We talk of the speed of an aeroplane annihilating time and space, and fast camera movement will do something similar. When the camera moves at a moderate pace, the intervening space and the time of its movement will have the same value as they do in everyday life. But the faster the camera moves the more it compresses the intervening space and shortens the time, until with the fastest movement (zip-pan and zoom) we approach annihilation of space and time. All this goes to show again that time and space in the cinema are not corporeal but mental coordinates having an illusory physical appearance.

To summarize the argument of this section: we have said that the cinema can repeat, prolong, abbreviate, or reverse the events on the screen. Past, present, and future time can be mixed in any order. A film breaks up the continuity of time in the real world, and out of the physical time of reality creates an abstract *film time*. Again, a central theme is demonstrated: the cinema's inability to express time may be an artistic advantage.

PSYCHOLOGICAL TIME

We have seen in the discussion so far that the cinema can either imitate exactly the time of the physical world, or can modify it radically. By modifying it, the cinema can, as Robbe-Grillet suggests, assemble on the screen, by various means, but principally by montage, something more like the time of our mental than our physical life – a mixture of future, past, and present, passing over some events in a flash, dwelling on others, returning to others. Something less continuous, less predictable, less inflexible than the time of the physical world.

We have included this roving of the mind under physical time because although a psychological phenomenon, it is one which the cinema can manifest physically on the screen. And we have reserved the term 'psychological time' for another mental phenomenon – our subjective sense of duration. Most of our knowledge of the universe comes, in one way or another, through our senses; but our knowledge of duration seems innate. We are still conscious of the passage of time even when we are alone in dark and silence, and virtually without any tactile sensations.

Our feeling of duration may be connected with subconscious awareness of bodily rhythms – heart-beat, pulse, breathing. Over longer periods, our feeling of time may be connected in some way with the knowledge of our own age and expectation of life. Perhaps it is significant that our feeling for rhythm and tempo, which is related to our sense of time, is also something innate and dependent on recurrent bodily rhythms.

Being subjective, our sense of duration varies considerably in comparison with clock time. If we are preoccupied and happy, 'time goes quickly'. If we are bored, idle, and unhappy, 'time hangs on our hands'. If we are looking forward to some future event, whether with apprehension or with impatience and longing, that is, if we are in *suspense*, time will 'go slowly'.

Variation is even more pronounced in abnormal states such as dreaming, fantasy, madness, or on the borders of sleep or unconsciousness.

In the real world, our mental state determines the way time goes. In the cinema, it is the other way round: the way time goes on the screen will affect our mental state. By making time go quickly – using quick cutting, loud or lively music, dynamic composition of the images, and rapid action (comic or thrilling) – the film-maker can induce in the audience moods of exhilaration and laughter for a comedy, excitement for an adventure film, horror and dismay for a tragedy. By making time go slowly – depicting quiet uneventful scenes, using soft, soothing music, static composition of images and slow cutting – he can induce moods of lyricism, contentment, sadness, nostalgia, or grief; the exact mood evoked will depend largely on the context and nature of the film.

Suspense

Our sense of duration is affected in a special way when we are held in suspense by a work of art. Suspense does not follow the general rule given above, for although time goes slowly, unbearably slowly, we are still highly excited – held and absorbed by the tension of the situation. Suspense consists in delaying the resolution of a situation so as to arouse and maintain the spectator's interest, and it is something common to all the narrative arts. It will be useful to quote a classical example from Scott's *Ivanhoe* which illustrates very clearly the use of long-drawn-out suspense.

In Chapter 22 of *Ivanhoe* the wicked Norman, Front-de-Boeuf, is about to torture the Jew, Isaac, in the dungeon of his castle when he is interrupted by 'the sound of a bugle, twice winded without the castle'. In Chapter 23, instead of telling us who blew the bugle and why, we go to another part of the castle where De Bracy (another wicked Norman) is trying to

seduce Lady Rowena, a beautiful Saxon – until he also is interrupted by 'the horn, hoarse-winded and blowing far and keen'.
One might think that Chapter 24 would bring us to the bugle
and its blower but, again, we move to another room in the
castle where Brian de Bois-Guilbert (*another* wicked Norman)
is making advances to Isaac's daughter Rebecca, a beautiful
Jewess. He also has to break off at the end of the chapter because, as he says, 'that bugle-sound announces something...'
Not until Chapter 25 do we discover the true role of the bugle
first mentioned in Chapter 22 which is, of course, to bring help
to Isaac, Rowena, and Rebecca. Scott could very well have
left all mention of the bugle until Chapter 25 but by bringing
it in earlier, he creates a situation which requires resolution,
and retains the reader's interest.

Another literary device is to end a chapter at a crucial point
and carry on in the next chapter with another part of the story
as, for example, in Charles Morgan's *Sparkenbroke*. This device
is very similar to the parallel cutting of the cinema which
takes us from the heroine in the hands of the thugs to the hero
trying to get the police to take up the chase. Suspense may consist in withholding something (in a detective story the identity
of the murderer) from the reader or the audience; or it may
consist in withholding something from one of the characters
in the film – *we* see the policeman ready with a big stick but
Charlie Chaplin does not, and we wait with bated breath for
him to get beaten.[1] In Hitchcock's *The Secret Agent* two British
spies are waiting to meet another agent in a Swiss church. There
is an organist playing somewhere in the background. Gradually
the audience realizes (long before the characters in the film do)
that there is something wrong – that the organ is playing one
long-drawn-out, unchanging note, that the organist must be
dead. We have given other examples of suspense in Chapter
Three which depend on framing. It should be pointed out that

1. Plate 24.

these examples involve a time as well as a space element and are relevant here also.

Our subjective sense of duration is partly a relative matter. A flurry of quick cutting, of violent action, of loud music or noise will be all the more effective if it comes after a slow, quiet sequence and acts with a sudden shock. Slow cutting needs some variation to relieve it. Our sense of time will also be affected by camera movement and not only by the absolute rate of movement, but by a change in the rate and whether it is accelerating or decelerating. Generally, camera movements are held rigidly to a steady rate and there is something emotionally satisfying about this. But there seems no reason why the camera should not excite us by getting faster in its movements or soothe us by gradually slowing down. The same applies to cutting – the psychological effect of a sequence in which each shot is shorter than the last (*accelerando*) is more exciting than a whole string of short shots. Our sense of the duration of each shot will also depend on its dramatic content, its scale, its emotional significance, and the complexity of its composition; and all these will have a relative as well as an absolute value.

The objection may be made that, as the audience is mostly unconscious of shot-change, it will be unconscious of the duration of shots, and the intended effect will be lost. But the fact that they are not conscious of the duration of shots does not matter. Subconscious reactions may be just as important, if not more important, than those the audience is aware of. There are many effects in art which are appreciated without the audience being consciously aware of them – the rhythm of a poem, the balance of a painting and so on. There is indeed something in the view that analysis spoils a work of art, something in the complaints that enjoyment of Shakespeare is spoiled by studying his plays at school. Analysis which leads to better understanding will in the long run increase appreciation and hence enjoyment, but at the time, in respect of the particular thing being analysed, it will tend to limit emotional participation, because of the concentration on reasoning which is necessary. Several film examples discussed here are from sequences which are erotic in their effect when seen in the cinema – but they lose their eroticism under analysis.

Rhythm and Tempo

Our mental sense of the passage of time can be affected by the rhythm of any work of art in which time is an integral element – music, dance, poetry, drama, film. But rhythm exists also in static arts – painting, sculpture, and architecture. It is a different rhythm in a way, but there are affinities – certainly movement and time are concerned. For, although a statue or picture does not move, we who look at it do not grasp it all in one moment. We take time to explore it, to move round it, or around inside it – movements which may be merely sub-conscious or imaginary, but can also be the actual movements of the eye. If the building does not move, *we* move – mentally if not physically – when looking at it.

The remarkable thing about film is that it works in both space and time, and combines static and dynamic rhythms. As Léon Moussinac[1] says:

If the cinema, a plastic art, hence an art of space, derives part of its beauty from the form of its images . . . it is also an art of time depending on succession, and the rest of its beauty depends on the duration and relationship of its images.

It is the relationship aspect which should be predominant. Each shot should augment and complete the previous shot and is useful only for its contribution to the total effect. The fact that a film is necessarily a dynamic construction, of forms and movements in a constant state of *becoming*, prevents the direc-tor from conceiving his shots statically for their isolated formal

1. 'Le Rythme Cinématographique', *Le Crapouillot, Cinéma*, 1923.

or dramatic content. Every shot should be seen in the perspective of a constant development of images, sensations, emotions, and rhythms. Here we have approached from the time aspect the same problem which we considered earlier from the space aspect (see Chapter Three, p. 87).

As in other arts, rhythm in film is a matter of relationships: proportions, and equilibrium. In a very general way rhythm will grow out of the content of a film. The duration of shots for instance, will depend on their visual and dramatic content.[1] A simple image needs less time to grasp than a complex one; a close-up less than a long shot; a fixed frame less than a moving frame; a strongly dramatic image less than a neutral one; a shot in strong contrast with the previous one less than one similar to it. But these are only very general guiding principles – a vast amount remains to be decided by personal intuition. In a film the number of rhythmical elements is very large. Quite apart from music, dialogue, natural sound, colour, all of which may have rhythms of their own, there is the composition of lines, masses, light, and shade, the movement of persons, objects, and light, the movement of forms caused by shot-change or by camera movements, the duration and relationship of shots, the rhythm of the narrative, and variations in dramatic intensity. As Eisenstein pointed out, each of these elements will form both a 'melodic line' of its own, and also be related simultaneously in harmony or discord with all the others. One could compare film to a piece of counterpoint containing a dozen or more 'voices', all on different instruments. René Clair distinguished three factors which, he said, would make the metre of shots as strict as that of Latin verse: the length of each shot, the alternation of scenes, and the movement within each shot. But he saw at once that none of these factors was capable of definition or measurement, and that it was impossible to lay down laws. Film rhythm could not be

1. Shot duration – time – is therefore affected by spatial considerations, another interrelationship of time and space.

achieved by reason; it was a matter of sensibility, flair, and taste. 'I am resigned', he concluded, 'to find neither rules nor logic in this world of images. The primitive wonder of this art enchants me.'[1]

The complexity of elements in a film is both an advantage and a handicap. The cinema's richness may make other art forms seem poverty-stricken, and the variety of its forms, the range of its styles, the multitude of its subjects, while they are something of which the average cinema-goer is generally un-aware, are a delight to those who are lucky enough to have access to them. But the film's complexity makes it (paradoxically, in view of its origin and growth as a popular art) one of the most difficult of all arts both to practise and to appreciate. We have already mentioned the viewer's difficulty in distinguishing the pure rhythm of movement amid the welter of other elements. It is just as difficult for the film-maker to control every element and achieve perfection in each. This is why simplicity, spareness, austerity, can be such virtues in film – the music should not be as rich as in a symphony, the dialogue not so copious as in a play, the visual composition not so subtle as in a painting, the plot not so involved as in a novel, the acting plainer than on the stage.

The rhythm and tempo of a film should be appropriate to its subject and to the audience. The rhythm of a teaching, a demonstration or a reportage film will follow its objective reasoning, and be such as to make the meaning plain before anything else. A fictional film, however, will follow an emotional pattern and a dramatic rhythm to suit the action. What matters in both cases is that the spectator should accept the film with his head or his heart, and that its rhythms should be effective and appropriate. *Lord of the Flies*, directed by Peter Brook, is a film which attempted strong rhythmic effects which were sometimes successful – the first appearance of the 'hunters' dressed in long cloaks and marching along the beach

1. René Clair, 'Rythme', in 'Les Cahiers du mois', *Cinéma*, 1925.

chanting *Kyrie eleison*, or the slow pan upwards from the feet of the rescuing naval officer – but at other times failed. One reviewer wrote that the film was 'too slow in the establishing shots, too flurried with action shots.'

The problem of rhythm in montage is seen from this angle[1] by J. P. Chartier,[2] who agrees that objective rules cannot be laid down. He describes various stages in the spectator's perception of each shot. Each shot is first identified and mentally related to what precedes it; then comes a period of maximum attention in which its full significance is appreciated; then attention flags, and becomes impatience and boredom if the shot is prolonged. If each shot is cut exactly when the viewer has had enough of it, his attention will be held continuously, and the film will have a satisfying rhythm. Thus, rhythm is not to be achieved by fixing a certain time relationship between the shots (although such relationships may emerge), but by ensuring coincidence of shot length with the attention it provokes and satisfies. It is a rhythm of attention rather than an abstract, temporal rhythm.

The psychology of an audience will differ from country to country and from generation to generation. Psychological rhythm is slower in Scandinavian and Germanic countries than in Latin and Anglo-Saxon ones. Consequently Swedish and German films often seem heavy and turgid to us. Russian films have been made with a special rhythm for certain provinces or for *moujik* audiences. The rhythm of Satyajit Ray's Indian films seems slow to Western audiences. Present-day audiences dislike silent films, not only because they are old-fashioned and the lack of dialogue makes them incomprehensible, but because their rhythm seems wrong. On the other hand, the pace of present-day films, American cartoons for

1. i.e. as a matter of relationships.
2. 'Films à la première personne', *Revue du cinéma*, No. 4, January 1947.

instance, is so fast that some spectators are unable to follow them.

DRAMATIC TIME

For thousands of years the tragedies and dramas of the real world have been re-enacted for the edification or entertainment of an audience. In the most primitive of these representations, dramatic time was very little different from the time which the events themselves would have taken in actuality. The interminable length of medieval mysteries indicates the difficulty which writers of the period had in altering the time scale. A drama which did not take virtually as long as the events it depicted would not have commanded the spectator's belief or attention.

In more sophisticated drama, some *condensation* of the time of actual events became permissible. According to one of the three dramatic unities, laid down in classical times and respected by classical dramatists of the seventeenth and eighteenth centuries (but not by Shakespeare), twenty-four hours was the maximum period which could be compressed into the three or four hours which a play lasted. Nowadays, the dramatist is entirely free and we have plays depicting different generations, or the life of a man from the cradle to the grave shown in a series of episodes.

The cinema has descended from modern, not medieval, drama and only a handful of films have tried to keep exactly the same time scale as reality: Hitchcock's *Rope*, Wise's *The Set-Up*, Zinnemann's *High Noon*, and recently Agnès Varda's *Cléo de 5 à 7*.[1] *Rope* is a curiosity – a film using camera movement exclusively and without a single cut from beginning to end. In fact it cheats and there are breaks caused by the camera moving to a dark surface and the screen blacking-out. In *The Set-Up*

1. Plate 25.

and *High Noon*, the fact that the events of the film take just an hour and a half is indicated by including shots of clocks which show the time. But these films cheat too and include a mass of incident occurring *in different places to different people* during this time which (if laid end to end) would in reality take far longer. In other words, space has been substituted for time. But these films remain an exception, and most films either condense or expand the time of everyday life.

Yet although the film director has freedom to deal with time as he likes, an attempt to distil too great a time period into a film can cause a loss of dramatic power. In Griffith's film *Intolerance* for instance, which ranges over the whole of history from the Babylonian empire to the present day, the various episodes never really form a single unity and the film is not as dramatically effective as the same director's *Birth of a Nation*, which covers the few years of the American Civil War. Preminger's *Exodus* would have been a better film if it had not tried to combine two entirely separate sections – one in Cyprus, the other in Israel.

In the case of a film whose story is in two widely separated parts, unity of time (and place) can to some extent be preserved by means of a flash-back. Instead of showing the beginning and then the end ten or twenty years later, the film can start with the second period, flash back to the first period, then return and finish in the second period. Thus the main containing action forms a unity based on the present, which covers only a short time span, the structure is more symmetrical, and the flash-back to past time is relegated to a subordinate role. There are innumerable examples – *Le Jour se lève*, *Le Diable au corps*, *The Lost Weekend*, *Citizen Kane*, *Hiroshima mon amour*, and so on. In some cases the present is limited to a few minutes at the beginning and end of the film, the whole of the story being set in the past, for example *Variety*, or *Le Crime de Monsieur Lange*. In this case, it is perhaps preferable to regard the opening and closing sequences as forming a prologue and epilogue to the main part of the film (a structure similar to Shakespeare's *The Taming of the Shrew*) rather than to regard the body of the film as a flash-back. Similar are films in which a series of short episodes is held together by some unifying device: men in a club swapping (Somerset Maugham's) yarns as in *Quartet*;[1] stories from books in an old book-shop (Alessandro Blasetti's *Altri tempi*); a woman visiting the men she danced with at her first ball (*Un Carnet de bal*).

We have already mentioned that cutting from shot to shot may be a means of shortening time and leaving out the inessential. Because a film is composed of hundreds of bits of time joined together, it can effect this condensation of time continuously from beginning to the end of the film. The theatre has steadily grown more flexible in this respect by abandoning elaborate stage settings, and allowing changes of place or time to be represented by moving a spotlight from one side of the stage to another, or by changing a cardboard tree for a cardboard street-lamp, and so making it possible to have far more changes of scene. But the theatre is still not so flexible as the cinema.

How much can be left out, how quickly the narrative can proceed, is something which the director must have continually in mind. If too much is left out, the sequence of events may be difficult to follow. As in the case of space, more can be left out between sequences than within the same sequence, and the various transition devices which have already been discussed (in Chapter Three, pages 65–9) just as they carry the spectator over a change of place, will carry him over a change of time.

Two unorthodox time transitions in John Schlesinger's first feature film *A Kind of Loving* are fitting examples. There is a long sequence in which the young man persuades his girl to make love to him. It ends on a quiet, a curiously quiet, note,

1. Directors: Arnakin, Crabtree, French and Smart.

both of them inwardly still. . . . Then suddenly by a straight cut we go with a bang into a raucous, violent dance scene – the band playing as loudly as possible, the girl being manhandled by a clumsy oaf of a partner. It is about a month later and the girl is worried that she is going to have a baby. The transition is very successful, no doubt because of the strong contrast in tone from *pianissimo* to *fortissimo*. Later in the film we see the same couple on their honeymoon. The camera (long-shot) is looking out from the hotel bedroom at them on the beach at dusk, as they turn to come to the hotel. Before this shot quite ends *we hear their voices in the hotel bedroom* in low intimate tones, and only then does the camera pull back and pan over to the couple lying in bed. This transition, achieved in a single shot, is a striking illustration of the cinema's ability to telescope time. Again, in Terence Young's *Dr No*, time is neatly telescoped in the following sequence. A beautiful spy plans to decoy James Bond by asking him up to her bungalow in the hills. She rings him up and as she gives him directions over the telephone we dissolve to Bond actually in his car driving and obviously following the directions which her voice goes on giving. . . .

Instead of condensation from real time to dramatic time there will sometimes be expansion. This can take two forms: either the film concentrates on a particular occurrence, repeats it, gives different aspects of it, stretches it out; or else there may be inserted a sequence which in thought takes place in a flash but in the film takes many minutes. An example of the first occurs in Michael Curtis's film *The Charge of the Light Brigade*, in which the famous charge lasts more than ten minutes, although in reality the horses had to gallop less than two miles.

An example of the second from *Death of a Salesman* has already been quoted. In the fraction of a second between Willy asking his wife a question and her answering it, he thinks of an affair with another woman; in the film the time is expanded to allow the love scene with the other woman to be played out.

There is an experimental film *The Last Moment* by Paul Fejos which opens with a figure struggling in the water and a hand reaching up. The film follows the chief character's boyhood, youth, first love-affair, war service, unhappy love-affair, decision to commit suicide. Then the opening sequence is repeated, the hand gradually sinks into the water and the film ends. Two films of this kind have been made from an identical Ambrose Bierce story: *The Spy* by Charles Vidor (1932) and *Incident at Owl Creek* by Robert Enrico (1961). A man is being hung under martial law during the American Civil War. The hanging takes place on a bridge and, as he drops, the rope breaks, he plunges into the stream, and by swimming under water, escapes. There is a long sequence of him making his way through the forest to his wife and home – then suddenly we are back at the bridge, the body dangling at the end of the rope. The main part of the film has occurred during the fraction of a second of his fall – a flash of wish-fulfilling thought.

This is a suitable point to consider the length of films. Bela Balazs held that films in practice could not last longer than an hour and a half because for physiological reasons the viewer could not watch for longer than this. 'This predetermined length', he wrote, 'is itself a style which the artist must master.' If ten thousand feet was the limit of length when Balazs wrote, it is certainly not so now, and the number of long films, two hours, two and a half hours and more, is sufficient to show that the spectator's physiology is no bar. Tyranny of length arises rather from commercial considerations and films are still cut down or stretched out to fit into programmes. Buñuel's son said of his father's latest film, *The Exterminating Angel*, that it was slightly too short for commercial exhibition, so he simply repeated a sequence at the beginning! The guests come into the hall of the house, mill around for a moment or two looking for the servants (who have gone) and then go up the grand staircase. Then the whole thing is repeated. Certainly it is an odd repetition without any clear symbolic meaning (as there is in other parts of the film) so the explanation given may be correct. Balazs is right in counting length as part of the style. It should be part of the total conception of the film and will largely depend on the content – what the artist has to say. Because of the pattern of commercial exhibition the most neglected form in the cinema is the short-story film and many short-story ideas are padded out to feature length. Short documentary films are not much seen in cinemas, either, but at least they flourish in other spheres – it is for the short fiction film that there is least place. Perhaps television will provide a medium, as it already has provided a medium for a great many documentary and cartoon films.

CHAPTER FIVE

Space-Time In The Cinema

HAVING for convenience of analysis discussed space and time separately, it remains to restore their fundamental unity and consider them together as cinematographic space-time. The space-time of the physical world forms a four-dimensional continuum in which all our sensory experience takes place. The space-time of the cinema is likewise composed of the same four dimensions and within them the film world, its people and events live and move and have their being. To this extent they seem to be the same. But we already know how different the components of the two worlds are. There are the same fundamental differences between film and reality when it is a question of space-time, as there are in the case of space and time separately. The differences can most conveniently be considered under two heads – within the shot and between shots. Under the first head the significance of cinematographic movement is considered, and the movement of the cinema compared with the immobility of the static arts. Under the second head the essential nature of montage is discussed.

SPACE-TIME AND CINEMATOGRAPHIC MOVEMENT

All movement in reality has space and time dimensions. However, in ordinary life, if the space dimension is comparatively very small, for instance in the growth of a plant, we think of it as something occurring in time only. Conversely, in the everyday world a rifle shot is just movement in space – the time it takes is infinitesimal and we disregard it.

Movement in reality is continuous but movement on the screen is discontinuous and is achieved by showing very quickly a series of still photographs. Because film movement is artificial in this respect, the dimensions of space and time can be manipulated (by slow and accelerated motion) in ways not possible in reality and so as to create new worlds of experience. In the case of a plant growing, the cinema, by increasing the relative value of the space dimension, shows us that this is movement in space as well as time. In the case of the rifle shot, the cinema, by increasing the time dimension relatively to that of space, can show the bullet moving slowly in time.[1] Slow and accelerated motion discussed in Chapter Four under time, thus have a bearing on space as well.

Of course, in these two cases both the time and space dimensions exist so far as science is concerned, and it is interesting to note that the cinema can demonstrate visually what science has discovered empirically or theoretically. We can say that a film, by varying the time dimension, in the one case substitutes space for time and in the other substitutes time for space, and thus the cinema is able to demonstrate that space and time alike are dimensions of the same continuum.

All movement has space and time dimensions, but what if there is no movement? This is a theoretical extreme in which the time dimension is infinity and the space dimension zero, and it gives us a new way of looking at the static arts. For they approach, at least, a state of perpetual immobility and their value in human eyes depends to some extent on this quality. They are immortal, eternal, unchanging. 'Forever wilt thou love and she be fair' wrote Keats of figures on a Grecian urn. Because of the sharp contrast with movement, this quality of 'frozen harmony' can be well appreciated in a still image suddenly occurring in the middle of a film.

Static Arts and Cinema

Because of their durability, sculpture and painting have been used from the earliest days for commemoration and for rep-

1. Plate 26.

resenting the immortality of gods. The Egyptian painter was referred to as 'one who keeps alive'. The Renaissance artist, commissioned to paint a crucifixion, put a portrait of his patron at the foot of the cross. However, since its invention in the last century, photography (the snapshot, the studio portrait) has largely replaced painting as a means of perpetuating the memory of the past.[1] There were several reasons for this: photography was cheaper than painting, it required less skill to get a likeness, and (human fallibility being more or less eliminated) it had greater authenticity. Painting, relieved of the need to provide an exact likeness of reality, has been set free to indulge in the abstractions and experiments of the last seventy years – expressionism, surrealism, cubism, and the rest.

It is worth noting that the cinema can go further than the photograph in preserving the past, for, although it presents a moving image, it is one which can be perpetually preserved and renewed. A film can perpetuate not only an instant but a period of time. Eight-millimetre home movies rival the holiday snapshot. Films of important people and events are an established part of historical record.

The advantage of being able to fix a period rather than a moment of time – or to make a durable record of movement – seems to have been appreciated millions of years ago, and throughout its long history static art has tried to imitate movement. Recent research, by filming and animating successive cave drawings of bison, has shown that put together they represent a continuous movement. The same technique applied to a Greek vase shows us an acrobat doing a somersault – a moving picture created over two thousand years ago! Then there are medieval and Renaissance paintings showing successive incidents in the life of a saint on the same canvas, paintings in series, (Hogarth's *Rake's Progress*), sporting prints of a day's hunt, and strip cartoons. An interesting experiment is Giacomo Balla's futurist painting *Dynamism of a Dog on Leash*,[2]

1. Plate 27.   2. Plate 28.

showing a woman taking a toy dog for a walk, a painting which may well have been influenced by the cinema.

This reaching out of static art for movement cannot in the nature of things be successful and in a sense it is not intended to be. Besides the advantage of being able to contemplate it at leisure and come back to it, the still image has a particular flavour of its own, which may even lead to its being used from choice in the cinema itself, as illustrated in the section on stopped action.

We see then that, even within the single shot, the space-time of the cinema is different from that of reality. It introduces us to a different world which may range from the immobility of the still image to accelerated motion as fast as the eye can follow. A world too which can vary the space-time dimensions of the real world for its own purposes.

SPACE-TIME AND MONTAGE

The differences from reality which occur within the shot illustrate the subjective nature of space-time in the cinema, but they are of less importance aesthetically than the differences which occur when switching from shot to shot. Here we are dealing with the predominant and characteristic technique of the cinema – montage.

In the ordinary world of experience every event occurs in a framework that is homogeneous, continuous, and irreversible. For example, if from his window a person sees two men talking in the street and wants to go near so that he can hear what they say or see who they are, he can walk outside and go up to them, but he cannot do so instantaneously. He has to go through the door, down the steps, across the street. He has to move through the space that physically separates him from them. He is dealing with concrete space. It is the same in the case of time. He cannot see what the men will be doing ten minutes later. He has to wait for the full ten minutes to pass.

In the cinema it is very different. Space and time can be divided, expanded, contracted. Scenes from different times and places can be brought together, distances abolished and time abbreviated, without the spectator being in the least disturbed. The observer mentioned above who is looking through the window, can be with the two men in the street in an instant. In the same instant he can be in Paris or Pekin. The film audience can see a figure in the distance and then close to, they can jump from one day to the next, see what happened yesterday then tomorrow. They may even be shown, in the same sequence, shots which, on the face of it, have no determined space-time unity whatsoever. The silent cinema would frequently use this method, depicting a spring morning, for instance, by a succession of images that showed: the sun rising over the trees; birds singing in a wood; a flower opening; a young woman pushing up her bedroom window with a smile at the new day. In a dramatic film the action can be split up, one occurrence alternated with one or more other events, or with past or future happenings. To do all this it is only necessary to join one piece of film to another. Thus unlike the physical world the cinema allows breaks in the continuity of space and time which give it an abstract character suitable for artistic creation.

There are limits to the liberty of montage. Complete freedom would result in chaos. It all depends on the film and what it shows. In normal movement from one point in a set to another, when both are visible on the screen, the whole action has to be shown. A sudden jump say from the door to the window would give a comic or a miraculous effect. No spatial abstraction is possible, and it is the same with time. The actor must be allowed the same time to go from door to window as he would take in reality. Likewise, in an ordinary film, montage does not make it possible to show realistically an identical action twice in successive shots. If a film were to show a man drawing a gun, once in medium shot and a second time in close-up, it would seem absurd to the audience.

Thus there are rules which limit the freedom of montage, but they will differ from one picture to another depending on the 'convention of reality' determined by the subject and style of the film. As, in mathematics, the nature of a theorem will depend on the initial axioms laid down, so, in a film, will the freedom with which space-time can be treated. For instance in a didactic film the abstract logic of the argument will determine the arrangement of shots and the space-time continuity of the film. As long as the argument justifies it, space and time can be split up without losing verisimilitude. To show that early training may inculcate militarism a shot of boys playing soldiers can be shown next to a battle scene. In the two shots, space and time are independent and the scenes are joined by a conceptual link. In a fiction film another convention of reality is adopted and the continuity is a dramatic and psychological one. Such a film can perfectly well show, in a few seconds, a man ringing a bell, a woman in a sitting-room who hears the bell, a servant going to open the door, and the man going into the house. This sequence is quite unlike any series of events which one human being could experience in the space-time of the physical world, but it follows a psychological continuity, a psychological reality, and it appears physically possible because there is a dramatic unity which justifies the splitting up of space and time. Finally, a third example. In a dream sequence or in a film whose whole action is subjective, reality becomes entirely mental and abstract. Space-time continuity can then be completely different from physical reality. A character in the film can move in a flash from one place to another, or one gesture can be endlessly repeated.

This diversity in the nature of cinematographic space-time is consistent with the rich and varied endowment of the cinema. In the first place a film is a form of expression both physical and mental. In the second place the cinema can represent equally well many different modes of experience –

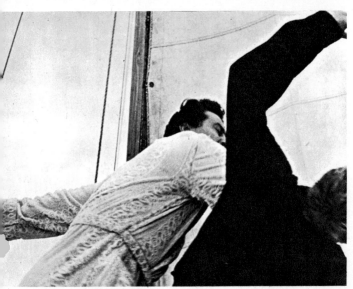

1. In a film, duelling, gunplay, or fist-fighting can take on the quality of a ballet (p. 17). (*Knife in the Water*)

2. Flaherty's films stem from direct contact with a way of life (p. 25). (*Nanook of the North*)

3. Film production is one of our heavy industries (p. 25). (*The Diary of Anne Frank*)

4. The first film-makers were content to register mechanically the actual world (p. 33). (*Peek Frean Biscuit Factory*, 1906)

5. The fantastic imagination of Méliès (p. 34). (*The Magic Head*, 1905)

6. The director may include human beings to give a relative scale of size (p. 39). (*Scott of the Antarctic*)

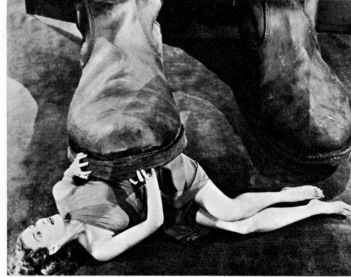

7. Human beings can be represented as giants or midgets (p. 40). (*Dr Cyclops*)

8 and 9. Shooting angle can bring out an object's essential nature (p. 40). Above, used to express the authority of the Church (*Léon Morin, prêtre*), and, below, the strength of bullocks (*Earth*)

10. The only way to show a crowd's number is by ... shooting at a downward angle (p. 41). (*Prisoners of War*, 1918)

11. The camera's exaggeration of contrasts in size can combine realism and symbolism (p. 50). The judge is huge, the pleaders tiny, in *A Matter of Life and Death*

12. In *Citizen Kane* scene after scene uses setting in depth (p. 57)

13. Distortion gives an opportunity to interpret reality in terms of a personal vision (p. 62). (*Überfall*)

14. The cinema can show actors' faces large enough for us to see every detail of their expression (p. 71). (*Ivan the Terrible*)

15. In *Les Parents terribles* Sophie steals out of the drawing room and the camera backs away with her (p. 79)

16. The frame forms a basis for the composition of each shot (p. 80). (*Battleship Potemkin*)

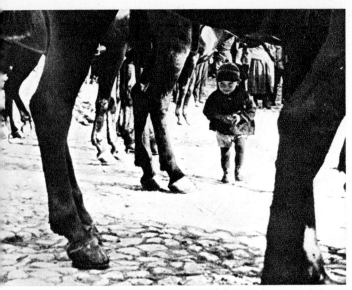

17. By extracting a fragment from the chaos of nature the cinema helps us to see it with new eyes (p. 81). (*Strike*)

18. A framing which deliberately excludes the central action (p. 82). A scene of childbirth from *Stage Coach*

19. In *October* oblique framing is used to make crowd movements more dynamic (p. 86)

21. Film can multiply objects or scenes (p. 89). (*Top Hat*)

20. A famous example of slow-motion (p. 95). (*Zéro de conduite*)

22. Film has no tenses – it is something happening now (p. 101). (*Sinking of a U.S. Warship*, 1943)

23. We see the little girl Julie and her mother (past) in the same shot as the grown-up Julie (present) (p. 104). (*Miss Julie*)

24. We see the policeman ready to make an arrest but Charlie does not (p. III). An example of suspense from *The Kid*

25. Only a few films keep the same time scale as reality (p. 117). (*Cléo de 5 à 7*)

26. The cinema brings out the time aspect of a rifle shot (p. 123). A bullet breaking an electric bulb. Taken at one millionth of a second

ranging from the real to the imaginary, the concrete to the abstract. Hence the necessity for a variety of conventions following sometimes the pattern of facts, sometimes the logic of ideas, sometimes the flow of the emotions or the flight of the imagination. Thus, in the hands of the film-maker, cinematographic space-time is a medium infinitely adaptable to the widest range of artistic creations.

Theories of Montage

Montage is considered here as basically an artistic use of space and time, and as a central technique of film-making which creates and determines the various modes of cinematographic space-time. However, in order to form a coherent artistic medium – in order to form this plastic, infinitely adaptable material for the film-maker – the separate shots when joined together must combine into a meaningful synthesis, an artistic whole. The process by which the separate shots combine in montage has attracted the attention of film theorists from Kuleshov onwards. In previous chapters we have considered, from an analytical point of view the fact that a film is made up of single shots, using the word 'cutting' to describe the process. Now we are to discuss briefly how shots combine to form an integral whole, looking on the process as a synthesis and calling it 'montage' rather than 'cutting', from the French word, 'monter', 'to assemble'.

Eisenstein, in one of his books, explains montage by analogy with Japanese character writing in which the whole is more than the sum of the parts. For example, the Japanese character for 'dog', plus the character for 'mouth', together make, not a character meaning 'dog's mouth' – which would be simple addition – but a character meaning 'bark' – a new concept. Put in exactly this form, Eisenstein's explanation is open to two criticisms. Firstly, it does not apply to all forms of montage – for example, to a simple time sequence. Secondly, there can be association of two separate elements to form a new meaning without montage and within the shot itself – the lovers embracing in one corner of the screen, the face of the jealous husband appearing at the window, or the contrasting expressions of mother and son in Cocteau's *Les Parents terribles* given in Chapter Three as an example of framing. Again, an association of this kind can be made by camera movement.

Nevertheless, having made these reservations there is no doubt that Eisenstein's analogy illustrates an important aspect of montage. The *gestalt* psychologists insist that we react to organized wholes which are something more than the sum of the parts into which they can be analysed. As I. A. Richards says in his book on criticism 'it is the organized whole which has artistic communicability'. A novel is a living whole not a series of unrelated words drawn from the dictionary. In a film the isolated image is not perceived and does not function by itself; the individual shots are brought to life by their context. Thus in every film there is enrichment of meaning by mental association, and this enrichment is achieved predominantly by montage.

Pudovkin's view of montage was very similar to Eisenstein's. He too stressed the carry-over in the mind which made it possible to obtain effects of sympathy, emphasis, contrast, or irony by juxtaposition of single images. Only if an object is placed together with other objects and 'presented as part of a synthesis . . . is it endowed with filmic life'. In a famous passage he described how the expression of an actor in identical shots was variously interpreted as hunger, grief, or tenderness according to the shots which preceded and followed it. Eisenstein said that Pudovkin stressed the mental linkage between shots while he himself emphasized rather the mental clash between them.

Carrying analysis a stage further, Marcel Martin in *Le Langage cinématographique* distinguishes between narrative montage and expressive montage. *Narrative montage*, in its simplest form, is putting individual shots together in chronological order to tell a story. *Expressive montage* is putting shots together with the purpose of producing a particular, immediate effect by the clash of two images. This is a useful distinction in the present discussion because Eisenstein's views can be applied most readily to expressive montage. In the case of narrative montage which is less colourful, less artificial and for most of the time 'invisible', there is not the same striking formation of new concepts.

Expressive montage adds colour and life to a film and many examples could be given. In François Truffaut's *Tirez sur le pianiste* one of the gangsters uses a stock phrase 'may my mother die if I'm telling a lie' and the film cuts momentarily to a shot of his mother collapsing. A character in Hitchcock's *Murder* says 'I miss my little tit-bit' and there follows a shot of cheese and a glass of beer. Another says sadly and hungrily 'Can't I stay at the Red Lion?' and the film cuts to a close-up of a roast chicken.[1] In expressive montage the contrasting shot that is used to achieve the effect may have nothing to do with the action of the film. This is the famous *montage of attractions*, the word 'attractions' being used in the sense of one thing being attracted to, i.e. having an affinity with, or similarity to, another. In Chaplin's *City Lights*, the film shows a crowd of commuters, then a flock of sheep; in Lang's *Fury*, we see women gossiping, then hens cackling; in *Strike* we see workers being shot down, then oxen slaughtered. A recent example is in Robert Enrico's *Au coeur de la vie* (from Ambrose Bierce's *In the Midst of Life*), in which wounded soldiers crawling along the ground in swarms are compared by a single, arresting shot to beetles scrabbling in the dirt. In Eisenstein's *October*, Kerensky's soldiers are compared visually to wine glasses and tin soldiers, the *ancien régime* symbolized by shots of medals and uniforms, and Kerensky himself compared to a peacock.[2] When used

---

1. In *The Fallen Idol* the director cuts from a woman in a raging temper to a lioness at the zoo.
2. Plate 29.

repeatedly, as it is in *October*, expressive montage can have an artificial effect, but it is by no means outdated. A visual metaphor, simile, or symbol can strike to the heart of things. It all depends on how it is handled. In *King and Country* (director Joseph Losey) the camera cuts away from the hero, Hamp, in the mud of the trenches, as he describes his peacetime background, and illustrates his words with brief shots of characters in England. These shots are too short for flash-backs and are a visual illustration of his thoughts, a kind of expressive montage. They succeed brilliantly in the film because they contrast strongly with the main sequence and also because they have a 'primitive' pictorial quality which illustrates a central theme of the film, the naïve simplicity of Hamp's character.

It is clear that in using expressive montage the film-maker is working in a medium as far from the reality of sense-data as the words of the novelist. By comparison, narrative montage may seem more natural, but it should be pointed out that narrative montage does not consist merely in juxtaposing separate successive shots of action, or even in changing from one scene to another. The fundamental characteristic of narrative montage, which radically differentiates it from reality, consists in the use of a mobile point of view *in the course of the action*. Recording an event by separate successive shots was at one stage a new technique, but it was the representation of the same event from different points of view or in a different time order which created a new art. Cutting *during the action* created a new optical, psychological, and dramatic world very different from the world of reality, for it meant that the event filmed was not reproduced objectively, but analysed and reconstituted subjectively. The film-maker imposed his personal vision and with the intervention of human agency artistic factors came into play.

ASSIMILATION OF SPACE AND TIME

As explained in the first section of this chapter the cinema can, by slow and fast motion within a shot, substitute space for time or time for space. Even more so from shot to shot. As a result of montage a complex assimilation of space and time values occurs. This peculiar space-time structure of montage forms a characteristic, most curious feature of the cinema. Even more than other characteristics it corresponds to the scientific assimilation of space and time into a space-time continuum. In scientific thought a hundred years ago time was quite apart from space and the two belonged to different orders – space solid, Euclidian in structure, time an endless flow. In science today, space and time are combined to form a framework on which the universe is built; we may move about in time much as we can in space, and space has some of the flowing quality of time. 'Physicists have been forced, by virtue of the character of their own subject-matter, to see that their units are not those of space *and* time, but of space-time.'[1] Mainly by means of montage, the cinema reflects these characteristics in artistic form.

Firstly the cinema leads to a *temporal organization of space*, a term originated by Erwin Panofsky.[2] In real life, in the plastic arts and on the stage, space is static, motionless, unchanging. It stays put while we move about in it, either physically or mentally. In the cinema, space loses its static quality and acquires a time-charged dynamic quality. Parts of space are arranged in a temporal order and become part of a temporal structure with a temporal rhythm. The close-up for instance is not just a large scale picture of a part of space – it is a stage to be reached in time just as much as a *fortissimo* passage in a musical composition. In any composite film picture (of an individual, a group, a landscape) shots of different aspects of space follow each other in an order in time and could be put together in a different time-order to give a different result. Pudovkin pointed out that

1. John Dewey, *Art as Experience*, Allen and Unwin, 1934.
2. Erwin Panofsky, 'Style and Medium in the Motion Picture', *Critique*, 1, New York, January 1947. Reprinted in full in *Film, an Anthology* by Daniel Talbot, Simon and Schuster, New York, 1959.

alteration of the order without any alteration in the shots themselves could radically change the meaning of a sequence. *One of the most important aspects of a composite film picture of space is its time dimension.*

We could say that montage in the cinema leads to the *temporalization of space*. The other way round it results in the opposite phenomenon, the *spatialization of time*. As Arnold Hauser[1] says, time in real life (except in dreams), in literature, and on the stage, has a definite directional trend of development. In the cinema, time loses this directional trend and (as will be apparent from what we have said in the chapter on time) in a film we are free to move about *in* time, as in real life we are to move about in space. A film can go backwards and forwards, can show separate events together, can show simultaneous events separately. Time loses its un-interrupted continuity and irreversible direction. A play cannot mingle brief moments and phrases of time as a film can.

There is an interesting passage in a novel of the thirties, *Winged Pharoah* by Joan Grant,[2] which describes a spatialization of time different from that of the cinema, but different also from the orthodox view of time as an irreversible flow. The novel is based on mystical experience and in certain mental states the author describes herself as being at the centre of a time circle. Time past, present, and future is disposed round the circumference of the circle and can be reached and experienced at will from the centre. It is also relevant to mention J. W. Dunne's book *Experiment with Time*.[3] The author claims to have experienced future as well as past time in dreams, and explains this on the theory that there are different dimensions in time which enable us in certain states to reach time we could not otherwise know. To repeat: in a film, time is spatialized because we can move about in it as we can in space.

1. Arnold Hauser, *The Social History of Art*, Routledge, 1951.
2. Methuen, 1939, rev. edn., 1948.
3. Faber, 1939.

There is another way in which the cinema spatializes time connected with the fact that in film every shot is in the present tense, that is, every picture we see is just something happening. Our sense of time is different from other senses in being direct and subjective. Most of our knowledge of the world we acquire through specific sense organs but our sense of time is innate. As soon as we wish to objectify time or measure it in concrete terms we can only do so in terms of space – clock, hour-glass, sun, stars, tide, growth, etc. This is exactly the case with the cinema. The cinema expresses different times by showing us different parts of space. As Élie Faure said: 'The cinema makes duration a dimension of space.'[1] It may show us a similar part of space (i.e. the same room) but something will be moved, changed, developed – so that essentially it is different in spatial terms. If absolutely nothing moves then we are back to the static arts – photography or painting and are not dealing with the cinema. Although, as we have seen, these arts have tried to imitate the film, they are quite different from it.

The fact that cinema shows us time by a series of different positions in space, brings us back to the basic principle of moving pictures – that they consist of a series of still photographs of space which – the other face of the coin – *are arranged in time*. Since a film is a series of still photographs, it follows that (from certain points of view) the difference between the succession of each frame within the shot, and the succession from shot to shot is a difference of degree rather than one of kind. In fact in an animated film which is created frame by frame, a cut from position to position of a single movement is exactly the same technically as a cut from one scene to another.

In this second way then, the cinema spatializes time, expressing duration by a series of positions, both from shot to shot and also within each shot. The latter case (within a shot) will include camera movement; and camera movement has the additional property of showing a series of different parts of

1. *L'Arbre d'Éden*, Éditions Crès, Paris, 1922.

space even if the subject is completely motionless. Normally in camera movement, say a panning-shot, the different parts of space will be related to a continuous period of time – successive instants immediately following one another. But camera movement can also be used by the artist to make large and dramatic time changes, e.g. from the present to the past as in the examples from *Miss Julie* and *Death of a Salesman* discussed in Chapter Four. There is also a striking example in Ingmar Bergman's *Wild Strawberries*. The camera swings to another part of space, and discloses the people and events of twenty years ago. We may even have – in thought or dream – the man and the-boy-the-man-used-to-be in the very same shot. In both these cases also, different periods of time are clearly expressed by different parts of space.

The two fundamental aspects of film, space and time, thus intermingle, interchange, interact. On the one hand the spatialization of time, on the other the temporalization of space. What a film shows us is space and nothing but space, so that this space has perforce to be used to express time. And yet on the other hand this space has to be *disposed* in time, has to be fitted into a temporal pattern. Again this temporal pattern is a continuously flexible one and enables us to move about in time as though it were space. These characteristics, at any rate, occurring so continuously and so flexibly, are peculiar to the cinema and make it something new and different both from reality and from any other art.

There is yet another way in which the cinema substitutes space for time, that is by multiplying, intensifying, and enriching the time the film runs, by deployment of space. It is rather like travelling on a holiday whose few days or few weeks may contain as much as months of ordinary life because they are crammed with experience – new places, new sights, new sounds. We try when on holiday 'to make as much of time as we can'. The time we spend in watching a film is similarly supercharged; it is ninety minutes of intensive experience. This is something common to all the arts, but the means are different and in other arts it is not space that is used to enrich time but other things – in the theatre as much as anything it is the force of personality, in literature it is the magic of words. The cinema cannot match the words of literature or the personal presence of the theatre – but its command of space and all that it contains (sights and sounds) is unsurpassed.

One last point. Quite apart from all the considerations we have been discussing, there can be an emotional flavour about time and space as we experience them in the cinema. From this aspect the variations from reality which occur in time and space are not of such direct significance, and what matters will be the feeling they give us. John Dewey in *Art as Experience* makes the point of art in general when he says:

As science takes qualitative space and time and reduces them to relations that enter into equations, so art makes them abound in their own sense as significant values of the very substance of things. Up and down, back and front, to and fro . . . *feel* differently . . . fast and slow as experienced are qualitatively as unlike as noise and silence, heat and cold, black and white.

The important thing here is the communication of experience, the *feeling* of spaciousness, of claustrophobia, of a rush of events, of the dragging tedium of ennui, of the choking unease of suspense. We remember the slow sequence of shots of country parched by drought in Victor Turin's *Turksib* with the repeated subtitle 'waiting, waiting, waiting', or the split-second cutting of the murder in Graham Greene's chilling gangster story, *Brighton Rock*, directed by John Boulting. We remember their *feeling*. Space and time in the cinema compared with science and everyday life are, like every other element, emotionally charged. We come back to the point made at the end of Chapter One that art is something anthropomorphic and bound up with the artist's experience.

The film is an art of time and space and, as Pudovkin says, the director builds up his own 'filmic' time and 'filmic' space. As Marcel Martin says, film grinds down space and time until one is transformed into the other in a dialectical interaction. The cinema's freedom is based on a double mobility: that of the camera in space and that of shots in order and duration. The film is free to work with endless variations of physical reality in which the laws of time and space become 'tractable and obedient'. George Bluestone suggests that 'time is prior in the novel and space prior in film ... the film renders time by going from point to point in space', but he also says 'time and space are ultimately inseparable'.

One may sum up by saying that, while the spatialization of time and the temporalization of space are useful concepts, the two are finally inseparable. One of the achievements of the cinema is that it can effect an ideal synthesis. It divests space and time of their everyday, commonsense (but not scientific) characteristics and, investing them conjointly with the immateriality of thought, associates them together in a new whole – *cinematographic space-time*. Despite appearances this is a mental rather than a physical entity and one which the artist can work with as freely as, say, the words of a language. It is this which makes the cinema truly an art and one of the richest and most developed of them all.

CHAPTER SIX

The Surface of Reality: Soft–Focus, Double-Exposure, Negative Image; Décor, Costume, Make-Up; Colour, Lighting

In the previous chapters we have been dealing with space and time as they make up the structure of reality, the space-time continuum, and as they are modified and used, selected and arranged, by the artist, to form an artistic space-time. In this chapter we wish to consider not the *structure* of reality, but the *surface* of reality – the surface quality, the texture and colour of things. These characteristics constitute the flesh which clothes the bones of length and breadth and depth and time; the texture of the image, the beauty that is only skin deep, the bloom on the peach, the polish on the furniture. In the cinema the features corresponding to this aspect of reality are: soft-focus, double-exposure, negative image; décor, costume, make-up; colour; and lighting. Like other distinctions we have made, this one cannot be pressed too far, and lighting and soft-focus, for example, may affect the structure as well as the surface of the film world. Ultimately the surface and the structure beneath it exist together and form a whole. But, nevertheless, taken for what it is worth the separation of the two is useful, and corresponds to a significant difference.

We shall find that the general characteristics of the surface of the film world are the same as those of its structure: that the film world falls as short of reality in its surface presentation as in its structure, but that these shortcomings are again of advantage artistically; that the artist projects his personality here also, renders the world as he sees it, charges it with feeling and meaning; and that appropriateness, fitness to purpose, restraint, and sincerity will produce the best artistic results.

On its surface, as in its structure, the film world has certain characteristics common to other arts, but some which are peculiar to itself. These surface characteristics of the cinema fall into three broad classes. First, there are those which depend on photography and are peculiar to the cinema: soft-focus, double-exposure, the use of the negative image, and optical distortion. Second, there are surface characteristics which depend on the *mise en scène*, characteristics which are common to the theatre and the cinema, although they take different forms and play rather different roles in the two media: décor, costume, and make-up. Finally there are two surface characteristics, colour and lighting, which are dependent partly on the setting, partly on the process of photography.

PHOTOGRAPHIC CHARACTERISTICS

Soft-Focus

Soft-focus is perhaps the clearest example we have yet had of the possible artistic value of a technical defect. In the real world if it occurs at all it occurs as a fault, as a defect of eyesight, which we go at once to the oculist to correct. The haze of mist and the haze of distance are not quite the same thing and the camera can render these by direct sharp-focus photography. Most beginners in camera work, through bad focusing, obtain soft-focus results which are unintentional, inappropriate, and inartistic. The important thing about soft-focus used for artistic effect is that the lens is deliberately faulted – just as the important thing about a drawing by an artist like Topolski is that the clear lines of nature are deliberately muddled and complicated or, in an impressionist painting, that the lines of nature are deliberately broken into dots or dazzled or left incomplete. All these three represent an escape from physical reality, an abstraction which allows the spectator's imagination freer play. There is of course in all these cases, a world of difference between the deliberate and calculated distortion of the master artist and the inartistic, ineffective mistakes of the beginner.

Like lighting, soft-focus affects both the surface and the structure of reality. Used over the whole of the image it blurs the shapes, softens the sharp lines of the composition and affects the surface appearance of the image. But used over only part of the image, say the foreground, it will draw attention to the sharply-focused background, emphasize the third dimension, and in this sense affect the structure of reality.

Soft-focus first became popular at the beginning of the century in still photography. It produced a flattering portrait and introduced a greater degree of personal aesthetic interpretation in the mechanical copying of nature. It has been suggested that impressionist painting also had an influence. Colombier and Manuel in *Tableau des arts du XXième siècle*[1] wrote:

> The photographer's supreme achievement is to make his work look less like a photograph of the sitter, than a photograph of his portrait painted by Gandara ... ; he no longer produces photographs, but etchings, pastels, Jules Bretons, Bongereaus, Henners – and even signs them.

Many of these effects were produced by soft-focus.

Film directors first used soft-focus as a means of visual idealization comparable to the vaporous style of the 'artistic portrait'. It became common in sentimental or religious films to surround romantic heroines and sacred characters with a supernatural aura. In expert hands it achieved more valuable results. In several of Griffith's later films, e.g. *Dream Street* (1921), it is used with close-ups and allegorical compositions to heighten the pathos or the symbolism. In Scandinavian films it helped to create the mystical atmosphere proper to Norse legend. In German expressionist and French impressionist work it is used to make reality more poetic or create an atmosphere of fantasy. In Gustav Machaty's *Extase* it is used to idealize shots of nudity which realistic treatment would have made vulgar. But perhaps the most successful use of soft-focus for this purpose is in

1. Denoël, Paris, 1933.

Man Ray's *Starfish*. Some of the shots of this famous film are among the most beautiful of the cinema: the woman Ondine or starfish, glimpsed as if through the waters of a dream, irresistibly evokes a Renoir painting, and the soft-focus by its richness and perfection attains a high degree of suggestion and stylistic value. Once again the film-maker claims the right to transform nature and create on the screen an original visual entity.

Soft-focus is also used to express subjective states of fainting or unconsciousness, for example in Hitchcock's *Notorious*, when Ingrid Bergman is overcome by a drug put into her coffee. In Marcel L'Herbier's *Eldorado* it is used while the dancers are being introduced in the Grenada cabaret. The heroine, Sybilla, starts thinking of her childhood, absents herself in thought from the others and momentarily becomes blurred in soft-focus. Brought to her senses by the shouts of the audience, her image comes back sharply into focus. In 1923 Dimitri Kirsanoff in *Brumes d'automne* expressed visually the thoughts of a young girl recovering from an unhappy love affair by accompanying her emotional upsets with a succession of soft-focus shots. In Paul Czinner's *Dreaming Lips* there is a scene in which Elizabeth Bergner, carried away by the personality and playing of a great violinist, sees only him clearly and the rest of the scene in soft-focus. In Orson Welles's *Macbeth*, in one of the soliloquies in which Macbeth, haunted by the memory of his crime, is prey to a delirium of doubts and remorse, a series of soft-focus shots followed by a return to a clear image is used again and again. In Alexander Singer's *Psyche 59* soft-focus and distortion of the image are used to express the visual sensation of a blind woman recovering her sight.

Soft-focus is frequently used also to introduce a flash-back. It can be regarded as the visual equivalent of the slight disturbance of spirit which accompanies the invasion of our mind by memories of the past. It is used very effectively in this way in Claude Autant-Lara's *Le Diable au corps*, and there are many other examples. It can also be used for humorous scenes. In Harold Lloyd's *The Freshman* when Lloyd walks nervously on to the stage to make a speech the audience goes out of focus. In an amusing scene in Robert Mulligan's *Love with the Proper Stranger* the hero is in his girl-friend's flat when he makes a remark that she takes as an insult: 'What did you say?' she asks him with an angry gleam in her eye; then the scene goes out of focus and we cut to a shot of him walking disconsolately down the street with his bag, having been thrown out of her flat. Another use of soft-focus is demonstrated in Richard Leacock's *The Chair*, in which the characters are introduced by the camera being pulled out of focus for an instant.

Finally, we come to soft-focus over a part of the image only, frequently used so as to strengthen the contrast between background and foreground and emphasize the depth of the picture. As André Bazin wrote

As soon as film space ceases to be homogeneous and is split into intellectual and dramatic parts, the art of mise-en-scène consists as much in hiding as in revealing. Soft-focus is a means of stressing the plane on which the camera is focused; it translates in terms of plastic composition the dramatic relationships which montage expresses in terms of time.[1]

A good example of this use is in an Argentine film *The Sad Young Men*, directed by Rodolfo Kuhn. The heroine is rejoining her friends after a shattering interview which has turned her upside-down emotionally. She walks along the beach where they are playing deck-tennis. A shot in depth shows us her face in sharp-focus and the others in the distance in soft-focus. Then as she looks at them the focus changes and they become sharply defined. The shot clearly expresses her gradual concentration, her effort, in pulling herself together, to meet the other people with outward equanimity. In a film about American politics, *The Best Man* by Franklin Schaffner, there is a very subtle example. The film depicts a struggle between two men, William Russell and Joe Cantwell, to win the

1. Plate 30.

'primary' election and be chosen as presidential candidate. Cantwell, an oppressive bully, is planning to 'smear' Russell by publicizing an exaggerated report of a nervous breakdown he had a year ago. The President of the United States who is campaigning for Russell interviews and draws out a witness who can prove that Cantwell is a homosexual. In a situation rapidly growing tenser, the President and the witness are talking on a couch, while Russell stands pensive, saying nothing, in the foreground. Suddenly the President and the witness go out of focus and the camera concentrates sharply on Russell. It seems at the time completely wrong. Surely the key people are the President and the witness who, in effect, control the election, and the camera ought to focus on *them*. But as the plot develops we find out that Russell's conscience will not let him use the evidence against Cantwell *and it never is used*. The camera, in focusing on Russell struggling with his conscience and ignoring the others, has given us a glimpse of things to come.

Double-Exposure

Like soft-focus, double-exposure is a common mistake among the beginners in photography who have forgotten to wind on the film in their camera, and therefore get one picture on top of another. In the way it appears in the cinema, it is a 'fault' peculiar to photography but, once again, in the hands of an artist, a very useful one for certain artistic and dramatic effects. However, although true double-exposure is peculiar to photographs, an equivalent effect is used not infrequently in graphic art, in drawing or painting, when part of a picture is seen through another part that would in nature be solid and opaque. The only time the phenomenon occurs in the real world is with glass (for example when, in a railway carriage, we see the landscape superimposed on the reflection of the faces inside the carriage) or in a mirage (where a freak reflection is superimposed on the real landscape). There is a very effective scene at

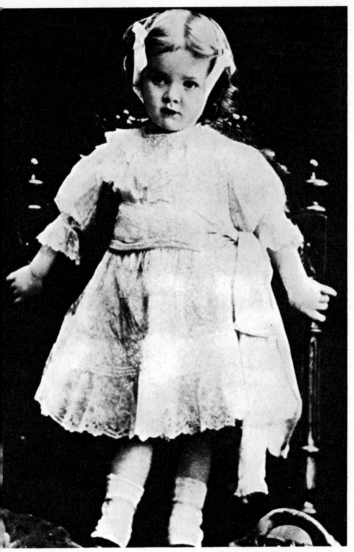

27. The photograph took over the function of recording the past (p. 125). Marlene Dietrich aged three

28. Painting has tried to copy the movement of film (p. 125). *Dynamism of a Dog on Leash*, Giacomo Balla, 1907

29. Montage of attractions. In *October*, Kerensky is compared to a peacock (p. 131)

30. Soft-focus as a means of stressing the plane that is sharply focused. (p. 143). (*Léon Morin, prêtre*)

31. Double-exposure was first used dramatically to represent the supernatural (p. 145). (*Nosferatu*, 1922)

32. Orson Welles uses upward-angle shots in which the ceiling is an important element (p. 151). (*Citizen Kane*)

33. Natural scenery constitutes the appeal of certain films (p. 150). (*The Seven Samurai*)

34. On the other hand the cinema can make use of formalized décor (p. 152). (*The Cabinet of Doctor Caligari*)

35. 'Star' make-up raises daily beauty to the level of a superior, radiant, unalterable beauty (p. 155). (*Rancho Notorious*)

36. Black-and-white is a form of painting with light (p. 158). (*Whistle Down the Wind*)

37. Black-and-white may soften reality (p. 160). (*Le Sang des bêtes*)

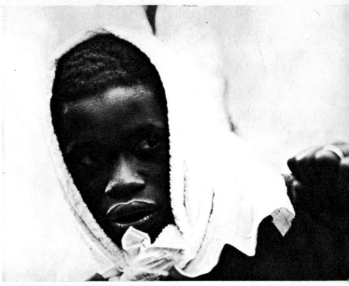

38. The brutal reality of boxing is expressed in black-and-white (p. 165). (*Un Coeur gros comme ça*)

39. Bathed in a clear limpid atmosphere (p. 171). (*Jour de fête*)

40. Lighting can give strong effects of depth (p. 172). (*Love Me Tonight*)

41. Side lighting gives relief and solidity to a face (p. 172). (*La terra trema*)

42. Poster for the first sound film *The Jazz Singer* (p. 175). (Note how, in the hands, the artist has reproduced the camera's exaggeration of perspective)

43. Poetry is suitable for a film (p. 178). 'This is the night mail crossing the border/Bringing the cheque and the postal order' – W. H. Auden. (*Night Mail*)

44. Early sound equipment was heavy and inflexible. Filming the first Vitaphone shorts (p. 180)

45. War reduced to its filthy reality (p. 203). (*Kanal*)

46. The end of *Le Procès de Jeanne d'Arc* is dominated by the sound of a conflagration (p. 208). Also an example of a close-up (p. 73)

47. Our imagination is at full stretch, stimulated by the film-maker's emotionally-charged material (p. 225). (*Strike*)

48. A film like *Kameradschaft* exists also as a composition in black-and-white (p. 234)

49. A period setting can be more convincing in a film (p. 215). (*The Leopard*)

50. The abstract, formalized expression of a film like *L'Année dernière à Marienbad* (p. 159)

51 and 52. A film can express abstract ideas if they are in concrete terms. Above, the hectic atmosphere of the stock exchange in *L'eclisse* and, below, religion in the modern world from *La dolce vita* (p. 216)

53. The realism of photography can give force to fantastic elements (p. 235). (*Un Chien andalou*)

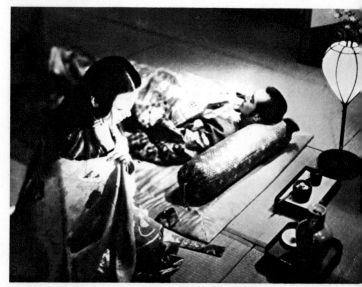

54. The most effective ghosts are the most realistic (p. 235). (*Ugetsu Monogatari*)

the beginning of Polanski's film *Knife in the Water*, where a shot of a man and a woman taken through the windscreen of a car has the reflected, moving pattern of the trees they are driving through superimposed on it. This scene makes use of the natural phenomenon, but transforms it (by tracking with the car and by using an unusual angle) into something cinematic, artistic.

Like reverse motion, double-exposure began by being a simple visual curiosity before it became a fully-fledged means of artistic expression. It was first used in still photography, in which there was a great vogue about 1865 to 1870 for the 'spirit photograph', obtained by double or multiple exposure. Georges Méliès used it in his films from 1908, for example in *Le Dédoublement cabalistique*, but in his hands it remained at the level of magic and fantasy.

It was first used dramatically to evoke the supernatural spirit world – ghosts, angels, demons, and spectres.[1] In an early film of *Uncle Tom's Cabin* we see little Eva's soul going to heaven. It is used in Victor Sjöström's *The Phantom Carriage*, in Murnau's *Nosferatu* and in Dreyer's *Vampyr*. In showing a ghost, double-exposure, as used for years, has a technical weakness. We can quite properly see the kitchen table through the ghost when he stands in front of it, but we can also (this time improperly) see the ghost through the kitchen table when he stands behind it. There is now a process (the Dunning process) which eliminates this anomaly, and enables us to see the table through the ghost but not the ghost through the table. The new system may be accepted as an improvement, but its artistic importance is to be doubted. The old method was entirely successful in suggesting the supernatural, and its logical confirmation seems supererogatory.

The second common use of double-exposure is to suggest an inner life: thought, feeling, imagination, dream. One of the most difficult problems for a director is how to express the

1. Plate 31.

emotional or mental life of his characters in terms of cinema; how to move from the outside to the inside of a character by the objective medium of film; how to give a picture language that faculty of introspection which the written or spoken word naturally commands. The answer may be to show a close-up of the hero's face and, dimly showing through it, his thoughts and feelings: a tender love scene with the heroine who now spurns him; a fight and victory over the villain who has supplanted him; a premonition of disaster as, in his mind's eye, he sees the heroine drowning in the boat that has been holed by the villain. Sjöström used it in *Masterman* and in *The Secret of the Monastery*. Delluc used it in *Fumée Noire* and in *Le Silence*. Käutner uses it in *Romanze in Moll* when the heroine at the concert is mentally distracted by thought of the assignation she has just come from.

Used like this, double-exposure could effect valuable economy of means in the silent film and avoid cumbersome subtitles. It is less essential in the sound film and it is currently much less used. In Truffaut's *Jules et Jim* there is a shot in which Jeanne Moreau's face moves over the forest scenery of the district she lives in, while her voice comes over the sound track reading out a complaining, introspective letter. The means seems excessive for the requirements of the film – a case of misplaced virtuosity

Double-exposure may be used to introduce a symbol or visual metaphor. In Abel Gance's *Napoléon* a stormy session of the Convention is accompanied in double-exposure by scenes of a great tempest. When Napoleon is leaving for the Italian campaign there appears, through a map of Europe which fills the screen, the haughty silhouette of Napoleon and the enigmatic visage of Josephine. Some close-ups of Bonaparte are decorated as if by a watermark, with shots of an eagle. Double-exposure can also be used to show violence. It is used in Christiansen's *Witchcraft through the Ages* to show a young priest's body torn in two by flagellation. It is also used in Metzner's

Überfall with a distorted image in the sequence when the hero is set upon and sandbagged by thugs.

Finally, double-exposure (as a mix or dissolve) may be used as a means of transition between the past and the present. In Autant-Lara's *Le Diable au corps* soft-focus is used for transitions from present to past and dissolves for transitions from past to present – sometimes in a mirror, sometimes on water. Also, the visual dissolve is accompanied by a mixing on the sound track from one sound to another. In Carné's *Le Jour se lève* it is the other way round, and dissolves are used to introduce flashbacks. Both methods are effective and, as with soft-focus, the confusion of image caused by double-exposure is representative of a mental confusion between past and present. Delluc[1] who used dissolves freely to depict memory and interior states, wrote: 'this confrontation in pictorial terms of present and past, of reality and memory is one of the most attractive aspects of film art ...'

Double-exposure splits up the world represented on the screen into, on the one hand, a physical world with flesh and blood characters and, on the other, an immaterial world inhabited by beings of dream or memory. It works by a tacit convention – the acceptance by the spectator of two levels of reality: the concrete reality of the primary image and the abstract reality of the secondary image.

The Negative Image

The use of the photographic negative is too extreme an effect to be very often possible. Nothing could be farther from reality. It presents a world with colours eliminated and then the resultant values of light and shade reversed. The only things comparable in the world of graphic art are the strong, artificial effects obtained by the bolder black-and-white media such as lino-cut, wood-cut. In plastic art one may compare it with the powerful effects obtained in modern sculpture by the

1. Louis Delluc, *Drames de cinéma*, Éditions du Monde Nouveau, 1933.

reversal of shapes, concave for convex, as in breasts that are expressed by the gouging out of the metal or stone, or in buttocks that become holes like the holes in the pelvis. This anti-reality of the negative image indicates the sort of use for which it is most suitable – to express mystery, fantasy, un-reality; and the history of its use in actual films more or less corresponds to this view.

It seems first to have been used in 1920 in *Le Lys de la vie*, a film made by a famous dancer, Loie Fuller, whose ballets and illuminated fantasies were popular after the war. The film was hailed by some critics as a remarkable attempt at poetic, avant-garde cinema, but it is interesting to note that some journalists claimed the negative sequences were included in the show copy by error. Among films with striking negative effects are Ivan Mosjoukine's *Le Brasier ardent*, Man Ray's *Les Mystères du Château de Dé*, Eugène Deslaw's *La Marche des machines*, Henri Chômette's *À quoi rêvent les jeunes filles*. An interesting use is in *Third Avenue El* in which it is used subjectively to represent the confused thoughts of a drunk man. As the film is in colour, the method takes the form of shots with most of the colour filtered out of them giving a similar effect to a true negative.

As we might expect, the negative is particularly suitable for evoking the other world, a spectral realm in which living things become skeletons,[1] a demonic, macabre anti-world. F. W. Murnau used it in *Nosferatu* for the arrival of the hero, in Count Orlock's strange carriage with black curtains, in the country of ghosts. Cocteau used it in *Orphée* for the arrival of the motor-car in the no-man's land of death. At the end of *The Rickshaw Man*, when the unhappy, drunken hero is dying in the snow, there is a beautiful sequence in negative image composed of shots in delicate shades with most of the colour drained out. The sequence reviews the key incidents of the

1. Note the resemblance of the negative to an X-ray photograph. One is led to think also of a painter like Francis Bacon who paints the *inside* of the human body.

film – that is, the events of the dying man's life – and the reference to death is made more strongly and effectively by the use of negative images as symbols both poetic and realistic. As a lover of visual antiphrasis and shock imagery, Godard has made use of negative sequences in such films as *Une Femme mariée* and *Alphaville*, but his employment of the technique is sometimes gratuitous. In his films the negative recalls the presence of death among the living or the void behind the inhumanity of modern civilization.

Optical distortion cannot be classed solely as a surface characteristic, and it has been mentioned already in the chapters on space in discussing camera perspective and the distortion caused by the exaggerated size of parts of the image very near the camera. However, it may be mentioned here for completeness, since there are forms of distortion which affect length and breadth only and not depth. One example has already been given from *Jules et Jim* of normal-ratio film stretched to cinemascope width. In other cases a distorting mirror or a distorting lens is used with effects which can be either comic or macabre. Examples from Metzner's *Überfall* and Singer's *Psyche 59* have already been given in other connexions in the two previous sections. In Polanski's film *Repulsion* we see the heroine's distorted image in the polished surface of a kettle: a visual symbol predicting the destruction of her personality by madness.

MISE-EN-SCÈNE CHARACTERISTICS

Décor

There is no doubt about the artificial nature of stage settings which have grown up out of a long tradition – from the amphitheatre of Greek drama, to the apron stage of the Elizabethan theatre, the wooden platform of the mystery plays, the room with one wall missing of the realistic stage (realistic chiefly in including actual furniture and bric-à-brac), and the stark props and lighting effects of the modern theatre. The stage is in essence simply a convenient place for the players to perform, and it is dressed with props and scenery, and lit, partly for decoration and for the rest merely to symbolize or suggest a real place.

In the cinema it is rather different, and it is the particular property of the camera that it is able to give us a photographic reproduction of real locations, real bits of nature.[1] The first films ever made, those of Lumière, had no set décor. The camera man merely set up his camera and filmed what was there or had his characters enact a simple story in a garden or a field. Then came the elaborate theatrical settings of Méliès and his imitators, but they proved to lead to a dead end. The American film-makers Porter and Griffith led the way back to natural settings and started the vogue of the Western – a *genre* in which magnificent natural scenery is sometimes the best thing in the film. Similarly the appeal of a film like *Three Coins in the Fountain* depends very much on the beautiful photography of Rome, and that of *The Knave of Hearts* on candid-camera photography in London streets. Modern film-makers, influenced by British documentary, by Italian neo-realism, by British 'free' cinema and by French *cinéma verité*, and with the help of much lighter and more flexible apparatus, make far more use of location shooting for interiors as well as exteriors. Examples are such films as Morris Engel's *Weddings and Babies*, Bryan Forbes's *The L-Shaped Room*, Jean-Luc Godard's *À bout de souffle* and *Vivre sa vie*, Clive Donner's *The Caretaker* or the films of Jean Rouch.

Nevertheless, despite its leaning towards realistic scenery, the cinema makes considerable use of studio sets and is likely to go on doing so. A very rough generalization is that two-thirds of the average commercial feature is shot in the studio and the rest on location. In the studio, however faithfully the settings in the finished film may seem to copy reality, the re-

1. Plate 33.

semblance is almost entirely illusory. To start with, they have different dimensions; to strengthen perspective and the impression of depth, it is an advantage to make screen sets of abnormal dimensions. Moreover, studio sets are invariably made of light, easily-worked, easily-handled, easily-dismantled materials – wood, hardboard, stucco, plaster, cloth, etc., and this different texture, together with the fact that they are only an approximate copy of real settings, has to be allowed for in lighting them. Also, they are painted in artificial shades with light values (for black-and-white film) or colour values (for a colour film) corresponding to the photographic effect which is desired. Finally, to make it easier for sound engineers and electricians to set up their apparatus, studio sets generally have no ceilings. This means that some habitual upward angles of vision are ruled out. An exception to this general rule is Orson Welles, who frequently uses striking upward-angle shots in which the ceiling is an important element in the composition of the shot.[1]

All these differences mean that the world represented on the screen is a new creation, not just a copy of reality, and they frequently compel the film-maker to make changes and inventions in composition which give scope for artistic ingenuity. Trauner, the French art director, has said:

A room which is suitable to live in would not be suitable for a film. Décor ought to be realistic but not naturalistic. Any décor which is an end in itself is not good décor for the cinema.[2]

There is one kind of artificiality in décor which can be jarring unless it is extremely well done. This is the use of various traditional forms of faking – glass shots, model shots, the Schuftan process, photographic backgrounds, back-projection and the like. For the interested reader a good account of the

1. Plate 32.
2. Quoted in *Les 1001 Métiers du cinéma* by Pierre Leprohon, Éditions Jacques Melot, Paris, 1947.

techniques involved is given in *The Cinema Today* by Spencer and Waley.¹ Most of them involve substitution of a photograph for the whole or part of the image. Back-projection, for instance, involves projecting a picture of, say, a mountain, forest, building or street scene so that it shows on a screen in the studio. This screen with its picture then forms part of the set and is photographed with it when the actual film is shot. Even when competently done, back-projection is not as good as actual location shooting. The actual location has an authenticity difficult to describe, and just as difficult to imitate.

We have already noted the cinema's advantage over the theatre in its ability to use natural scenery and, even in the studio, film décor can be far more solid and realistic in appearance than that of the theatre because it does not have to be moved and can therefore be built on the spot. But, at the same time, the cinema can make very successful use of settings just as formalized and abstract as in the theatre² – from Robert Wiene's *The Cabinet of Dr Caligari* to Dreyer's *La Passion de Jeanne d'Arc*, or to a recent film made by Ted Zarpas from a performance of *Electra* in an amphitheatre in Athens. For a fantasy like Lang's *Metropolis* or a ballet or a musical film, film scenery can successfully be as artificial and formalized as any stage setting or any painting. It is when the artificial is posing as real that the camera is liable to give it away.

Costume

In everyday life, costume is utilitarian, the word '*utilitarian*' being understood widely to include functions like attracting the other sex and conferring prestige, as well as warmth and protection. In the cinema as in the theatre or in painting, it has a predominantly aesthetic or dramatic function. It can even become an integral part of an actor's personality. Film clothes,

1. Oxford University Press, London, 1939.
2. Plate 34.

Nicole Védrès says,[1] 'have little or nothing to do (directly at least) with changes of fashion, model gowns, historical costume, folk dresses or the everyday work of *couturiers*'. The supreme example is Charlie Chaplin. One need only draw a cane, a hat and a pair of shoes to know who is intended. The clothes which Buster Keaton wears differ from film to film, but his style of costume is unmistakable. The identification of a man with his clothes or accessories occurs to some extent in real life in the case of politicians (Churchill and his cigar, Baldwin and his pipe, Chamberlain and his umbrella) or in the case of music-hall comedians (Jimmy Edwards with his moustache, Maurice Chevalier with his hat tilted on his head). But it seems stronger in the cinema. The reason perhaps is that, in the black-and-white shadow world of the screen, there is less difference in kind between a man and his clothes and it is easier for the two to coalesce in a unity in the mind and eye of the spectator.

It is interesting to note that in the costuming of musical films realism is better avoided. Cowboys or farm workers (Donen's *Seven Brides for Seven Brothers* and Zinnemann's *Oklahoma*), factory workers (Donen's, *The Pajama Game*), New York gangs (Wise and Robbins's *West Side Story*) – can all be glamorized to the extent of wearing the gaudiest colours and *outré* styles. Lawrence Langner in *The Importance of Wearing Clothes*[2] suggests that, if shows of this kind were costumed realistically, the audience would be critical of incidents which, in the fairy-tale atmosphere created by the costume, are passed over and accepted.

Nicole Védrès holds that directors should not necessarily dress the actors in the clothes that suit them best, but should 'use the clothes to create an image'. Edgar Morin in *The Stars* points out that, in the special case of the film-star, clothes are an ornament, an idealized version of the real thing, however lowly the real thing may be.

1. 'Vêtir les images', *Intermède*, Rombaldi, Paris, 1946.
2. Constable, London, 1959.

In the heart of the wild West the star changes her gown for each sequence. Elegance takes precedence over verisimilitude, artifice over realism. A star can be modestly dressed in a raincoat or even in rags. But raincoat and rags will be made by a master *couturier*.

It is not difficult to conclude that costume in the cinema is not a copy of costume in reality but a contribution to the total artistic effect.

Make-Up

Make-up in the cinema fulfils a different and perhaps more important role than it does in the theatre. In the vast amphitheatres of the Greek theatre, an actor was a tiny figure whose expression would have been lost to most of the audience. Masks larger than life-size and with emotions depicted in the most striking possible lines were an obvious advantage. Masks have been used, too, with resonant mouthpieces which amplify the human voice. Modern theatre make-up is the heir to this dramatic tradition, and invests the actor with a special authority and a personality suited to the role he is playing. It aims particularly at bringing out the expression, and stressing the lines of the mouth and eyes. While the contemporary theatre may have diminished the role of make-up, it still to some extent perpetuates the hieratic function of the antique mask.

In the cinema, actors can be presented in a great variety of styles ranging from no make-up at all, to a make-up far more elaborate than anything used in the theatre. At its most elaborate, in other words, in the case of 'star' make-up, the cinema also provides the actor with a mask, a mask which is invisible but more complete than anything known to dramatic art, a mask which may require wig-makers, dentists, and plastic surgeons as well as the usual *coiffeurs*, make-up men, and colourists. It is also a mask with a different function, idealizing, beautifying. In both respects film make-up is nearer that of ordinary life but more skilful and carried to a higher pitch of perfection. The function of stressing expression is not required in the cinema since this can be brought out in other ways, particularly by the close-up. Cinema make-up can afford to be more elaborate than theatrical since there is only one performance. It also requires to be more flawless since the camera will look closer and more searchingly than a theatre audience, but, at the same time, with the aid of flood-lighting and perhaps soft-focus, it can achieve a more complete illusion.

As Edgar Morin says, star make-up in the cinema

does not oppose a sacred vision to the profane life of every day; it raises daily beauty to the level of a superior, radiant, unalterable beauty. The natural beauty of the actress and the artificial beauty of the make-up combine in a unique synthesis.[1]

Star personality and hence star make-up are unalterable in different scenes of a film and even from film to film.

In darkest Africa as in the filthiest hovel, at grips with hunger, thirst, frostbite, the marvellous Max-Factorized faces bear witness to the presence of the ideal at the heart of the real.

Star make-up is unalterable because it is divine and stars are the gods and goddesses of the modern world. But instead of God making man in his own image, man has fashioned these gods in an idealized, human image to fulfil a dream – a material, juvenile but perhaps a necessary dream – of fabulous wealth, of everlasting love, of effortless success. Star make-up means depersonalizing the face and creating an unchanging super-personality.

This ideal nature of star make-up, as of star costume, is more clearly visible if we contrast it with the other end of the scale – the films made without any make-up at all, the films of Eisenstein, Flaherty, Dreyer's *La Passion de Jeanne d'Arc*, Visconti's *La terra trema*, de Sica's *Umberto D*, Bresson's *Pickpocket*, Welles's *Citizen Kane*. These views in close-up – showing the grain of the skin, its shadows, its relief, its thousands of

1. Plate 35.

wrinkles – tranform the face from the star's smooth mask into the richest and most expressive of terrains.

But, even here, the face is still a mask, although an infinitely richer, more expressive one. For it is the property of the camera to turn whatever it touches into a *film object*. The most important thing for an actor in a film is to be photogenic – acting ability, beauty, elegance and the rest – all come after this, as less important desiderata. This is realized and has been said most often in relation to the glamorous end of the scale. The young starlet knows instinctively that, in taking a screen-test, the ability to photograph well counts more than dramatic talent. To make a good impression on the film, to be a good foundation for make-up, for lighting, for camera-angles, for all the visual artistry of the operator – this is what is needed. But it applies just as much to the non-actor at the 'realistic' end of the scale. The word 'photogenic' can be understood in a wider sense than that of the merely attractive, glamorous, or pretty. The face of Falconetti in *La Passion de Jeanne d'Arc*, a tragic pattern of suffering, seamed with grime and sweat, can be called photogenic. And, again, the artistic value of a shot like this is in its success as a film object, as an artistic entity in its own right, not as a copy of reality. For these film close-ups show us the human face as we would never see it in reality.

Because of the greater control over an actor's appearance which can be achieved in the cinema, it is possible to effect far greater physical transformation than on the stage. A star never changes, because it is part of his appeal to be always the same. But an actor like Lon Chaney, in his many roles, or like Alec Guinness, who played seven different parts in Robert Hamer's *Kind Hearts and Coronets*, can change far more in appearance, in voice, in gesture and mannerism. Double-exposure can enable the same actor to appear twice in the same shot and talk to himself. Throughout film history there have been examples of famous actresses playing double roles, from Mary Pickford in an early silent film to Bette Davis in the film *Dead Image*.

Here we touch on the more synthetic nature of screen acting. The cinema brings us so much closer to human beings that stage acting would be overpowering. 'Don't act, think' is what one film director[1] advised his actors. Again, a film performance is far less than on the stage a controlled total effort of the actor, but more a picture painted, stroke by stroke, jointly by camera man, actor, director, and the rest. A child's smile of welcome to its mother may be directed at an ice-cream. Spencer and Waley[2] tell of a film in which the heroine had to register ecstasy at the return of the hero she supposed dead. The best of the many takes was found to be one caused by the camera over-running after the tea-break had been announced. Although some purist directors, like Rossellini, are said to eschew these methods, the fact that they are non-naturalistic does not matter, provided that the result will move and convince us.

PHOTOGRAPHIC AND MISE-EN-SCÈNE CHARACTERISTICS

Colour

One of the most important of the surface characteristics of film, as of reality, is colour. From the earliest days of the cinema, the inability of the original photographic processes to re-produce colour was considered a serious drawback. Compared with other more subtle deviations from reality this was such an obvious disadvantage. As a result, a great deal of research has been undertaken from the very beginning in an attempt to in-vent a workable colour process. In addition, the world's film archives are full of productions, which were common forty or fifty years ago, made on tinted film-stock: blue for summer days and for idylls; green for landscapes and seascapes; red for fires and murders; and mauve for night scenes and romantic agonies. There are also reels of film which have each frame

1. Friedrich Murnau.
2. *The Cinema Today*, Oxford University Press, 1939.

coloured by hand – the work of thousands of hours and of armies of anonymous workers. The first processed colour film, shown in 1910, was in Kinemacolor, a two-colour additive process, which proved unsatisfactory in use. In 1925–6 a Technicolor two-colour subtractive process was introduced, the only surviving film which used it being *The Black Pirate*, with Douglas Fairbanks in the lead. In 1935 came the first successful three-colour picture in Technicolor: *La Cucaracha*.[1] From this date onwards, the colour film was established commercially; improvements followed, and various other systems were developed: Agfacolor, Ferraniacolor, Dufaycolor, Sovcolor, and so on.

Early attempts at colour were abandoned partly because of failures and financial disasters, but also because the black-and-white film proved a complete success and was more and more accepted. Furthermore, as in the case of other imperfections of the cinema, it was found that, far from paralysing the artist, the black-and-white image set him free from the need to imitate nature slavishly. As in other arts, the film director began to create on the screen artistic realities which were not copies of nature but valid in their own right. The photographic image was not just a picture that *lacked* colour. It was something positive with positive artistic qualities of its own. The still photograph and the black-and-white film developed together as new forms of visual art. They were new because the half-tones of the photograph are just as different from the black-and-white of any of the graphic arts – whether etching, woodcut, pen and ink, charcoal or chinese brush drawing – as they are from reality. Photography was a form of painting with light,[2] particularly in the case of film, since film with its method of projection could achieve a more luminous image than photography. The early silent classics, especially some of the early Swedish and Norwegian films, showed what beautiful results could be achieved.

1. Directed by Robert Edmond Jones.
2. Plate 36.

At the same time continuous technical improvement played its part – better lenses, better lighting, better film-stock. The film image showed a higher degree of delicacy in rendering tonal values, and the range of intermediate shades between black and white became richer and more subtle. On the screen there flourished a fairyland of light and shade creating those symphonies of chiaroscuro which enchanted Bardèche and Brasillach[1] and formed some of the greatest triumphs of the young art. Black-and-white is able to reveal the world as a film in full colour cannot do. Peter Ustinov, in a recent interview in *Film*, gave as his reason for creating *Billy Budd* in black-and-white: 'Colour beautifies everything and I never feel you get the conditions of people in colour.'

When colour was introduced widely on a commercial scale in the late thirties it was expected to kill black-and-white film stone dead, just as sound had made the silent film into a historical curiosity. But today, twenty years later, despite the improvement in range and quality of colour films, black-and-white is as popular as ever, both with film-makers and audience, and by no means entirely because of the lower cost of producing a film in black-and-white. An interesting thing is the way in which black-and-white has turned out to suit the cinemascope screen, and has crept into a form of presentation which started using colour exclusively. The black-and-white film is beautiful in its own right, not because it is like nature. It enables the director to achieve a formalism, a stylization of the image. In Resnais's *L'Année dernière à Marienbad*, the abstract, formal, universalized atmosphere would have been impossible in colour.[2] The striking last shots of Renoir's *La Grande Illusion*, with the black dots of human beings against the white loveliness of the snow, and the faint hint of symbolism, would have been less effective in colour. The harsh, unreal, science-fiction atmosphere of Stanley Kubrick's *Doctor Strangelove* is

1. *History of the Film*, trans. Iris Barry, Allen and Unwin, London, 1938.
2. Plate 50.

dependent on its use of black-and-white. In Orson Welles's *Macbeth*, the sombre tones are needed to conjure up a brooding air of medieval conspiracy, and, in Bergman's *The Silence*, the use of black-and-white helps to create the stifling emotional climate of the film and underline the morbid psychology of the characters. Black-and-white, again, can be used to blunt the edge of reality.[1] The brutality of Franju's *Le Sang des bêtes* would have been unbearable if the film had been in colour. The examples of *Kanal* and *Fires on the Plain* are given in Chapter Eight.

A director is sometimes able, by artistic means, to suggest colour in a black-and-white film. Nicole Védrès quotes the example of William Wyler's film *Jezebel*, in which Bette Davis causes a scandal by wearing a red dress at a ball. Her dress shows on the screen as a darkish grey, hardly different from the costumes of the other women. But the effect of her entry into the ballroom, of the daring cut of the dress, of her defiant air, of the stir caused among the other guests – these are such that in our minds *we see the dress as red*.

One might expect to find the visual magic of black-and-white only in the most beautiful of the cinema's early films before the introduction of colour: *Sir Arne's Treasure, Siegfried, Battleship Potemkin, Earth, Turksib, Moana*, made at a time when black-and-white was the only medium available. The remarkable thing is that there are just as many recent examples: *The Informer, The Grapes of Wrath*, Orson Welles's *Othello, Pather Panchali, Les Amants, La terra trema, A Taste of Honey, L'eclisse*. All in all, the black-and-white medium is producing just as great art today as ever in the past, and it is no more likely to be superseded by colour than black-and-white forms of graphic art have been superseded by painting.

All this is true. But when all this has been said, it is just as true to say on the other side that the advent of colour opened a new

1. Plate 37.

chapter in film history, a chapter which as yet is hardly begun. Colour has gone a long way from the early days of its introduction, when audiences went away bilious from a surfeit of oversweet, over-emotional colour ladled on like syrup over a trifle. Since then colour systems have grown subtler, and directors have learned to handle them with more discretion. Under these conditions, colour can add a new richness to the screen, can open up new possibilities.

What is important to realize is that colour in the cinema is no more 'natural' than black-and-white. None of the colour systems in use can reproduce the range of the spectrum with accuracy. A system which gets close to the range of reds reproduces the blues badly. Another cannot exactly render shades of green or yellow. Nor will the system which is most accurate necessarily be the most beautiful – in fact the contrary may be the case.

However, supposing there were colour systems which obtained a perfect correspondence of tone with natural colour in the finished positive film, the result on the screen would still be nothing like nature. In the first place, conditions of viewing in a darkened cinema are quite different from those of everyday life. In the second place, colours on the screen have a luminous quality because they are produced by light shining through a translucent material. It would not be possible to get on the screen the solidity of pigment used in painting though it is possible to *suggest* this – as in Pintoff's *The Old Man and the Flower* or in *A Short Vision* directed by Joan and Peter Foldes. Visual textures and the quality of surfaces, which in real life combine with colour, cannot possibly be reproduced on the screen. But, again, they can be suggested, as Pudovkin suggests the texture of the fur in *Storm over Asia* (see p. 208).

The proper use of colour lies not in natural imitation but in human expression. A painter will not try to reproduce on his canvas the profusion and incoherence of natural colour. Consciously or unconsciously, his first care is to compose a harmonized range of shades which will form an artistic unity and express his personal vision.

Bela Balazs has pointed out that the black-and-white image is more homogeneous, and cutting becomes more difficult with colour because the colours have to be harmonized between shots. In George Cukor's *Heller in Pink Tights* there is a transition from a stage scene with powerful reds to a white, outdoor snow scene. The transition leaves a momentary awkward impression because for several seconds the snow is tinged with red – an after-image from the previous sequence. Also the dissolve based on shape becomes difficult because it is the colour rather than the shape which predominates. Colours merge into each other less easily *unless* a dominant colour is chosen and the composition of the sequence based upon it. In Visconti's *Senso*, the closing scenes in the dusk, with the cream uniforms faced with red against the dark brown of the stone barracks, are quite breathtaking because the colours are few and soft. Again, the colour in Ophuls's *Lola Montès* is rich but subdued, and is based on one predominant shade, often purple or maroon. In another fine colour film, Renoir's *Le Déjeuner sur l'herbe*, the greens of high summer dominate the long, outdoor picnic sequence. In Hitchcock's *The Trouble With Harry*, the dominant note is the red-and-gold of a New England autumn. In *Lawrence of Arabia* David Lean has flooded the screen with the blood-red and sulphur of the desert. In Jacques Baratier's *Goha*, the colour is mainly in pale greens and blues and shades of white. Against this light, airy background the director uses vivid splashes of deep red, orange, brown, or gold. In *The Rickshaw Man*, directed by Hiroshi Inagaki, as in many of Ozu's films, there is frequent use of beautiful blue shades.

Again, in *Heller in Pink Tights*, which is about a theatrical troupe in the wild West, the colour is based on the vivid stage sets, whose sombre vermilion and orange mix at times with the sinister black of the professional gamblers and the stormy blue of Sophia Loren's costume. These violent stage colours are at times contrasted with the burnt umber and yellow green of the prairie, especially in a fantastic sequence of Indians looting the wardrobe-wagons of the stage company's caravan. Although undeniably one of the most effective of colour films, its colour could never be called natural. It is significant perhaps that in Anthony Mann's *El Cid* the colour is more effective in rendering the splendour of medieval jousting, battle array and court ceremonial than in some of the outdoor scenes. In the case of some of the early colour systems which resulted in a predominance of red, chestnut, or blue, some directors were able to achieve harmonious compositions, for example Rouben Mamoulian in *Becky Sharp* or Josef von Baky in his delightful *Münchhausen*.

An indication that successful colour in film-making is not to be found in mechanical reproduction of nature, lies in the fact that colour is most frequently and most effectively used in the musical and in the ballet film. In this field it *has* ousted black-and-white. Partly for the reason that a musical demands the gaiety of colour, but also because the musical is a highly artificial form in which all the factors can be completely controlled. The colours of the décor, the costumes, the properties, can all be chosen to film well, and to combine into an effective colour composition. One can almost go so far as to say that in the cinema (perhaps because we are so accustomed to photographic reproduction, not only in films, but in books, newspapers, and snapshots) colour is, in itself, somehow more artificial than black-and-white. This gives another reason why, the musical being what it is, the association of colour with it is so appropriate. *On the Town*, *Singin' in the Rain*, *An American in Paris*, *Gigi*, *The Pajama Game*, *Black Orpheus*, *The Red Shoes*, the *Bolshoi Ballet*, *Porgy and Bess*, *The King and I*,[1] *West Side Story* – one can think of many other similar films in which the handling of colour is a major part of their appeal. Just as some

1. Directed by Walter Lang, 1956.

black-and-white films are inconceivable in colour so these musicals are inconceivable in black-and-white.

Colour suits a comedy like *Genevieve*, a light romance like *Breakfast at Tiffany's* or *Tom Jones* (in which some of the scenes seem designed to obtain the effect of old colour-prints), a farce like *The Pink Panther*. Colour is generally used for big spectaculars such as *Around the World in 80 Days*, *Giant*, *The Pride and the Passion*, *The Guns of Navarone*, *Spartacus*, *The Fall of The Roman Empire*, or *Cleopatra*. Laurence Olivier chose colour to represent the historical pageantry of *Henry V* and *Richard III*, but black-and-white for the tragic drama of *Hamlet*.

The colour of many Japanese films is outstanding, for example Kinugasa's *Gate of Hell*, and Japanese directors have been particularly successful in using colour to re-create the romantic, heroic atmosphere of ancient Japan. In John Huston's *Moulin Rouge*, about Toulouse-Lautrec, and in Minnelli's *Lust for Life*, about Van Gogh, colour is appropriate because it brings the film closer to the world of the painter. Colour is of course an essential element in most present-day animated films, although cartoons are a different art form and one which falls outside the scope of this book.

Just as all the artistic elements we have mentioned so far (cutting, camera movement, framing, and the rest), if skilfully handled, blend and are accepted unconsciously by the spectator as part of the total effect, so it is with colour. Colour should not be obtrusive although it is such a strong element that it may be difficult to keep it in check. A good many films recently have mixed colour with black-and-white, which is a good way of keeping it from being overbearing and yet, at the same time, stressing the particular quality or importance of the scene in colour.[1] In Jerome Hill's *The Sandcastle* there is a short colour sequence to show the magic (real magic, as it is part of a little boy's dream world) of a beautiful, iridescent awabi-shell. In

1. This is a different approach from that of early film-makers who included one section only in colour simply because of the expense.

Agnès Varda's *Cléo de 5 à 7* there is only one shot in colour, the tarot cards by means of which the fortune-teller divines that the young heroine is suffering from a fatal disease. In a film by Bernardo Bertolucci, *Prima della rivoluzione*, there is a sequence in colour preceded by the key word 'magic'. In it a boy and girl look out from a dark pill-box to a bright square and pretend that the rectangle framed by the window of the pill-box is showing them 'cinema variety in colour'.

In François Reichenbach's *Un Coeur gros comme ça* there is a sequence of a boxing match in long-shot, framed by the concentration of the lights on to the ring, and glowing with colour as rich and rare as a jewel. This is the romantic, glamorous view of boxing, to be contrasted later in the film with the brutal reality – in black-and-white.[1]

Dramatic Use of Colour

Colour may be used emotionally for its symbolic or dramatic effect either in a single scene or to help give a tone to the whole film. Eisenstein said that 'we should think of the *meaning* of colour.' Mention has already been made of the tinted film-stock of the early days in which the whole scene took on a shade appropriate to its character: blue for summer days and idylls, red for fires and murders, and so on. A more recent case of colouring the whole film occurred in *South Pacific* (directed by Joshua Logan) in which certain sequences are tinted in violent shades. Although the film was very popular, it is doubtful whether these scenes were a complete success with modern audiences. The *Wizard of Oz* was mainly in colour, but had an introductory sequence in sepia showing a tornado. This nicely held the balance between black-and-white and colour, and formed a bridge for the translation of the young heroine (Judy Garland) from the everyday world of her home to a land of fairy-tale.

It should be recognized that colour can be related to

1. Plate 38.

emotions only in the most general way. Much will depend on the context and meaning of the film, much on other elements such as music and tempo. Red may be just as suitable for the gaiety of a musical, the excitement of a battle or the violence of a murder. In Hitchcock's film *Marnie* the heroine is violently affected by red, and the red of a storm, a sunset or a dress causes her to have a nervous upset. This strange reaction turns out to be due to a violent childhood experience buried in her subconsciousness. Her mother had been a prostitute and the child, molested by one of her mother's customers, attacked him with a poker and (as she thought) killed him, her principal memory of the event being the red of his blood. However, in Vadim's *Les Bijoutiers du clair de lune*, the red flash of Brigitte Bardot's car among the slagheaps of the Spanish hills is used with a very different effect. Again quite different is the red of a cheek flushed by a slap in Veit Harlan's *The Golden City*. In many cartoons, green is used as a comic effect to symbolize incipient seasickness or nausea. But in his remarkable first feature film, *The Boy with Green Hair*, Joseph Losey uses green very successfully to symbolize peace and the importance of international understanding. Far from being comic there is a grave seriousness and charm about the boy's green hair. Another example of symbolic use of colour from *Marnie* is the bag carried by the heroine in the opening sequence of the film. It is the bright yellow colour of gold and turns out, as we might expect, to hold money which the girl has stolen.

Examples have already been quoted of colour giving a dramatic tone to a whole film or a whole sequence. The opulent colours of *Lola Montès* or *Heller in Pink Tights*, both with theatrical backgrounds, are very different from the innocent blue skies and greens of Renoir's *Le Déjeuner sur l'herbe* or *The Greengage Summer*, another film with effective scenes in colour. Pure colour is used in some of the scenes of Kon Ichikawa's *Alone on the Pacific*, and a sequence depicting calm sunny weather at sea contains a shot in which there is no image whatsoever, and the whole screen is simply drenched in bright golden light which vividly evokes the appropriate mood. In *Giant* there is a cosy, picture-postcard effect about the colour of some of the sequences in the Virginia home of Leslie Benedict (Elizabeth Taylor), and this is very different from the harsh sweep of colour in the Texas scenes.

West Side Story uses colour with striking effect in many sequences. Early in the film there is a transition from the hero, Tony, working in the street, to the heroine, Maria, in a dressmaker's shop, which depends on the shimmering colour of semi-transparent material. In the street scene, the washing on the line grows gradually more glamorous in colour and texture, the camera concentrates on it and then dissolves to the dress material in the shop. The transition is made by a pure colour dissolve. After the lyrical dress-shop scene, and before a violent dance scene, there is a brief sequence, in abstract reds and blacks, of figures turning and changing, which helps the transition from one mood to another and presages the conflict to come. In the dance-hall scene Maria wears the only white dress, which both stands out prominently against the other strong colours, and also conveys an obvious symbolic meaning. During the dance, the hero and heroine are picked out in sharp focus, while in the background, in soft-focus, the colours swim together and are blended. The contrast between the two planes is not only a matter of outline, but of colour and texture as well. Then there is a quite different, fairy-tale effect as the couple dance against a dark background, shot with green and red lights, and the violent pace changes to a slow tempo. One of the scenes after the dance is given a romantic tone by the use of a purplish-blue background and the black silhouettes of couples kissing on the stairs. In another scene in which Maria and Tony stage a make-believe wedding, a rich golden light suffuses the screen and gives an other-worldly radiance to the two lovers. Then, when the couple are parted, the mood changes, and the camera switches to a shot of black chimney-pots against an angry red sky and to scenes of the warring gangs. Even the heroine singing at her window is now bathed in red. Then there is a shot of a wire barrier bright red, then a single shot of pure colour with the whole screen one blood-red. These sequences lead up to the central fight scene in which two boys are knifed and killed. The scenes after the fight are in drab, sombre colours, suiting the mood of mingled dismay, remorse, resentment. Then at the end, when Tony is shot, a flashing red light from the revolving lamp on the police car shines intermittently on the gang as they stand round him – a recurrent memory image, as it were, of the violence which has ended so tragically.

In the second part of Eisenstein's *Ivan the Terrible*, a short colour sequence carries a symbolic meaning when the pretender to the throne, who dresses up in the Tsar's robes, realizes that plotters are lying in wait for him and that he is about to be killed in mistake for the Tsar. The previous banqueting scenes are in strong tones of red but, at the same time as the expression on the pretender's face shows his fear, the colour changes to a bluish tinge. Pudovkin's *Harvest* is an early Russian colour film in which the natural colours of the landscape were chosen to suit the moods of the characters. In *Le Carrosse d'or*, Renoir uses colour to create a romantic mood, and, in *The River*, with the double purpose of evoking the rich life of India and contrasting it with the paler, lighter 'colour' of a young girl's affection for an older man. In *Muriel*, Alain Resnais uses colour symbolically and dramatically in many of the scenes.

In Antonioni's first colour film, *Il deserto rosso*, the colour has an important dramatic role to play. The story is about an unhappy woman shut inside a mental prison of nightmare and agony, and the film is dominated by cold shades of green, grey and blue, which occur in almost every scene and give an emotional tone of sadness, unease and troubled dreams. Antonioni himself has said that his film was 'born in colour' and he intended that 'the colour should serve the ends of the story'. At the same time, it has been suggested by one critic that the director and his team have become drunk with the beauty of colour, and that the pictorial loveliness of many of the scenes painted in virtuoso style is such as to inhibit the use of colour as an emotionally meaningful element.

As a final example, one can mention the successful use of colour for poetic and dramatic ends in Albert Lamorisse's *Le Ballon rouge*. The balloon is the chief character in the story and, to ensure that it has the principal dramatic part, it has to occupy the most prominent place on the screen. The director achieves this by painting it a splendid red and, what is more, showing it against a background of neutral greys and biscuit colours. Besides the dramatic emphasis given by the contrast, the colours also have a symbolic function. The neutral backgrounds represent the poor district in which a little boy lives, the unromantic, ordinary workaday world. The red balloon on the other hand stands for the splendour and magnificence of the life he aspires to, the fairy-tale world he floats towards at the end, carried up to the sky by a whole collection of gaily-coloured balloons. The film should be noted both as an artistic and as a technical achievement for, as in all colour films, the effect is not finally obtained until the film leaves the laboratory. A recent illustration of this last point was Visconti's *The Leopard* which was praised for its colour in the original Italian prints, but criticized for the colour of subsequent prints made by a different process for exhibition in England.

No doubt this field of the symbolic and dramatic use of colour will be more explored by the film makers in the future. The present treatment does not pretend to be exhaustive, but enough has been said to indicate some of the possibilities.

Lighting

In the cinema, lighting is a method of composition and what has already been said about graphic composition will apply. The photogenic quality of a scene is rather an illusion to be created than a reality to be copied, and the camera man will not only light a scene adequately to give a good exposure, but will try to obtain a quality of light to suit the dramatic atmosphere. Also, as Pierre Leprohon says, 'Lights and shades react not only on the objects but also on each other, complementing, contrasting, accentuating or softening the total effect'. Unlike painting or photography, film-lighting is not static. The film-maker has to solve a dynamic problem and ensure lighting harmony in a constantly moving perspective of space and time.

Maurice Barry, in writing about his film *Les Gîsants*, described the importance of correctly lighting Germaine Pilon's double tomb-statue so as to bring out the very subtle sculptural effect. The statue shows two naked figures, one dead, one alive – Henry II killed in battle, and Catherine de Medici, who chose to spend the night lying beside her dead king. To bring out the difference between the dead and the living body, the lighting had to match the sculpture in skill and subtlety.

Lighting can ensure that a composition has a unified structure and can bring out its meaning, concentrating attention on what is important and leaving unimportant detail in the shade. In early films lighting tended to be flat and uniform so that the spectator became lost in visual chaos. Later, reacting against this tendency, which came from the theatre, directors favoured more dramatic lighting with part of the scene high-lighted and the rest in shade. But, carried to extremes, this impressionist method can become monotonous and fail to hold the spectator's interest. Nowadays there is a tendency to return to better balanced lighting with the centre of interest emphasized more discreetly.

Another property of lighting is to invest the actors, décor, accessories and costumes with the appropriate character and set the emotional tone of a scene – what may be called the key. In *Les Portes de la nuit*, *The Third Man*, *Le Journal d'un curé de campagne*, *L'Année dernière à Marienbad*, the lighting creates a stifling

morbid atmosphere in which the slightest dramatic effect will
react very powerfully. In quite another mood films like *Chapayev* or *Une Partie de campagne* are bathed in a clear, limpid
atmosphere[1] which lends itself in the one case to excitement and
action, and in the other to bucolic romance. The second part
of Renoir's *La Grande Illusion*, in the chateau prison, has quite a
different emotional tone (confined, dark, cramping) from the
third part when Jean Gabin and his companion have escaped,
and this difference is partly a matter of lighting. In Renoir's
film *Le Caporal épinglé*, which on the surface is a kind of macabre
comedy about a French soldier, a prisoner-of-war of the Germans, who cannot cease from continual attempts at escaping,
the underlying grief of the film is indicated by the lighting
which is continually grey. There is hardly a light, bright shot in
the whole film.

Generally speaking, dark lighting is used for tragedy or
drama and bright lighting (high-key) when the scene aims at
giving a warm, sunny impression with an optimistic emotional
tone. However, if the lighting is pressed beyond a certain point
and the scene overlighted, then an unreal, ghastly effect is obtained which is suitable for dreams, visions, or nightmare
memories. There is an example in Ingmar Bergman's *Sawdust
and Tinsel*, in which a flash-back depicts a humiliating memory
of the circus clown, Teodor, of an occasion when he found his
wife bathing naked with a regiment of soldiers and carried her
back to their caravan through a jeering crowd. This is contrasted
with the rest of the film by being overlighted and also by being
filmed silent. Another striking example is in the dream sequence
of Federico Fellini's *8½*, a film which uses unusual lighting a
great deal. The same means is used to give a harsh, satiric effect
to a scene from *Doctor Strangelove* in which the air-force general,
Buck Turgidson, is summoned from his quarters, where his
secretary is basking under a sun-lamp, to attend a midnight
meeting in the Pentagon.

1. Plate 39.

The character of a face can be greatly changed by lighting. The following is a general description of the various effects but context can modify these considerably. Lighting from above spiritualizes a subject and gives it a solemn or angelic look (religious characters) or an air of youth and freshness. Lighting from below imparts a feeling of unease and gives a wicked or unearthly appearance. Lighting from the side gives relief and solidity to a face,[1] but may make it ugly and show the lines. It may indicate an ambiguous personality, half good, half bad, symbolically half light, half shade. Lighting from in front blurs any faults, flattens relief, softens modelling, makes the face more beautiful but takes away its character. Coming from behind, lighting idealizes a subject, giving it an ethereal quality. This sort of lighting is a modern version of the halo of saints or the aura of a medium.

Finally, lighting affects not only the surface but also the structure of reality by helping to create pictorial and scenic space. By skilful use of light the camera can give the strongest effects of depth.[2] In John Ford's *The Long Voyage Home*, we see one of the sailors in flight through the Cardiff docks at night after being mixed up in a brawl. The scene is filmed facing a strong light, a beacon or light house, which creates very strong counter-illumination. The fugitive runs from the foreground at full speed towards the central light point and seems to be swallowed up by it, while his shadow grows out of all proportion, stretching along the ground to the spectator. The strong effect of distance is emphasized by using a wide-angle lens. Ford had already used a similar shot when Henry Fonda flees towards the setting sun in *Drums Along the Mohawk*. Lighting appears to be much more successful in emphasizing depth in a black-and-white film than in a colour film. On the whole colour tends to flatten the image, presumably because the shading of black-and-white is obscured by the colour. How-

1. Plate 41.   2. Plate 40.

ever, if colour is treated in a certain way using very strong black shadows, if, in fact, the film-maker produces something half-way between colour and black-and-white, then strong effects of depth can be obtained.

Lighting in the cinema is generally quite artificial. Two-thirds of the average film is shot in the studio, using floodlights, and artificial light is also very often used for the remaining exterior scenes which are shot on location. It is rare for camera men working in the open not to use reflectors and often lights as well, in any except the sunniest weather, either to accentuate the contrast of light and shade or to reduce it, or to concentrate attention on an important detail which might otherwise be unobserved. In the studio the director is in complete control and can mould, fashion, compose, and distribute the light as he wishes, aiming both at an atmosphere suitable for the scene and a consistent style for the whole film. The arc-lamps and mercury-lamps used in the studio have light and colour values different from those of natural lighting. Shadows do not come out in the same way. Relief looks different. Moon-light on the screen is something quite other than natural moon-light; it is usually shot in daylight with special filters. Thus the conditions of lighting on the screen vary enormously from those of physical reality. However, once again the deficiency of the camera compared with the human eye, that is, the need to supplement natural light sufficiently to make good photography possible, can be put to good account artistically and dramatically.

CHAPTER SEVEN

The Fifth Dimension: Sound

THE first six chapters have been devoted to analysing, in terms of sight alone, the film's artistic version of the four-dimensional space-time continuum re-created on the cinema screen. But, besides this, there is the world of sound, another dimension, another aspect of reality, the most significant thing about it perhaps being that it comes to us through a different sense organ which determines the nature of our experience of it. Differences in its artistic use in the cinema will stem from differences between the two senses of sight and hearing, but the general picture of the artist expressing his experience through a medium in which he cannot accurately reproduce physical reality, and which thus offers opportunities for the exercise of his art, will still hold good.

Next to sight, hearing is the richest and most complex of our senses. Sound is the basis of one of the greatest of the arts, music. As speech it forms a medium for thought, and is the most important means of communication among human beings. As one can imagine, those who hoped the cinema would create a total illusion of reality were not likely to be satisfied with sight alone, and from the very beginning of the cinema every effort was made to incorporate sound. The history of sound in films is broadly similar to that of colour: early attempts and failures; the realization that the silent film was a valid art form and acceptable to audiences; technical progress in, and eventual perfection of, workable sound systems.

The mechanical reproduction of sound was invented as early as, or earlier than, the mechanical reproduction of moving pictures on a screen, and between 1892 and 1910 Edison, Pathé Zecca, Henry Joly and Léon Gaumont tried out many different combinations of the phonograph and the film projector. But none of them were successful for public exhibition. The final solution, reached in the late twenties, was a system of 'optical' sound. It is worth while explaining simply the principles involved. Variations in sound waves are recorded as variations in light and shade on a separate sound track, but on the same strip of film as the visual images. A light shining through the sound track as the film is projected turns these optical variations back into sound waves, which the audience hears through loudspeakers at the same time as they see the pictures on the screen. The first sound film to be a popular success was *The Jazz Singer*, directed by Alan Crosland, in which Al Jolson made such a hit. It used a slightly different system, but the optical system we have described was introduced and became established shortly afterwards. *The Jazz Singer* was not shown until 1927, and sound films (talkies) were not general until 1930 or later.[1]

Thus, for half its history to date, cinema has meant the silent film, and in this form it has produced great art. So much so that those who had the art of the film most at heart were dismayed by the introduction of sound. One has only to see some half-a-dozen films, say *Intolerance*, *Greed*, *Battleship Potemkin*, *Earth*, *The Last Laugh*, *City Lights* and Gance's *Napoléon*, to realize the range and authority of the silent film. The limitation of expression caused by the lack of sound forced the 'silent' director to describe, to depict, to narrate in pictures and nothing but pictures, and enabled the silent film to develop a purely ideographic, powerful visual magic. Even today, in the partnership of sight and sound, sight is the predominant one of the pair. A great many short films and occasional feature films are still made without dialogue – in effect silent films. One such, a Japanese film, *The Island*, director Kaneto Shindo, won the Grand Prix at the Moscow Film Festival in 1961. The only sound addition to the totally adequate visuals is a rather poor musical accompaniment which, if anything, detracts from the film.

1. Plate 42.

Thus, while visuals without sound are still perfectly valid after thirty years of sound films, we cannot even imagine sound without visuals being able to make a film. This illustrates an important difference between the film and the theatre, for almost any play can be adapted to the radio, and given in sound only, without too serious a loss. On the other hand, radio programmes about the cinema can only reproduce songs, excerpts from the dialogue, comment and interviews. Again, for an actor to talk in a play without intending to be heard would be as unreasonable as silent music or pictures painted to be looked at in the dark. But this often happens in a film – we see people talking behind glass, or in a crowd; it is the 'look' of them talking that interests the film-maker, and this can be better conveyed if words are not present to interfere with and disturb the image. In other cases, a film gives us the sound of speech not the actual words – or not enough of the words to have any meaning: the buzz of conversation at a party, the menacing shouts of a crowd, the bustle of a market, the gabble of the loud-speakers on the railway station at the beginning of *Les Vacances de Monsieur Hulot*, the music of a strange dialect or a snatch of conversation in a foreign language. The examples have a different significance: in *Monsieur Hulot*, the meaninglessness is a joke which is funny because railway loud-speakers frequently are incomprehensible; in the case of the crowd, a menacing meaningless sound can be more frightening than actual words; and in the other cases the music and rhythm and the sensuous feel of the conversation, can be better conveyed without the interference of meaning.

Even when we do hear the words and their meaning matters, the sound and intonation and the appearance of the characters as they say them may also be of as much or more significance. That is why dubbing is generally so unsatisfactory – because the appearance of the actors as they speak bears an organic relationship to the sound and rhythm of the words, and dubbing inevitably disrupts this. Subtitles preserve the original sound-visual combination but at the cost of interfering with the image on the screen. There is, at present, no system in general use which gives a good translation of a foreign film, but at the same time leaves the original unspoiled. Perhaps the most promising is a system in use on the Continent which shows subtitles on a separate screen. Another method is in use at the National Film Theatre in London: the original film is shown undisturbed, but for those who want it, a spoken translation is given through earphones. It is interesting to note in passing that performances of plays in foreign languages of which most of the audience will not understand a word (Russian, Modern Greek, Swedish) are occasionally given in London theatres. One wonders whether the fashion may not have grown in favour with audiences used to watching films in foreign languages, and have sprung from a realization, born of the cinema, that there is beauty in speech and acting apart from the meaning of the words.

DISADVANTAGES OF SOUND

The advent of sound brought with it disadvantages and advantages. One of the greatest of the disadvantages, although only temporary, was connected with this very difference between the cinema and the theatre in the use of dialogue. Just as, in its beginnings, the cinema had copied the scenery and static viewpoint of the theatre, so, when it was able to combine speech with its pictures, it copied the continuous dialogue of the theatre. As for the silent film, so for the sound film, development meant escaping from theatrical influence.

In the theatre, dialogue is continuous and may serve the functions of creating an atmosphere, describing events offstage, revealing a character, and so on. All these things the cinema can do visually, and if they are also conveyed verbally there will be audio-visual pleonasm, as bad as or worse than the pleonasm and repetition of poor writing. Again, dialogue on the stage is generally not ordinary language. It is often poetry or poetic prose and, even if it aims at a realistic effect, even if it uses slang or peasant idiom, it is still far from common speech. Film scripts also often use an enriched dialogue, and poetic prose or poetry (as in the British documentary *Night Mail*, directed by Harry Watt and Basil Wright, or in the many films of Shakespeare plays) is perfectly suitable for use in a film.[1] But, at the same time, many documentary films and more recently, feature films (for example *Un Coeur gros comme ça* or *Weddings and Babies*) use a 'candid' camera style and the flat, repetitious, untidy speech of everyday which would not suit the stage. Harold Pinter started as a playwright but his laconic dialogue is well suited to the cinema. Nevertheless, the film made from his play *The Caretaker*, for all its virtues, remains a filmed play, and is very different from his screen writing for *The Servant* or *The Pumpkin Eater*, which were conceived as films. We have already mentioned the point that stage dialogue, even with naturalistic acting, must be spoken clearly and loudly enough to be heard even if it means talking in a 'stage whisper'.

It might be mentioned in passing that one of the preferred methods of *cinéma vérité* (a new movement in the documentary field) is to record a great deal of actual conversation, possibly private conversation taken with a hidden microphone, select the best of the sound material and only then proceed to shoot the visuals to accompany the sound. This is a reversal of traditional methods, by which either images and sound are recorded together or the images are recorded first, and it gives the film-maker the fullest opportunity of making the dialogue casual and authentic. *Cinéma vérité* depends also on improvization and the unconscious humour of non-actors. The resulting films gain in authenticity and spontaneity, but may lose artistically; they tend to be journalism rather than literature. Examples are Zavattini's *Mysteries of Rome*, Jean Rouch's *Chronique d'un été*, or Chris Marker's *Le Joli Mai*. They offer

[1]. Plate 43. Verse is aptly used also in Gance's *Cyrano et d'Artagnan*.

further evidence that film (especially as influenced by television) can be a more casual medium than the stage.

Another difference between theatre and cinema is that in the former the dialogue *is* the play; it exists as a valid independent literary form in its own right, and forms the basis of an indefinite number of performances and interpretations. In the cinema, on the contrary, there is only one original, authentic film, and the shooting script is a technical blue-print for putting together bits of sight and bits of sound (of which speech is only one element among several) to form a celluloid mosaic. For some films the script can be published in a modified form for reading, but, much more than a published play, this is a reproduction of the film mosaic in another medium. Any script will be as different from the actual film as a book of architect's plans and drawings is different from an actual building. Also, visualizing a film from a script may be as much of a technical accomplishment as reading a musical score.

Before ending this comparison, it should be said that the cinema can successfully adapt the theatre in the form of a filmed play. Various examples can be given in which the original theatrical form is more or less worked into a film. Cocteau's *Les Parents terribles*, Asquith's *The Importance of Being Earnest*, Clive Donner's *The Caretaker* and Sidney Lumet's *Long Day's Journey into Night* are cases in which most of the dialogue is retained but much else is added by film technique. Zarpas's *Electra* and Jean Meyer's *Le Bourgeois Gentilhomme* are more film records of superb stage performances. There are many examples of filmed opera, from Menotti's *The Medium*, which is true cinema, to Czinner's *Der Rosenkavalier*, which is merely a film record of the opera. Again, there are adaptations of ballet as in Czinner's *Bolshoi Ballet* and the point has already been made that the film can analyse paintings and drawings (as in Basil Wright's *The Drawings of Leonardo da Vinci*) and create something new from them. The point to stress here is that, though film adaptations of plays which retain on the screen all the dialogue of the play may be successful in their own terms, they form only an annexe to the art of the film – they are special cases, which do not affect the fundamental difference between play and script which we have stated.

The disadvantage of overwhelming dialogue was connected with another handicap which also gradually disappeared. The original sound-recording apparatus was heavy and inflexible.[1] Visual and sound shooting were generally inseparable and even music was recorded at the same time. This meant studio sets, an almost static camera, and serious limitations in the cutting of the film. For instance, as Karel Reisz says, 'In a dialogue scene, the editor is constantly tied down by the continuity of the words . . .' The free camera movement of the last days of the silent films was lost, and the novelty of dialogue soon failed to compensate for interminable fixed shots. However, gradually the camera and the microphone became independent of each other, more subtle and more flexible. The camera recovered its mobility, and (as discussed in the next section) sound vastly increased its range.

It was not only dialogue that was overdone. In early sound films, directors, intoxicated with the new medium, deafened the audience with a meaningless multitude of noises: striking matches, creaking hinges, gurgling bottles, chinking glasses. In addition the reproduction was often inaccurate so that (for instance) the rustle of a dress sounded like the crackling of paper.

A more permanent disadvantage resulting from the addition of sound was that it made an elaborate art out of a simple one. The silent film was a comparatively pure and homogeneous form. The domain of sound possesses a multiplicity of kind which that of vision does not. There are not different kinds of image as there are different kinds of sound – music, speech, and noises. Thus the introduction of sound meant the introduction not of one new element but of three, and a tremendous increase

1. Plate 44.

in the complexity and consequently the difficulty of the art. Also there can be three different kinds of sound simultaneously competing for the spectator's attention. Not only images and sound, but images, commentary, music, and noise effects can assail the audience all together throughout a film with an almost intolerable effect.

ADVANTAGES OF SOUND

To offset its drawbacks, sound brought important advantages. The silent cinema was silent only in name, for it had from the start been accompanied by music. In fact, to watch a silent film altogether in silence is a curious, incomplete experience. Often the accompaniments were bad, inappropriate or hackneyed. Sometimes, for an important film, special music would be chosen or even composed for the occasion, but, although many large cinemas had orchestras, these would mostly play music of their own choosing. Many cinemas had a special kind of cinema organ installed which was used to accompany all films regardless. Most of the music was trite and unimaginative, sometimes it was excruciating. This did not matter so much as one might have thought. As Kracauer says in *The Nature of Film*: real life is filled with sound, and a completely silent cinema would have been disconcerting. The music was not intended to increase the reality of the mute image by adding sound nor, although it did increase the spectator's emotional receptiveness, was it absolutely essential for this purpose. Its main function was 'to affirm and legitimate the silence'. Thus, provided it was not actively offensive, the music could to a great extent be disregarded; it was the visuals that mattered.

All the same, inferior music, if it did not invalidate silent films, did nothing to help them, and film music nowadays is very much better. Because the sound track is an integral part of the sound film the music can more easily be created as part of the total concept of the film, and may be the work of a great composer. Another point is that music does not have to be continuous, and directors have learned the value of restraint. In most films today, music is used only intermittently, to heighten the mood at keypoints. One sees documentaries and even feature films in which extraneous music is avoided entirely, and the only music in the film is that which arises necessarily from the action or the actual setting. Music not motivated by something in the image occurs only twice in Renoir's *La Grande Illusion*. Again, since the music is on the same track as the visuals, it can be precisely timed to fit them, and can be used to stress a rhythmic beat (a train or a galloping horse), to reinforce the noise of an angry crowd, to sublimate a noise or a cry (the shriek of a tortured prisoner or the cry of a woman in childbirth) which merges into a musical phrase. In an American comedy, directed by Garson Kanin, *My Favorite Wife*, the music is used to echo and mock the cry of a boy paging Cary Grant in an hotel where he hoped to pass incognito. In *City Lights*, a pompous speech turns into the wah-wah of a saxophone. In Hitchcock's film, *Strangers on a Train*, a girl is murdered in a fairground while, very prominent in the sound-track, there is distinctive, hurdy-gurdy music. Later in the film, Hitchcock uses the same hurdy-gurdy music as a memory image to recall the murder.

So far as type of music is concerned, one can say generally that the best film music is that which is composed by a sensitive artist to fit the film. All kinds of concert music have been used for films, from Byrd to boogie-woogie, but, however good the music in itself, it may be inappropriate for the film concerned. Several 'new wave' French directors have used Vivaldi, Bach, and Diabelli, but such formal music as this, with so strong a shape and rhythm of its own, tends to take too prominent a place. Of the three, Diabelli, the most light-weight musically, was probably best for the film in which it was used – Peter Brook's *Moderato Cantabile* – since its prominence was legitimated by the fact that it played an integral part in the action. It is worth quoting as a special case, a Polish film,

Requiem for 500,000, by Jerzy Bossak and Waclaw Kazmiercak. The visuals show Nazis deporting children to concentration camps; the sound-track consists of some of Bach's greatest music. In this case, the deep humanity of the music renders the visuals far more heart-breaking, and the director, in an interview, said he wished to stress the fact that the same nation was responsible both for such ignoble deeds and for such noble music. This example is relevant also to the section on audio-visual montage which comes later in this chapter.

Film music is necessarily 'canned' music and as such cannot attain the delicacy and richness of the actual concert hall. But it assorts with the rest of the recorded sound-track, and enables the highest standards of performance to be universally current. Because of the control given by recording, with its amplification and modification, a film can produce artificial music which could not be made by normal means. The zither in *The Third Man* was transformed by amplification to sound like a new instrument. The film also seems to suit electronic music and *musique concrète* – at least, in the sense that the general public will accept difficult modern music and music of this kind as part of a film whereas nothing would persuade them to listen to it alone as music in its own right. It is even possible for the film-maker to compose his own music or something like music by making marks directly on the sound track of the celluloid film.

Another advantage of the introduction of sound was that it freed the image to be itself, in other words relieved it of the need to try and express sounds in visual terms. In the silent film there was something particularly strained about shots of a factory siren blowing, a train whistling madly, a woman singing, or even an impassioned speech intercut with meagre sub-titles. In cases when a sound had a key role to play in the action it could henceforth be conveyed more directly, more effectively and less obtrusively.

The possibility of using words at all was a third great advantage. In silent cinema, the written captions were always an alien element and never combined with the visuals into an artistic whole. The difficulty seems partly to have been that the captions came after the images in time, and simultaneous captions on a different screen, or even (like present subtitles) on the same screen, would have been much better. By comparison, in a talking film the words and images blend perfectly. They are naturally complementary and we can register them simultaneously without the one interfering with the other. In the case of captions it was necessary to stop the film and, as it were, make an announcement. The talking film meant that the audience were once and for all freed from this irritating interruption. Unfortunately, there is still the initial interruption of voluminous credits, which would be better conveyed on a programme or at the end of the film.[1]

The coming of the sound film also enabled the artist to use silence in a film with a positive dramatic effect. Bela Balazs develops this point fully. Silence cannot have a positive value for instance in a radio play because this consists of words only, nor in a silent film, because this contains no words. On the stage the effect of silence cannot be drawn out or made to last as it can in the cinema. In a film the effect of silence can be extremely vivid and varied and a silent glance can speak volumes. Two examples from *La Grande Illusion* illustrate the point. In one scene a group of men are gathered round, opening a case which has been sent into their German prison and which they expect to contain food delicacies; there is bustle, chattering, excitement, expectation. Then the lid bursts open and shows the case full of books. Suddenly there is complete silence – more effective than any comment. It is a silence which each spectator will interpret differently to suit himself, and which should

1. More and more in recent years film-makers have tried to give the credits artistic distinction, to make them appropriate to the subject, and to integrate them with the film by showing them after or during an introductory sequence. Saul Bass is the first person to have won a reputation solely for his film credits.

no doubt be interpreted differently for each prisoner. Another example occurs earlier in the film, when the prisoners are dressing up for a concert, turning over piles of costumes; there is the same bustle, a buzz of conversation, a coarse laugh at some women's corsets. Suddenly one of the prisoners appears dressed as a girl – he is a pretty young man and the impersonation is well nigh perfect: he looks like a young, appealing girl. Gradually (this time) the noise stops; conversations die away; the men turn to look at him – each busy with their own precious thoughts. . . . Silence is used by Abel Gance in *Un Grand Amour de Beethoven*, perhaps rather obviously, to illustrate Beethoven's deafness. It is also used effectively in a short film – *Together*, directed by Lorenza Mazzetti – about two deaf mutes in the East End of London. A most important example is Ingmar Bergman's recent film *The Silence*, a picture of two sisters and a little boy staying in an hotel, and waited on by an old man. The film is silent for most of the time, but this silence conveys the strangest and most varied meanings; in different situations it expresses lust, boredom, drunken stupor, agonized unhappiness, the wonder of childhood, the resignation of old age. Long periods of silence, particularly at the beginning of the film, are also most effectively used in Pier Pasolini's *The Gospel according to St Matthew*.

Another point in favour of sound is the way in which visuals and sound can reinforce one another. The combination can be more powerful than the sum of the two would be. And they can be combined in various ways, either to harmonize or to contrast with each other. Then there is the beauty and interest of sound, simply for its own sake. These last two points we shall consider further in the next section.

SOUND AND REALITY

The various distinctions we have drawn between film and reality in relation to space and time, can be fruitfully applied to

sound also. In the first place, isolation of a sound and its reproduction in a film has an effect similar to the isolation and framing of the image – it makes possible an artistic selection. Thus,
since the introduction of sound, it has been a function of the
cinema not only to make people see but 'to make people hear'.
The sound cinema has given us more sensitive hearing, taught
us to appreciate the quality of natural sounds – the wind in the
leaves, tyres crying on the pavement, the deep breathing of a
sleeping man. There is the panting of the fugitives in the submerged forest in King Vidor's *Hallelujah*, the noise of trains
during the fight in *Sous les toits de Paris*, the savage growling of
the storm in *Man of Aran*, the ticking of the police commis-
sioner's watch in *The Informer*, the whistle of the express in *Brief
Encounter*. Again there is the slow poetry of the old-fashioned
American speech, beautifully spoken by Burt Lancaster in *The
Kentuckian*, the charming Negro voices in *Shadows*, the feast of
Indian music in Ray's *The Music Room*, the gossamer musical
sequence in *Cléo de 5 à 7*, the ringing of the church bells on the
roof in *L'avventura*, the irresistible beat of Auden's verses in
Night Mail. One could go on instancing examples of how the
sound film has given us new ears.

Secondly, as with vision so with sound; in real life we hear
what we attend to, what interests us; but in the cinema just
the opposite happens – we attend to what we hear, what the
director makes us hear. A mechanical and utilitarian mental
process is replaced by an operation which aims at releasing an
artistic emotion. In the real world our hearing is selective in
much the same way as our vision. If we had to listen to everything we should hear nothing. The sound engineer must
achieve this selection in the cinema much more clumsily by
artificial means. As Robert Ivonnet[1] says

. . . the extreme sensitivity of modern equipment has its disadvantages
. . . sounds are given full intensity which normally would be shut out

[1]. *Le Cinéma par ceux qui le font*, edited by Denis Marion, Collectif,
Paris, 1949.

by the brain. Thus in a country scene the chirping of grasshoppers does not interfere with conversation; but reproduced on the screen it is insupportable and must be reduced in volume by artificial means.

But the apparent disadvantage is at the same time an advantage, for the process of selection while according with realism can achieve an endless variety of artistic effects. There is a striking example from Renoir's *La Bête humaine*, analysed in detail in Ernest Lindgren's *The Art of the Film*. The principal character, played by Jean Gabin, has been at a dance-concert with a young married woman (Simone Simon) with whom he has a liaison. They leave the music of the dance-hall and return to her flat, where they plan to murder her husband. The husband fails to appear, but Gabin in a fit of sadistic madness strangles the girl. But for a few words of dialogue and the girl's screams, this scene is silent. We then cut back to the dance-hall, where a tenor is singing, and the people are asking where Gabin and the girl have got to. The camera then comes back to the flat, with Gabin, sane again, realizing with horror what he has done. This time the flat is not silent but is filled with the sound of the song from the dance-hall. We realize that the music of the dance-hall must have been audible all the time, but the couple in the flat have been so absorbed by passion, violence, and fear that they did not hear it. The song is also dramatically effective, because it relieves the tension created by the murder, and at the same time (it is a love song) forms an ironic commentary on the girl's fate.

The film-maker is able to make use of the artificial registration of sound, not only to choose the sounds he wants and to attenuate or eliminate unnecessary ones, but also to multiply, intensify, transform and orchestrate sounds as if they were invented musical material. Distortion of sound may be artistically effective. There is, for example, the use of an echo-chamber, so telling in the Trust Library scene of *Citizen Kane*. In Olivier's *Hamlet*, electronic distortion is used for the ghost's voice. In *Psyche 59* (directed by Alexander Singer) there is a scene in which a mother is harshly jabbing her blind daughter's nerves; we hear the mother's wounding remarks first loud and jangled, with the mother in blurred close-up (as the blind daughter hears them), then in a clear, quiet voice in sharp medium shot (as they really are). In a film by the Swedish director Rune Hagberg, *After the Twilight*, the principal character in a fit of madness strangles his mistress, who, in the silence of the night, utters a truly inhuman, terrible cry. Asked in an interview how she managed it, the actress of the film admitted it was not her voice: 'We tried all sorts of animal noises,' she said, 'and finally hit on a seal!' In Sacha Guitry's film *Les Perles de la couronne*, by running the sound track backwards the French actress Arletty was able to give the impression of talking Abyssinian! In Karel Zeman's inventive *Baron Münchhausen*, the director uses distorted sound to enable the Baron to talk 'diplomatic language'. In an East German film attacking neo-Nazism in West Germany, *Holiday on Sylt* (directed by Annelie and Andrew Thorndike), there is a scene of a Nazi meeting to which a faked effect has been added for propaganda purposes. On the sound track a single cheer has been repeated again and again, so that it sounds like a savagely reiterated *Heil! Heil! Heil!* and gives the meeting a far more sinister, more aggressive character. In a Bulgarian film, *Sun and Shadow*, directed by Ranghel Vulchanov, a girl playing on the beach plucks a fishing-net and produces liquid musical notes from it. In the film the effect is over-conscious and does not perhaps come off successfully. Here we merely note it as an example of the power of film to combine realistic and fantastic elements.

Although the method has become a film cliché and has been used many times before, there is a sequence using added sound in *Judgment at Nuremberg* which is effective in this particular film. Spencer Tracy wanders alone in the empty stadium where the Nazis staged their rallies. On the sound-track we hear Nazi songs and violent, ranting speeches echoing in the vast emptiness of the arena. In Edward Dmytryk's *Give Us This Day*, an

Italian working-man brings his wife home after a magical honeymoon to the slum apartment in Brooklyn where they are to live. By added sound, the atmosphere of the place is vividly evoked – a bedlam of shouting, swearing, and quarrelling, of dustbins being banged on the pavement, of doors slamming, of babies yelling, of rowdy kids playing in the yard – and the all-pervading noise conveys an atmosphere of being 'overwhelmed by the environment, of not calling one's soul one's own, of being driven half-crazy'.[1]

In *La Nuit fantastique* Marcel L'Herbier obtained a rich effect by doubling the sound-track. In *Lumière d'été* Jean Gremillon is said to have combined together two hundred sounds to obtain the 'thickness' he wanted. In *Le Tempestaire* Jean Epstein has reconstructed a complete new world of sound out of natural and musical elements. By slowing down or speeding up the recorded elements, by a grouping of mass effects and individual sounds, by having the composer highlight the sound montage by musical phrases, he has integrated the elements of a storm into a great orchestral composition. Pudovkin writes of his film *The Deserter*:

> For the dock sequences I used only natural sounds: heavy hammers, pneumatic drills at different distances, the noise of rivetting, sirens, falling chains. All these noises I recorded on location then mixed them altering their duration and intensity like notes of music. As a finale I showed the ship nearing completion, while the sound in a complex orchestration mounts to its peak. It was real musical composition: I had to feel the length of each sound-shot as a musician feels each note.[2]

SOUND MONTAGE

The independent recording of sound allows montage effects within the sound-track itself, and also between the sound and the images. Although we use the same word, 'montage', for

1. Claude Roy in an article in *L'Écran français*, October, 1949.
2. Authors' translation.

sound combinations and for visual combinations, there is a fundamental difference between the two. The essence of visual montage is that we see one image after the other and mentally combine or contrast them. There may be montage in this sense in the case of sound: a high-pitched voice may alternate with a deep voice; or the sound of pneumatic drills may contrast with that of the wind in the trees; or (as in Thorold Dickinson's *Men of Two Worlds*) the music of an orchestra in London may be followed by native African music. There is an example of this consecutive montage of different kinds of sound in Paul Rotha's *The Life of Adolf Hitler*. A scene of a victory parade in Berlin with a loud and plummy military band playing *Deutschland über Alles* is immediately followed (*bang*) by the noise of guns on the Russian front with ragged German soldiers retreating and surrendering. The ironic contrast of the visuals is strongly reinforced by the ironic contrast of the sounds.

But this sort of combination is not (as with visuals) virtually the only combination, or even the most important. What is generally meant by sound montage is either similarity or contrast between different types of sound or between sounds and images, *which occur sometimes after one another, sometimes together, sometimes with an overlap (partly together, partly separate).* In the cinema, except for double-exposure used for dissolves and special effects, the audience is not expected to look at more than one picture at the same time although of course there may in effect be two elements combined in the one frame. Almost the only film which has made creative use of more than one screen is Abel Gance's *Napoléon*.[1] But in the case of sound, not only do we naturally see and hear at the same time, we can also listen to more than one kind of sound (music, speech, noises) and more than one noise at the same time. Only with music and speech are we unable to take in more than one composition

1. There is a triple-image effect by way of a joke in Truffaut's *Tirez sur le pianiste*. There is also Gance's *Quatorze juillet*, which is entirely in 'polyvision'.

or more than one person talking at the same time.

The important question concerning audio-visual montage, debated when sound was introduced, was whether there should be synchronism or non-synchronism of sound and image. Clearly synchronism gives the natural, realistic, reproduction-of-actuality view of things. We see a man talking: we hear what he is saying. We see a man chopping wood: we hear the sound of his blows. In view of this, it is a remarkable thing that, as early as 1930, Eisenstein, Pudovkin and Alexandrov drew up a manifesto which contained this passage:

... only the method of using sound in counterpoint with the visuals offers new possibilities for developing and perfecting the art of montage. Experiment with sound should be concentrated on using asynchronism between sound and visuals. This approach will lead in time to the creation of a new orchestral counterpoint of visual and sound images.

This passage indicates that the Russians recognized at once that non-natural asynchronism was likely to be more interesting artistically than the more natural synchronism. Speaking as a practical film-maker, Anthony Asquith pointed out in *The Cinema 1950*[1] that an audience can grasp the meaning of visuals much quicker than that of sounds. Consequently, in any sequence in which the cutting of the visuals is rapid, the appropriate sound for each visual, when these are changing every split second, could not be used without completely confusing the audience. 'Further, there is no underlying unity in the sounds as ... in the movement of the images.' The use of one sound, very often music, to cover a variety of rapid images is essential.

Kracauer in *The Nature of Film* gives a complex and exhaustive analysis of the different combinations of sound and image and distinguishes three different contrasts of image-sound in

1. Ed. Roger Manvell, Penguin Books, 1950.

combination: (*a*) synchronism – asynchronism; (*b*) parallelism – counterpoint; (*c*) actual and commentative sound. *Synchronism* is the same combination of sound and image as we would experience in real life (we look at a person and hear him talking). *Asynchronism* is a combination of sound and image we would not experience in real life (we look at an empty nursery and hear the voices of the children who have just been playing there). *Parallelism* is a combination in which sound and image repeat one another and one of the two is redundant – parallelism implies audio-visual pleonasm. Parallelism can be either synchronous or asynchronous. If a character in the film mentions London and the visuals show 'Big Ben' this might be an example of asynchronous parallelism. René Clair gives an example of synchronous parallelism: 'It is not important to *hear* the sound of applause if one *sees* the hands which applaud.' *Counterpoint*, on the other hand, is a combination in which both sound and image make an essential contribution to the total effect and can also be synchronous or asynchronous. In Rossellini's *Paisà* we hear the cry of a forlorn child wandering among the bodies of those killed by Nazis, both before (asynchronous) and after (synchronous) the infant appears on the screen. In both cases the wailing sound adds to the effect of the visuals. The third contrast is between sounds which naturally belong to the world shown on the screen (*actual*) and those which do not (*commentative*). In one travelogue, for example, all the commentary may come from tourists and others naturally present in the scene (actual). In another there may be a disembodied commentator (commentative).

The reader may find it difficult to get a clear picture from this brief summary, and if he wishes to follow the classification in more detail, should consult the original. The scheme has been given here, albeit briefly, because it seems the only complete analysis yet attempted, but it is far from perfect. For instance, the three opposites and the distinctions they stand for are determined from different points of view, and the categories they represent are not mutually exclusive but overlap and merge with one another in a confusing manner. Also there is a gradual progression from one extreme to the other and there will be border-line cases difficult to assign to one side or the other. For instance, in the case of parallelism there will be many different degrees and types of redundancy and it may be very much a matter of opinion whether a particular shot or sequence illustrates parallelism or not. In the case of counterpoint the contributions from the visuals and the different sound elements may differ widely both in kind and value. Similarly there will be cases also which are not clearly either synchronous or asynchronous – suppose, for example, we see one person's face and hear another person speaking. This is a combination which could occur in real life and could therefore be synchronous, but used as it mostly is on the screen it does not seem right to call it synchronism. In the third contrast, what about an interior monologue? Is it to be classified as actual (people do talk to themselves) or commentative? In general, sounds and visuals overlap and intermingle in so many ways, that satisfactory classification is most difficult and neat divisions do not accord with the facts. A further difficulty is that there is no clear-cut beginning and end of a sound as with the straight cut of visual montage, and sounds are faded in and faded out – or faded down until they are just perceptible.

Kracauer reaches two general conclusions which are interesting but he might have arrived at them without his scheme of classification. First, he is persuaded that image-dialogue combinations are more likely to give rich and varied artistic results when the images predominate over the dialogue than when the dialogue predominates over the visuals. Secondly, he points out that constant visual illustration of dialogue (one of the characters mentions Paris and the film cuts to a shot of the Eiffel Tower, etc., etc.) can be extremely redundant and boring, even although it is asynchronism of sound and image. Thus, in this analysis, counterpoint is by definition better than parallelism, but asynchronism may or may not be better than synchronism. Kracauer's classification may give us a complete logical structure, but it becomes so complex in application that it seems more of academic than practical interest.

Rather than continue the discussion in such abstract terms it will be more profitable simply to discuss examples of some of the many ways in which sounds and images can be combined. Besides those which follow, examples from other sections of this chapter will also be relevant.

A primitive example (which, like the visual illustration of dialogue, became a most boring cliché) comes from one of the earliest sound films, *The Jazz Singer* (director Alan Crosland). During some of Al Jolson's songs, the camera leaves the singer to wander among the places he sings about. Richer, more subtle examples are to be found in the films of the British documentary school of the thirties, many of which have extremely complex sound-tracks. In Basil Wright's *Song of Ceylon* the visuals show us romantically beautiful tropical scenes, while the sound-track prosaically quotes from business letters, enumerates the contents of old bills of lading or gives the prices of copper, tea, rubber, and other commodities. This both provides an effective contrast and also relates the seemingly remote forests to our own everyday existence.

There is a good example in *Citizen Kane*. When Kane's second wife, Susan, has a disastrous début singing opera on the stage, we see first the actual scene, hear the thin voice failing disastrously on the high notes, listen to the meagre applause. Then on the screen there appear notices in Kane's own newspapers, praising the performance, celebrating an imaginary triumph. But on the sound-track the pathetic voice goes on and on, giving the lie to the visuals and creating an ironic contrast. In an interesting Canadian documentary about a 'pop' singer, *Lonely Boy*, there is a sequence in which we see the 'lonely boy' doing one of his numbers. Instead of the sound-track carrying the almost inescapable 'pop' song, we hear the boy's husky voice commenting on his own performance. 'I know just what actions I'm gonna make' (we see him making them); 'I know just how I'm gonna put it across' (we see him putting it across). The audio-visual montage is effective in several ways: firstly, we escape the boring, many-times-seen-and-heard, routine combination of image and sound and instead have something unusual and unexpected; secondly the comments are apt and penetrating, and add to our knowledge both of the person and of his art; thirdly, the visuals without the sound possess a new quality and give the actions a ballet-like air; fourthly, the silent, gesticulating figure has a pathetic, appealing look – he really does seem a lonely boy.

In John Ford's *The Long Voyage Home*, the story of a cargo-boat carrying dynamite across the Atlantic during the war, there is a sequence of an air-attack treated entirely in counterpoint. The camera remains on the bridge of the ship and shows the panic of the crew. We see nothing of the planes except their shadows sweeping across the deck, but we hear the roaring of their engines, the whistling of their dive-bombing, the crackle of machine-guns, the crump of bombs. The effect is terrific and the danger seems worse because it is not seen. Also, as the camera never looks up, the treatment suggests a person so terrified he dare not raise his head. In Clouzot's *Le Corbeau*, towards the end when the nurse, condemned by public opinion, is running away through the town, the streets are deserted, but we hear the shouts of the crowd as if they were coming after her.

There is a charming example of audio-visual montage in an Indian film, *Wedding Day*, director Mrinal Sen. The hero earns a living by peddling his wares to daily commuters on a railway train. His stock-in-trade includes a red dye for women's feet, an Indian equivalent for lipstick. In one sequence, he wakes in the night and sits lovingly contemplating his beautiful young bride. Into the stillness on the sound-track there breaks the noise of the train and his voice in an interior monologue saying,

'When you cannot sleep at night and sit awake looking at the one you love, think how much a little present of red dye for her feet would please her.' Before he has finished speaking, the visuals catch up with the words and we cut to the train with him now actually speaking the words. This is a brilliant example of economy: the words start off as a reverie and finish as an actual sales talk. Also the dialogue forms a perfect transition: in the night scene looking forward to the next day, in the day scene referring back to the previous night. The sequence also combines and contrasts the two main aspects of the film and also of the hero's character: an idyllic love affair, on the one hand, in which his good qualities predominate, which is destroyed, on the other hand, by his weakness in business, his inability to earn a living and his gradual ruin.

It will be seen from the complexity and variety of these examples how difficult it would be to lay down rigid rules of audio-visual montage. Because sound is so complex, audio-visual combination and alternation is far more complicated than visual montage alone, since there can be interplay not only between the visuals and noise effects, music or words, but between each of these three elements as well. Each sequence, each shot, is a special case. But if the artist is faced with extremely complex and difficult material, at least there is the widest scope for invention and the exercise of imagination.

METAPHORIC AND SUBJECTIVE
USE OF SOUND

Audio-visual montage enables sound to be used independently of the visuals both symbolically and also subjectively. In cartoons the sound frequently represents a simple metaphor or a symbol; Pluto's tail vibrates like a tuning fork; Donald Duck turns corners with a scream of tyres; General McBoing-Boing gives his orders in a voice (literally) of thunder. In Georges Rouquier's *Farrebique* there is the impressive sound of a tree falling at the moment when the old farmer dies. The same sound is used quite differently in a stylish French documentary, *La Métamorphose du violoncelle* (director Dominique Delouche), in which, instead of symbolizing the end of a human life, it represents the beginning of the process of making music – a tree cut down to make wood for 'cellos. In *Citizen Kane*, as Susan Alexander, Kane's empty-headed second wife, goes out of the room after a silly quarrel, a parrot screeches aloud, making a pointed comment on her character. In an American film, Robert Mulligan's *Love With the Proper Stranger*, a rejected suitor goes out of the door pursued by the pistol shots of a television programme in the room behind him.

In a satiric, short Dutch film, *Ballad of a Theatre Tout* made by Max de Haas in 1937, there is a wedding between an old hag and a simple-minded fellow, in which we can hardly hear the official reading out the words of the ceremony for the noise of a pile-driver on a neighbouring building site. The discordant noise matches the incongruous couple. In Nicolas Ekk's *The Road to Life* there is a dramatic final scene in which a crowd is gathered to welcome the first train on a new line. When the train comes in, the body of a murdered man is lying on the front of the engine. The cheering which has started dies away, and the only sound left is the heavy beat of the engine – as if it were sobbing with grief. In *Okraina* (director Boris Barnet), there is a scene of an official send-off for a body of troops at a railway station. A Tsarist spokesman harangues the crowd, which cheers repeatedly, but in the film the cheers cannot be heard for they are drowned by the whistling of the train. The sound expresses symbolically how the grim reality of departure for the war predominates over the spurious patriotic enthusiasm aroused by the orator. Music can also be used symbolically as a leitmotiv. In Jean-Pierre Melville's film *Léon Morin prêtre*, a sequence of harsh chords is used to typify the German occupation forces. When, after liberation, the heroine and her little girl, accompanied along the road by two American soldiers, pass a wrecked German tank, the harsh chords come back on the sound-track irresistibly recalling the earlier background of the film. In the same film a quite different dancing bugle motif is used for the Italian troops. Organ music is used for scenes showing the heroine with the priest in church, but piano music for scenes in his flat. Hurdy-gurdy music is used to typify two gossiping old spinsters. In a scene where the priest (Jean Paul Belmondo) has brought the heroine a book on theology and is reading it to her, louder and louder electronic music is used to express the heroine's stronger and stronger obsessive sexual feeling for the priest, until she reaches out to take his hand.

Like images, sound can be used subjectively to express the impressions or state of mind of a character in the film. There is the famous scene from Hitchcock's *Blackmail* in which the words '*Knife, Knife, Knife*', are repeated in a frightened girl's mind. In *Jean de la Lune* (director Jean Choux) the heroine is going off with a smooth charmer to Brazil, leaving in Paris the man she loves. When the train stops at a country station, we hear schoolchildren singing the round 'Jean de la Lune' which reminds her of her former lover. When the train goes on, the music goes on (in her head) with it, until finally she changes her mind and goes back to Paris. In a film *Life is Very Good*, Pudovkin tried to use sound subjectively. At one point a mother mourns the loss of her grown-up son, but instead of hearing her sobs we hear a baby crying. This was intended to suggest that the woman still thought of her son as a young baby. In another part of the film a woman is having a brief moment's farewell conversation with her husband whose departure for the war is imminent. The poor woman is distracted and every minute keeps hearing (in her mind) the noise of the departing train, before it actually moves. Unfortunately audiences failed to understand this use of sound, partly because it was new, partly because the associations were too remote; they simply thought a baby was crying in another room and a train leaving from another platform. Pudovkin had to scrap the sound-track and the resultant silent film was called *A Simple Case*.

Allied to the subjective use of sound is the use of the interior monologue which sprang from the commentary. The commentary was at first confined to documentary films and, as in the example already given from *Song of Ceylon*, is a special case of audio-visual montage. Its first use in a feature was in Sacha Guitry's *Le Roman d'un tricheur*, in which the verbal element is a thread to tie the visual episodes together. The interior monologue seems first to have been used in R. Z. Leonard's film *Strange Interlude* (1932) based on Eugene O'Neill's play, in which the characters' thoughts as well as their conversation are heard. The idea was more successful in the cinema than on the stage, as on the screen the actors did not have to move their lips to make their thoughts audible. The use of interior monologue was proposed by Eisenstein much earlier in 1930, for a film to be based on Dreiser's book *An American Tragedy*, and he wrote at the time: 'It is clear that the correct thing for sound films is the interior monologue.' It is a great pity that Eisenstein's plans for the film came to grief. In a Bulgarian film already quoted, *Sun and Shadow*, a rather shy young couple are playing on the beach and we hear their voices saying sweet nothings without their lips moving. The girl's voice says: 'But you must not say such passionate, such intimate things. I hardly know you.' Then the boy's voice says: 'But these are only our thoughts. We can think these things even if we cannot say them.' The effect is quite charming. There is a different type of example in *The Paleface* (director Norman McLeod), in which Bob Hope is able to have an amusing argument with his conscience, a disembodied voice – as it were another self.

In *Terminus*, John Schlesinger's film about Waterloo Station, pop songs are used as a kind of commentary. When the boat train from South Africa comes in and there are reunions after long parting, we hear the song 'I Wouldn't Have Known You.' A train full of West Indians brings the song 'Jamaica Boy', while rich, sophisticated American tourists leave for the Continent to the tune of 'Paris, Rome, Madrid', In this case the songs merely support and comment lightly on the visuals. But a commentary can provide a strong ironic contrast. In an unfinished British documentary directed by Nazli Nour there is a sequence in which the camera shows us the most appalling slum interiors while the melodious, cultured voice of a house agent describes marble patios, swimming pools, reception halls, and so on – the effect is devastating. Devastating, too, is the effect of a sequence of Alain Resnais's film *Muriel* in which the young boy, Bernard, is showing his girl-friend a film of his soldier companions. The film in bright colour shows jolly shots of troops relaxing in camp, young men laughing and gay. To accompany it we have on the sound-track his flat voice describing how they tortured and killed an Algerian girl. Again ironic is a long section in Carl Foreman's *The Victors* which opens with a Christmas newsreel of soldiers playing in the snow. On the sound-track the happy Christmas songs go on and on, but the visuals change to show the execution, for desertion, of a soldier by a firing squad. There is also in this sequence a formalized ritual effect, obtained by careful composition of the image, by shooting in long-shot at a downward angle and by the strong black-and-white effect of the dark uniforms against the dazzling white snow.

Enough has been said to establish that sound, whether as speech, music, or noise, has become an integral part of the film even if it is still the visuals which predominate. The general principles which govern the use of sound in film are similar to those applying in the case of the images: economy, restraint, appropriateness, variety, variation from reality. The inferiority of recorded sound as compared with sound in reality, carries the compensating advantage of making all sorts of artistic uses possible. Here too art lies not in imitating nature but in creating a coherent, expressive world of sound in film terms.

CHAPTER EIGHT

The Other Senses: Taste, Touch, and Smell

WE have now discussed the cinema as it affects two of our senses – sight and sound. In fact this completes the review of the cinema as it exists and the film up to the present directly affects these two senses only, apart from the innate sense of time. But since we are making a comparison between film and reality we ought to take into consideration our whole experience of reality and this includes other senses besides sight and sound – smell, taste, touch, and the kinaesthetic sensations of our own bodily movement. Ought the cinema to include these senses? Is it possible? Is it desirable? Does their omission qualify, limit, or impoverish the film spectacle? These are questions we should briefly consider.

As might be expected, advocates of *cinéma total* would be glad to incorporate these senses also in the entertainment they offer and if it becomes technically possible to expand show-business in this way, it will very likely be done. Their use is mentioned, half in satire, in Aldous Huxley's *Brave New World*. In the United States, film performances have been supplemented by spreading different smells about the auditorium – new-mown hay, tobacco, and the scent of roses.

For entertainment of a sensational kind, the more that can be added the better, and we must look forward to the 'Sensation Cinemas' of the future. One day it may be possible to shut oneself up in a room in London and be transported on a trip to Japan, with all the sights, sounds, and scents artistically contrived: the taste of Japanese food, the feel of a breeze in our hair, a spray of cherry-blossom brushing our cheek, its fragrance in our nostrils, the hand of a friendly guide on our shoulder. Even then, although the spectacle would be carried so much nearer to reality, this could conceivably be an *artistic* experience (although perhaps only on the fairground level), in the sense of being different from a real experience. But the problem created for the serious artist (and the spectator), by the present complexity of the cinema which we have already mentioned, would be intensified many times, and there is much to be said against further elaboration. Although the point does not perhaps need proving, it is worth considering the arguments in a little more detail, as they will indirectly illustrate more fully the nature of the cinema.

In the first place taste and touch and smell are not senses particularly suited to communicating artistic experience. Physiology teaches us that, although they are far more delicate and complex than was once supposed, they are more limited than sight or hearing. They are certainly responsible for many sensuous pleasures, but pleasures which belong rather to the realm of our active experience, than to the more reflective kind of artistic experience. Much of the pleasure of sport and games is in the *doing* and we can hardly have kinaesthetic sensations for instance except by ourselves acting and achieving. We cannot enjoy the pleasures of taste without actively eating and drinking. This very activity will interfere with the detachment that is necessary if the spectator is to participate as fully with his eyes and his ears as he does in an artistic experience. Wordsworth, for instance, defined the essence of poetry as 'emotion recollected in tranquillity'. Smell is more passive and it is perhaps significant that this is the sense which has been experimentally exploited.

Mostly also these senses are dependent for their full enjoyment on the contribution of sight and hearing. Every good cook knows how important it is for his dish to look attractive, and the best dinner is one at which there is good conversation. The perfumer is careful to make his flacons elegant in appearance. We judge whether a person has 'the skin you love to touch' by looking at it. It is only in their disagreeable aspects that these senses really dominate us – it is when we are racked with pain that we cannot escape from the tyranny of our sense of touch, and no visual magic will disguise a bad breath or the taste of foul medicine.

This brings us to the second argument against making the cinema all-inclusive: that the present limitation causes a desirable softening of reality. If it is done in the right spirit, it is proper for art to show us unpleasant things. Paintings show us the agonies of martyred saints, bloody battles, old age, suffering, ugliness, and death. Dickens's novels dwelt on poverty, slums, cruelty to children, and other evils of his time. But these experiences are transmuted by art into something very different from actuality; they become *artistic experiences*. We may be deeply conscious of the suffering and misery involved, indeed we may be more conscious of it than if we were actually implicated in the reality – but our involvement is intellectual and sympathetic. Because the senses are less involved and the imagination has free play, art can touch us to pity, shame, revulsion and can send us away reflective and conscious of an abuse that needs redress. If the audience are involved in too strong and crude a sense experience, the effect could be to deaden this power of sympathy. The impact of films is very strong as it is – a businessman, a hard-headed experienced person, complained that he could not sleep after seeing the ill-treatment and crucifixion of slaves in Stanley Kubrick's *Spartacus*. Another example is Wauda's *Kanal*[1] which has the grim setting of the sewers of Warsaw during the destruction of the city by the Nazis. Part of the tragedy and horror of the film is that, to carry on the war, to survive, to fight back at the Germans, the men had to live and die in excrement. It is the ultimate debunking of war, war reduced to its (literally) filthy reality, at the other end of the scale from the romantic heroics of many

1. Plate 45.

battle epics. Another film, *Fires on the Plain*, by the Japanese director, Kon Ichikawa, shows the tragic defeat of the Japanese towards the end of the Second World War, trudging through the mud, starving, ragged, half-naked, finally reduced to cannibalism or self-destruction. Both these films were shot in black-and-white. Association of ideas, which in these two examples would be crude and strong, would have diminished their artistic impact if they had even been shot in colour, let alone with other sensory effects added. In every medium, and particularly in the cinema, there is value in restraint.

Here we touch on the eternal problem of art and censorship, No society is without its taboos – religious, political, sexual, social, even artistic. No audience is without its prejudices. Art has always been subject to censorship, for one of its functions is to act as a field for social experiment, to promote and to reflect changes in the *mores* of a society; and another of its functions is to provide a release, a vicarious means of expression for feelings and impulses which cannot find expression in everyday life. At the same time censorship imposed by authority is by its nature approximate and often ineffective. An official censorship may be necessary, especially in order to try to protect those who are unable to protect themselves from crude political exploitation or gross pornography. But, finally, the most important censorship is that exercised by the artist himself as part of the discipline of his art, and by the audience itself in the form of discrimination against crude vulgarity and insincere sensation. This on both sides is a matter of good taste. The artist may quite legitimately attack the prejudices of his audience and the, audience may quite legitimately choose what they will accept, but in both cases there are certain indefinable standards of art and morality. For this sort of censorship there are no rules; it will depend on the audience, the occasion and the work itself. The trouble with the official censorship, for which rules often have to be laid down, is that it will frequently be unable to check the unscrupulous sensation-monger but may penalize the serious artist.

In many cases the artist is able to say by suggestion what he cannot say directly. A film director cannot show his audience a couple making love – not because it would be immoral but because it would be inartistic and ridiculous – but he can symbolize it in many ways. In Claude Autant-Lara's *Le Diable au corps*, when the lovers embrace each other the camera leaves the bed and stands still in front of the fire, with its symbolic flames, while the music swells out, transforming and exalting an episode that could not have been handled visually. Later in the film, when the girl is dead and the man, in despair, mopes about the scene of his love, the camera makes exactly the same movement round the bed – this time empty – and finishes on the same grate – this time full of ashes.

In Torre Nilsson's brilliant film *Summer Skin* there are three sequences of this kind, each handled differently. When the good-looking young invalid hero is seduced by an older woman servant, the circumstances leading up to this are harsh and unromantic – loud music on a gramophone, the boy getting dressed, the camera moving in to black-out against the back of a chair. There is an entirely different lyrical, tender feeling when the hero and his girl wander together in a pine-forest and, at the critical moment, the camera pans upwards to the soaring trees and the sky. A different and less idyllic atmosphere is suggested in a third sequence of rich young playboys and girls on a necking party on the beach at night. In another Argentine film *The Sad Young Men*, directed by Rodolfo Kuhn, the heroine picks up a little clockwork toy, winds it up and sets it on the floor before she holds out her arms to the young man she is passionately in love with. The camera then concentrates on the clockwork toy shuffling on the floor, slower and slower, until it runs down. In the morning, when the man goes off to work, the girl takes the little toy into bed with her in his stead. The symbolism could hardly be more direct, yet in the film it is natural and inoffensive. In *L'Année dernière à Marienbad* the seduction of the heroine is symbolized by a series of rapid forward tracking-shots, each fading into the other, as she stands facing the camera, enraptured. The music works up to a climax, the visuals to a blaze of blinding light with violent over-exposure. Then the tension relaxes completely with a dark, slow shot and a murmuring voice. There could hardly be a more candid film than Bergman's *The Silence* which suggests kinds of sexual behaviour many people would consider abnormal. But the behaviour is suggested, not shown explicitly, and so the film has been accepted by censors and audiences in most countries.

It is generally in fact much more effective to appeal to the mind and the emotions rather than directly to the senses. 'Heard melodies are sweet, but those unheard are sweeter.' The worst fears are those which exist in our imagination. The best meals are those we remember from our youth. We live in a mental world and the mind interprets the messages it receives from the senses sometimes incorrectly, always partially. This is a point to be returned to in discussing the nature of film reality. Suggestion may also be far more effective than full statement because it is more stimulating. In attacking a person, innuendo will penetrate deeper and have a more devastating effect on any intelligent listener than straightforward abuse. Suggestion demands a contribution from the listener, flatters him by demanding it, and involves him much more than if he is merely a passive recipient. The artist can say too much and become boring. Secondly, in supplying mentally the images that are omitted, each viewer will imagine something different, something to suit his own case. There is a story of a successful blackmailer who threatened strangers by accusing them of some un-named crime, merely saying 'I know all about you, everything is discovered.' If his success is truly reported, it is no doubt because the threat was couched in such vague terms that the details of their crimes were supplied by the victims themselves. The same applies to certain kinds of character-reading and fortune-telling in which past and future are put in the most general terms. In the hands of a skilful practitioner each client can almost be made to tell his own fortune. It is the same with a horror film: the most fearful monster is one we never see, the worst torture one whose details are withheld – we supply them to suit our own case. Thus by suggestion the artist can both deal with subjects that would otherwise be too shocking, and he can convey his meaning more pointedly, more wittily or more forcefully than he could by full statement.

There is a famous sequence at the end of Lewis Milestone's *All Quiet on the Western Front* in which the hero, Paul, a German soldier, is shot by a French sniper. The sniper is shown carefully aiming his rifle but all we see of Paul is his hand stretching out to try and touch a butterfly that has come to rest. We recognize it as Paul's hand because we already know he is a butterfly collector, and, because of the sniper, watch it stretching farther and farther in anxious suspense. Then there is a shot, the hand jerks, slowly drops, and lies still. Paul's death is as vivid as if we had seen a full picture of him dying. The same technique of suggestion, of letting the spectator use his imagination, appears in an incident in Satyajit Rays gentle film, *The Big City*. An old man has gone out visiting and he is shown labouring up a steep flight of stairs with the help of a stick. As he reaches the top, Ray cuts to a shot of someone coming to greet him, and we watch the expression on this strange face change to alarm. Then follows simply a shot of the old man's stick clattering down the stairs. We never see the old man collapse but for that very reason his accident impresses us all the more. Again in Buñuel's strong film, *Diary of a Chambermaid*, when the manservant, Joseph, proceeds to kill a goose with sadistic relish the camera turns away at the crucial moment. The way the scene is handled, and the camera averted as though from a deed too horrible to look at, actually strengthens its impact.

A final reason for not wishing to incorporate the other senses of touch or smell or taste is that the visual and sound resources of the cinema can, if they are sufficiently vivid, suggest other sense impressions by an association of sense memory similar to association of ideas. The cinema can suggest impressions of touch and taste without there being any actual sensory experience. Although our physical perceptions are independent of each other, the feelings they arouse in us are an interrelated whole. Baudelaire says in his poem *Correspondances*:

> Just as the sounds of far-off echoes blend
> Into a shadowy, soul-felt symphony
> Vibrant as night and colourful as day
> So colours, scents and sounds all interact.

The whole Symbolist school of French poetry following Baudelaire made this one of their aesthetic principles.

In a famous sequence from Pudovkin's *Storm over Asia*, the hero, a Mongol trapper, rouses the envy of a Yankee trader by showing him a magnificent silver-fox skin he has come to town to sell. A close-up of the pelt perfectly lighted, shows us the thick gleaming fur just as a slow ripple runs through it bringing out the closeness of the hairs and depth of the pile so vividly that the viewer can virtually *feel* the richness of its texture for himself. In *Une Partie de campagne* there is a sensuous tracking-shot of a rainstorm on the river in which we can hear the rushing, sweeping sound of the rain and *feel* the sharp, clean, stinging coldness of the drops. One could give many other instances, from luxurious beds whose comfort we can feel at a glance, to sumptuous repasts we enjoy with our eyes. Sound can have similar associations. The end of Bresson's *Le Procès de Jeanne d'Arc* is dominated by the fearful noise of a huge conflagration, until we can almost smell the smoke and feel the heat of the flames.[1]

The cinema can evidently give a good account of itself with sight and sound alone. Scents and flavours and Rupert Brooke's 'rough male kiss of blankets' can be left without too much regret to the showmen of the future.

1. Plate 46.

CHAPTER NINE

Reality and Artistic Creation

IN the introduction we said that art touches on reality at three points at least: it arises from the artist's experience; it has to be expressed in a tangible medium; it has to be presented to a real audience. The preceding chapters have been concerned with the second of the three stages: the manner in which the artist's experience is expressed in the tangible medium of a film. In this last chapter we discuss the impression of reality which a film makes on its audience and the extent to which the audience believes in a film and accepts it as something of truth and value. It has already been said that all the stages in the creation of a work of art are related to one another and, since the third stage (presentation to an audience) is related to the previous stage (expression in a medium), this chapter is not isolated from the rest of the book but will round off the argument of the previous chapters.

FILM AND REALITY

Although an audience in the cinema may be strongly affected by the things which happen in a film, they do not treat them like real events. To quote Professor Michotte Van den Berck in the *Revue internationale de filmologie*:[1]

. . . film performances give the audience a strong impression of the *reality* of what they see on the screen, stronger than other plastic arts can produce. However they do not react in the same way to film situations as to those they meet in everyday life. In real life an accident or a fight would cause an active reaction: running away, intervention, expostulation. In the cinema there is ordinarily no active bodily response and the reactions of the audience are largely confined to the expression of emotion. This raises an interesting psychological

1. 'Réalité des projections cinématographiques', *Revue internationale de filmologie* Nos. 3-4, October 1948.

problem. It is clear that there are different sorts of reality and we must distinguish between them.

The first reason for this difference in attitude is that when we go to the cinema, we go there to see a film, and this colours our subsequent behaviour. The persuasion of reality which the cinema exerts on our *senses* may be very strong: in a 3-D film when someone stabs at the audience with a sword, we may instinctively duck, or we may feel quite giddy during a sequence in Cinerama showing a bob-sled ride. But at once our mind rejects these instinctive reflex reactions and we feel silly, much as we would if we went up to a wax figure of an attendant in Madame Tussaud's and asked it the time.

This, of course, is *trompe-l'oeil* which occurs in many forms of art, and it may be enjoyable simply as a joke at the spectator's expense. It exists at one end of the scale in the plastic ink-blots, flies, spiders, and poached eggs of the practical joker. On a slightly higher level, in Roman Polanski's film *Mammals* the audience is fooled at the start of the film by being shown a blank screen which turns out to be a field of snow. In Bert Haanstra's *Fanfare* we see cows gliding mysteriously through the fields until the camera alters its angle to show us the barges which are carrying them. These are simple examples but there is an element of this sense illusion in more serious cinema. It depends on habit and our habitual way of looking at things and taking them for real – seeing is believing. As we saw in the example of the fairground 'Crazy Cottage', habitual reactions may be extremely strong, and there may be a situation in which we react despite ourselves – our mind knows it is an illusion, but our body is caught in a conditioned sensory reaction. We may very well enjoy the resulting surge of visceral feeling freed of the unpleasant concomitants of reality, and even deliberately cultivate it. This is the thrill of the scenic railway as well as the thrill of the adventure or horror film. People like to 'be scared to death' or to 'enjoy a good cry' provided it is in the cinema and not in real life.

Nevertheless it would be wrong, because there is an illusion, to say that the spectator is deceived by the artist. The spectator wants to be deceived and he himself contributes to the deception. The situation is more like a game with conventions which both parties accept before the game starts. If the artist observes the conventions the spectator will accept the reality (perhaps a better word would be 'validity') of what he sees.

The interesting thing is that, when the physical compulsion of *trompe-l'oeil* is at its strongest, our mental assessment of the artist's achievement is low. In cases where the physical reality is less strong our mental acceptance may be far stronger. These cases of an approximate physical version of reality are by far the more general rule, *trompe-l'oeil* being the exception, and we have studied the many ways in which film falls short of physical reality. It is clear that our sensory impression of a thing or an event and our mental belief about it, are two different things although they occur together, interact and combine. A better description of our mental attitude in most cases is, not belief, but 'suspension of disbelief'; and this includes recognition in a film of a mental truth, validity, reality – call it what you will – as important or more important than the physical reality.

The second reason why an audience reacts differently to film and reality is because the events on the screen are not happening 'here-and-now'. This may seem to contradict what has already been said and what is said later about the immediacy of film. In Chapter Four, for instance, it was said that in a film of the sinking of the *Lusitania* the picture on the screen showed the audience people drowning before their eyes. It is true that some forms of art have a greater immediacy than others and the film is one of those which give the spectator a powerful impression of 'being-present'. Nevertheless all art has a certain historicity and even with film we are still looking at a *picture* of the people drowning.

Kracauer in *The Nature of Film* credits the cinema with giving a very strong feeling of 'being-present', and says a film can give the spectator a sense that the events presented are, like life, not completed. He concludes that the construction natural to the cinema is an 'open-ended' one – meaning the kind of plot which is a slice of life, not the rounded, finished, inevitable ending of formally constructed tragedy or comedy. An artistic medium certainly has an influence on the type of construction which suits it best, but to rule out the formally-constructed plot is to restrict the film medium beyond reason. No doubt an 'open-ended' construction can give a more realistic impression, but it can equally well be used in a novel or on the stage even though they may be less naturalistic media. And there seems no reason why the cinema should not be used, as it has been hundreds of times, for the formally-planned, conclusive ending.

The historicity of art goes with its durability – *ars longa vita brevis*. It is a quality of art to last and many arts enable an experience to be perpetually renewed. As has been said earlier, one of the things which make people value and cultivate art is its everlasting quality. A novel or a film is capable of being re-read or re-seen *ad infinitum*. The events of real life, on the other hand, cannot be exactly repeated. History never repeats itself but art does.

It is interesting from this point of view to compare a film with a *personal performance* by a great musician or actor. The play or the music as written is, like the film, fixed for all time, but the actual performance itself is, like life, transient and incapable of exact repetition. Consequently such a personal performance will give the audience the very strongest feeling of 'here-and-now', of 'being-present', stronger than a film. It is noteworthy that the hysterical teenagers who react to Paul Anka the Canadian pop singer and to the Beatles usually go into hysterics only when their idols are present in the flesh, and the transports of the audience are modified when the appearance is only on the screen.

Although the 'being-present' feeling given by a live performance may therefore seem stronger than that of a film, one can perhaps say that the two forms are different not so much in intensity as in kind. In the case of a personal appearance the 'here-and-now' feeling belongs to the performance, to its manner rather than to its content, whereas, in the case of a film, the 'here-and-now' feeling belongs to the things portrayed, with their strong connexion with physical reality, not to the performance of the film itself.

There is a third reason why the spectators react differently to a film and to reality: because the events on the screen are happening to other people, not to them. This third reason for a difference in attitude will affect the film audience more or less strongly according to the type of treatment and the extent to which the spectator identifies himself with one or other of the characters. The novelist can take a detached attitude and write about his characters in the third person or he can write as if hero or heroine were telling the story in the first person. It is the same with a film. The spectator will be least involved with the most indirect treatment – for instance a film which is admittedly from the start simply a film of a stage performance or a ballet. He will be most involved when the camera becomes one of the characters, when he looks with the heroine at the blade of the circular saw coming nearer and nearer ... or when (in Hitchcock's film *Rebecca*) he follows with Rebecca's own eyes her approach to Manderley and hears her thoughts voiced in his ears. Again the more sympathetic the character to the spectator, the fuller will be his identification with it. The naïve identification involved in the star system is mentioned later in this chapter.

THE REALITY OF THE FILM IMAGE

It has been said earlier that film gives an audience a stronger feeling of reality than other arts. There are several reasons for this. Firstly, there is the ability of the cinema to reproduce movement. There is a fascination about movement in itself without any added interest, which automatically attracts one's attention. The natural sights which hold our gaze most strongly are such things as running water, passing clouds, the dancing flames of a fire, the flight of birds. It is the same with art. Ballet depends almost entirely on movement and the practised gestures of an actor or the precision of slapstick are part of the theatre's appeal. In the cinema, graphic composition in becoming mobile comes alive, and, both with cinema and television, movement lowers the spectator's critical resistance, enables the image to impose itself more forcefully, and gives a stronger sense of reality.

Secondly, there is the point, already mentioned, that the photographic image created by a mechanical process is more objective than other artistic methods of reproduction and therefore apparently gives a scientific assurance of authenticity.

A third reason for film's strong impression of reality is the feeling it gives of 'being-present'. We mentioned this in Chapter Four, when writing of film being in the present tense, and in the previous section we compared it with the effect of a real actor's presence in the theatre. It is connected with, even part of, the factor just given – the impeccable authenticity of the photographic image. It depends too on the mental attitude of the spectator rather than on the physical perfection of the reproduction, for it is strongest in the case of newsreels and documentaries regardless of the quality of the photography and hence regardless of actual likeness to the original. An old newsreel of the First World War with its grainy image, bad lighting, uncertain definition, and jerky movement – we believe in it implicitly, far more than we do in the theatrical studio settings of the thirties, glamorized by soft-focus and back-projection, although these may give a better imitation of the real thing. Nevertheless, we *do* believe in studio settings, in all the tricks of the cinema, and even in completely formalized décor; and this is very largely because they come to us through the medium of the same camera which gives us the newsreel. There is a transfer of belief from the documentary to the fiction film and our implicit faith in the one helps to make the other more real.

The *Kon Tiki* film is an example of an absorbing record which holds the spectator by its authenticity despite technical faults. Again, it is interesting to compare a film like Emile de Antonio's *Point of Order*, a plain film record of the 1954 Army-McCarthy hearings, with *The Finest Hours*, the film about Churchill directed by Peter Baylis. In the former film, the natural drama of the hearing (Joseph Welch, the lawyer and judge, who later appeared in Preminger's *Anatomy of a Murder*, takes a leading part) is allowed to reach the audience sparely edited and without studio additions; in the latter, documentary material has been padded out with staged sequences in lavish colour and a reverential commentary. There is no doubt which is the more effective. In Fred Zinnemann's *Behold a Pale Horse*, based on a Spanish Civil War theme, the verisimilitude of the whole film is increased by a pre-credit introduction of newsreel material taken during the war itself. This merges imperceptibly into the fictional material which is sufficiently similar in style to assimilate well with the newsreel shots. The same transference from newsreel to fictional material is used throughout Carl Foreman's *The Victors*, to increase the realistic impact of the film.

The recreation of a historical setting – for example the period atmosphere of Jack Clayton's *The Innocents*, Visconti's *The Leopard*, or even a farce like Hamer's *Kind Hearts and Coronets* – can be very much more convincing in a film than it would be on the stage.[1] A stage version of sober historical reality seems more artificial in some ways than a film of fantastic science fiction. Admittedly, the more remote a historical period the more difficult it becomes to represent it convincingly, but,

1. Plate 49.

properly handled, the cinema might make history come far more vividly to life. Renoir's film, *La Marseillaise*, is an indication of what might be done. Up to the present, classical and biblical history has been for the cinema little more than a prospecting ground for super-spectacles – musicals without the music. More generally, the cinema seldom shows the good historical novelist's care to 'think himself' or 'read himself' into the period. But it can be said in defence of the cinema that the historical novelist (or playwright) has the advantage of working protected by a cushion of words. An anachronism like Shakespeare's 'The clock hath stricken three' in *Julius Caesar* would be far more shocking if we actually saw the offending clock on a Roman mantelpiece.

The Concrete Nature of Film

This brings us to a fourth characteristic which makes film so real: the fact that it is composed of concrete images. This sets it in a completely different class from the novel or the play composed of abstract written or spoken words. This characteristic may not at first sight seem to be consistent with Astruc's phrase *'Caméra-stylo'* (already quoted), but his description is nevertheless quite apt. A film is a kind of writing, but a picture writing. It can even express completely abstract ideas provided they are adapted to the nature of the medium and formulated in concrete, pictorial terms.[1] Kon Ichikawa's film, *The Key*, is about an elderly man almost at the point of death, but relentlessly driven by sexual desire. On his knees he contemplates his wife's naked body and, as he gazes impotently at it, the golden skin dissolves into the curving sand-hills of a desert. This single dissolve says as much as a good many words, but in quite a different way. It is interesting to compare it with the lines which come at the end of Baudelaire's poem *Delphine et Hippolyte*:

> Jamais vous ne pourrez assouvir votre rage
> Et votre châtiment naitra de vos plaisirs.

1. Plates 51 and 52.

Both express with savage irony the bitterness of abnormal desire, both are extremely effective, yet the means are completely different. However, it seems to be the film which is likely to appeal more strongly to a wider audience. In Rodolfo Kuhn's film *The Sad Young Men* a young, single girl has been to the doctor, and the camera follows her as she walks through the town. She looks at a baby in a pram, at a baby in an advertisement in a shop, at a toddler clinging to its mother's skirts. The shots are not quite right; there is an awkward jolt to the camera, and something uneasy about its angle. The sequence tells us in concrete terms, but just as effectively as a novelist could by a 'stream of consciousness' soliloquy, the fact that the girl is upset and the reason for it. Buñuel's criticisms of conventional religion are conveyed with bitter force in concrete terms in *Viridiana* – for instance when, at the height of a drunken orgy, he groups rogues and vagabonds at a long table in a parody of Leonardo da Vinci's picture of the *Last Supper*.

There have been many films in which we see the gangster or the victim dying on a piece of waste land or a rubbish dump – Wajda's *Ashes and Diamonds*, Fellini's *Il bidone*, the little boy in *Los Olvidados* – indicating symbolically that here is a wasted life, a piece of human rubbish. (These shots also bring us back to the remark in Chapter One about the artist painting a derelict cottage; they demonstrate the ability of the camera to create beauty out of the most sordid reality.) Symbolism is used in one of the best scenes in Carl Foreman's *The Victors*: a weary, dirty group of soldiers, who have been looting in a bombed Italian town, are held entranced by an exquisite little musical toy with two tiny figures in evening dress dancing on a tinkling grand piano. The little musical-box perfectly represents the delicate luxuries and easy comforts of peace, a complete antithesis to the danger and hardship of the soldiers' present lot.

Nevertheless the film world pays for its vividness by a limitation. There is a universality of denotation about the word which the film cannot equal. We read:

Oh western wind when wilt thou blow
That the small rain down shall rain?
Christ, that my love were in my arms ...

In a film the words 'my love' have to be expressed as Brigitte
Bardot, Elizabeth Taylor or Gina Lollobrigida. The inability of
even these goddesses to match the simple words 'my love' illustrates the incomparable force of imagination. It is its very face-
lessness which gives the word such a power of evoking dreams,
as these lines have had over the centuries. One can give another
example from the theatre which uses both abstract words and
concrete actions. One might think that it would be more
effective for a violent murder to be shown on the stage, but in
Greek plays it most often occurs off-stage and then is reported
in words. There are special reasons for this in the ritual nature
of Greek drama – the use of masks would make violent
action unsuitable, and so on; nevertheless, the effect of this
indirect presentation, of saying the abstract word instead
of showing the concrete deed, can be tremendous. These
are further examples of the theme which runs through this
book – how departure from reality can be turned to artistic
advantage.

The nearest the cinema gets to the generalized expression of
words is in a film like *L'Année dernière à Marienbad*. Here the
characters have no history, no families, no professions, no
names even but letters instead; they wear a neutral uniform –
evening dress; the place is remote, without associations, we
are not quite sure where. The film approaches as near as possible to the universal reference of the words: 'man', 'woman',
'fear', 'love'.

There is a saying of Walter Pater which is relevant to this
point: 'All arts aspire to the condition of music.' Music goes
farther in the way of abstraction, in dispensing with particular
meaning, than any other art. Although it may successfully convey an incidental meaning, programme music even in the
hands of Strauss, Tchaikowsky or Beethoven is of secondary

importance. Also, although music combines so well with other artistic elements (e.g. in ballet, film, opera), it is generally (except in the case of the greatest opera in which the music overwhelmingly predominates) both lighter in weight and less deeply felt than when it is undiluted. Pure music is the freest of all arts and is able to communicate immediately and intimately with the listener.[1] It strikes through and beyond reason and emotion. It can stir us to the depth of our being without arousing specific thoughts or emotions and move us to a state of indefinable rapture.

Can we then from Walter Pater's saying draw any conclusion about the direction which film should take? Since he wrote, the development of abstract painting has provided another art form equally without particular reference or meaning, and many films have been made consisting entirely of abstract images. Should film-makers concentrate on films of this type? This would be to restrict the medium in a ridiculous fashion and to deny its heritage of vivid concrete expression. Walter Pater does not suggest that other arts should try and copy music by 'going abstract'. The value of comparison with music will be realized if it leads the film-maker on the one hand to give full weight to the abstract elements, the pure rhythm and form, which exist in all the arts intermingled with meaningful elements; and on the other hand to reduce the burden of meaning to a necessary minimum.

Compared with most other arts, film has a large proportion of realistic, meaningful elements to limit its freedom, but their prosaic burden can be lightened by artistic means. Lasker, the chess champion, recommended playing 'dangerously' to transport a game outside the areas of standard analysis and precipitate positions with richer possibilities of invention. Dewey

1. There is a moving sequence in Henri Colpi's film, *Une Aussi Longue Absence*, in which the heroine, Alida Valli, desperately tries to restore the memory of a vagabond she thinks is her husband by playing music to him – when every other means of communication has failed.

quotes Poe as speaking of 'a suggestive indefiniteness of value and therefore spiritual effect' and he also quotes Coleridge as saying that every work of art must have about it something 'not understood' to obtain its full effect. Herbert Read wrote that 'distortion of some kind is present . . . in all art'. All these are instances, in their respective spheres, of an escape from the trammels of reality. When reality can either be discarded as in music or when by various means it can be prevented from tyrannizing, then the artist's imagination is at its freest to reach out to the audience and they are at their freest to respond.

A fifth and final reason for the strong impact of the cinema lies in the conditions of viewing. One of the most important elements is the darkness of the auditorium. In *Les Cent Visages du cinéma* Marcel Lapierre[1] points out that it prevents comparison of size. On a screen surrounded by darkness, a person may be ten feet tall without any appearance of abnormality, because the spectator's attention is monopolized by the rectangle of the screen and there is no clash of proportions with objects outside the field of light. If one goes into a cinema in the middle of a performance, the screen seems like a huge picture hung on the wall, but this impression disappears after a few minutes and the spectator lives, as it were, in the midst of the images.

THE ROLE OF THE ARTIST

It is clear from what has been said that the reality of a film exists at two levels at least – the physical and the mental. On both levels the film-maker will best convince his audience by creating an artistic whole in keeping with the nature and purpose of the particular film, and broadly within the convention the audience will accept. It may be as important for the artist to avoid destroying the illusion as to do anything positive to

1. *Les Cent Visages du cinéma*, Bernard Grasset, Paris, 1948.

create it, and paradoxically this may involve him in avoiding a too-specific use of realistic details.

The physical level will include such things as décor, props, costume, appearance, habits, manners, customs, speech. For instance, belief in a historical film may be killed stone dead by intrusion of modern speech idioms. And not only slang. In Joseph Mankiewicz's fourteen-million-pound epic, *Cleopatra*, there is the following exchange between Elizabeth Taylor (Cleopatra) and Rex Harrison (Caesar) – *Cleopatra:* 'I seem to have rubbed you up the wrong way.' *Caesar:* 'I'm not sure I want to be rubbed by you at all.' *Cleopatra:* 'I shall have to insist that you mind what you say.' Later she says to him: 'We've gotten off to a bad start, haven't we?'

What is the audience to think of this? Quite apart from colloquialisms, the phrases themselves, the attitudes they represent, the flavour they convey, the associations they evoke – all are modern and all combine to destroy the feeling of period achieved in some of the ceremonial and battle scenes. As one reviewer dryly remarked: 'If the purpose of this dialogue is to reduce these awe-inspiring figures to human proportions, the director has been more successful than I think he would have wished to be.' There is no need and it is not possible to copy historical reality exactly. The audience knows (vaguely) that the Romans spoke Latin but they would not welcome a film with dialogue in that language. It is sufficient for the dialogue to have an archaic flavour. Scott in his historical novels deliberately cultivated a style different from the idiom current at the time he wrote, a neutral style without period associations. This is a problem the silent film did not have to meet. Dreyer's *La Passion de Jeanne d'Arc* has faults but it almost completely avoids modern associations. In Bresson's *Le Procès de Jeanne d'Arc* the Maid's beauty-parlour hair-style and, even more, the English voices with their cultivated, high-pitched accent, destroy the feeling of period. We do not really know how English was spoken in the time of Joan of Arc, but more neutral voices would have been more successful. Nor do we know how Joan did her hair, but the treatment in Dreyer's film was better: Falconetti's hair was simply hacked off, and avoided association with particular styles.

There are many cases in which the unique ability of the camera and microphone to reproduce a real location, real accents or the raciness of slang or dialect is a delight. The real backgrounds of *Bicycle Thieves*, *Man of Aran*, *We Are the Lambeth Boys*, *Un Coeur gros comme ça* convey something no studio set can match. Generally speaking, dubbing takes away from a film because an authentic native accent is replaced by something more remote. However, in cases where dubbing adds a touch of realism it can be successful: in French versions of their comedies Laurel and Hardy talk French with a strong American accent; in a French version of Richard Williams's cartoon *Love Me*, *Love Me*, *Love Me*, the commentary is spoken by an Englishman speaking broken French. Because difficulty in talking foreign languages is so real, it adds to the effect. No doubt the charm of an unusual but real accent has something to do with the popularity of Jean Seberg in France, and of Simone Signoret or Charles Boyer in England and America.

However, there are other circumstances in which it is important for the film-maker to escape from the limiting references of realism by formalizing, by abstracting, by simplifying, by leaving the spectator to fill in the detail with his own imagination. In the décor of a Fu Manchu thriller every detail may be obtrusively correct and yet the whole (more Chinese than China itself) fail to persuade us. Whereas *The Cabinet of Dr Caligari*, using only abstract angles, creates an immediately convincing world of evil. The advantage of suggestion over plain statement has already been discussed in Chapter Eight.

Also in a sense on the physical level, but different from the elements we have been discussing, are those which go to make the style of the film-maker: framing, camera-angle, lighting, cutting, use of music, and so on. These elements do not correspond to anything in the physical world, but are features of the medium in which the film-maker embodies his ideas. Thus there is no question, with these elements, of fidelity to reality; it is a matter of choice, arrangement, manipulation. We have considered each of these separately and come to the conclusion that rigidly applicable rules of universal validity cannot be formulated; but the most successful artists are those whose style is suited to the film and the audience. As E. H. Gombrich says in *Art and Illusion*:

The form of a representation cannot be divorced from its purpose and the society in which the given visual language gains currency.

Another point may be added: style will generally seem more natural when it is unobtrusive, when it is the art that conceals art. A display of technical virtuosity for its own sake, even when it is admired, will surely draw attention to the artificiality of the medium and act as a barrier between the spectator and what the artist wishes to express.

The second level on which a film exists is mental. On this level reality is a reality of ideas, of emotions, of behaviour, of character, of fundamental, universal truths. On this level the artist seeks to create an artistic whole which will convince by its emotional or ideological depth and verity. At this level, everything will depend on the intensity of the artist's experience and the sincerity of its expression. The physical components of a film may be treated with great sensitivity and the style may be excellent – but it may fail on the mental level. Jean-Luc Godard's *Vivre sa vie* is a stylish film, but some critics at any rate have found it hollow. As the film of a man celebrating the beauty of a woman he loves it has great charm, but its implicit claim to be a dispassionate account of prostitution cannot be taken seriously, and on this level it compares unfavourably with Luciano Emmer's *Woman in the Window* (also about prostitution) which impresses as more profoundly observed and mature. Again, Alf Sjöberg's *Frenzy* and von Sternberg's *The Blue Angel* are so much better than the average cheap sex film because the directors seem really to feel the terror and tragedy of the passions they express. The sentiments expressed in Wellman's *Oxbow Incident*, in Capra's *Mr Deeds Goes to Town*, in Sydney Lumet's *Twelve Angry Men* are impeccable, and the films carry us along with their pace and style, but ... but somehow a doubt remains. Films like *Greed, La Grande Illusion, Pather Panchali, Los Olvidados, Tokyo Story*, or *La terra trema;* all these are possibly less polished, less smooth (if more original) in construction and style than the other films just mentioned. But they leave us in no doubt about the film-maker's passionate sincerity and depth of feeling and they convince us more fully of their deep truth. False nobility, sentimentality, cheap sex, as opposed to real nobility, sincere feeling, true passion – all these may arise from the artist's failure to feel deeply enough, or from his inspiration becoming diluted and lost in the process of realization.

In art the mental level, which we may call also the level of imagination, is the more important. E. H. Gombrich writes in discussing Constable:

What a painter inquires into is not the nature of the world but the nature of our reaction to it ... his is a psychological problem.

If this is true of painting, the artist's account of the physical world, it will be even truer of film, dealing more fully and explicitly with feelings and ideas. Even in his ordinary life, an artist, like any human being, will be as much affected by his mental as by his physical environment. 'Nothing is either good or bad but thinking makes it so.' In his art, free from the immediate pressure of the physical world, the balance will tilt on the side of the mental.

There is another reason from the side of the viewer why the mental level or the level of imagination is particularly important in art. In ordinary life, for much of the time, all our senses and our body itself are very fully occupied in doing and reacting – our imagination, if it is active at all, is busy with utilitarian reasoning, anticipating, serving the needs of the situation. In the cinema, on the other hand, our body is quiescent and only two of our senses are actively engaged. But our imagination is at full stretch: directed and stimulated by the film-maker's emotionally charged, expressly-selected material and by his technique of presenting it.[1] Thus it may be that a film will succeed in taking hold of the spectator's mind in a stronger, deeper, possibly more lasting way than reality itself.

In practice, in the artist's work the two levels, physical and mental, will occur together, interpenetrate and interact and both are important. For the finest art, perfection of form must be combined with greatness of conception. It is also possible that the spectator's acceptance of the rational and emotional content of a film will be spoiled by a bad style or unskilful rendering of the physical details. But the other way round failure is more complete – if the film artist succeeds in creating the perfect receptacle, only for the spectator to find that either it contains absolutely nothing or else its contents are nasty, putrid, or void of nourishment.

THE ROLE OF THE SPECTATOR

It is the artist who creates the work of art and seeks to impress an audience, and the major activity is his. But the spectator is not merely a passive recipient. At one time it was thought that those who sat and listened or watched were quite passive. Education was a process 'of pouring knowledge into empty heads' and cinema-going was criticized because the audience were 'doing nothing'. In fact watching a film involves, or

1. Plate 47.

ought to involve, fairly intense sensory and intellectual activity, and in all arts the spectator must make some contribution for the communication of the artist's experience to be complete. Like the work of the artist the contribution which the spectator makes will also be on two levels, the physical and the mental.

It is scientifically well-established that physical sense perception consists not merely of taking an impression of an external stimulus but is a positive activity. As Thouless in *General Psychology*[1] writes: 'perception is an activity of the mind itself of which sensory stimulation is generally a determining cause, but not a necessary condition.'[2] Again, he says: 'a perception is not something produced by a stimulus, but by the activity of the organism itself.' When we see a film, a life-time of habitual visual experience operates to validate the illusion on the screen, and the viewer unconsciously corrects imperfections or omissions in the image, and will see it as perfectly real even when the likeness is no more than approximate. Our senses both of sight and sound also have a high tolerance for poor quality of reproduction, and automatic sense adjustments operate, without our being aware, to ensure a constant level of good vision or good hearing. Thus, up to a certain point, poor print quality or a bad sound-track will not disturb a cinema audience, particularly if they are absorbed in the film.

Because perception is an activity of the organism it is to some extent the organism not the stimulus which determines what the perception will be. It is like an activity being triggered off rather than an impression being taken. Our sense of cold, for instance, depends on special nerve endings which feel cold and

1. University Tutorial Press, 1945.

2. In the last phrase ('but not a necessary condition') Thouless refers to that part of an area of perception which is void of sensory stimulation but filled in by the mind following a pattern of expectation. For example, show a spectator an incomplete letter (R) and he will fill in the top part of the upright of the 'R' following a pattern of expectation although this area is void of sensory stimulation.

nothing else, and they will still register cold if they are touched with something warm. At a higher level a film image brings into play a complex of analogies and similarities determined by conditioned reflexes which outweigh any optical altera-tions from reality. Dr Oldfield, writing in *Revue internationale de filmologie*,[1] uses the phrase 'organic responses' and says that, even on the purely cognitive level

the strength of reality in a film depends less on the precision of detail and fidelity of the image to its original than on the appeal made by the visual narrative to the organic responses of the subject.

It follows that absolute identity of the film image with its original is superfluous. And it also follows that individual reactions to a film will vary from one person to another. Such variations, slight at the immediate level of perception, may be much greater when it comes to intellectual or emotional responses.

The contribution of the spectator is just as great on the level of emotion and imagination as on that of perception. 'The viewing of a film [writes Professor Michotte Van den Berck][2] releases many and powerful emotional reactions in the audience which are really felt.' This emotional participation frequently takes the form of identification with one of the characters in the film, the spectator feeling the emotions appropriate to the situations in which that character finds himself. Again, the total reaction of the spectator will result from the interaction and combination of sensory and mental responses. The sensory reactions give rise to ideas and emotions which in their turn facilitate the spectator's acceptance of the physical images. When the influence of a film is at its maximum the spectator's mental participation can be so intense that he is completely absorbed in the spectacle in a state approaching a day-dream or a trance.

1. 'Perception visuelle des images du cinéma', *Revue internationale de filmologie*, Nos. 3-4, October 1948.
2. Op. cit. p. 209.

Emotional Response and Star Worship

Emotional response to films is often regarded critically. But the cinema, by enabling us to enjoy vicarious experiences, provides an outlet, even a means of sublimation, for impulses which might be undesirable socially. It also forms a focusing point for dreams of wish-fulfilment, dreams which may help people to bear the disappointments and monotony of everyday life. The opium of the masses today is a compound of cinema and television, not religion. No doubt one factor in the decline of cinema attendance has been a rise in the standard of living which, besides making alternative forms of recreation more widely attainable, has also made the popular cinema's brand of oblivion less necessary – though many have found an alternative hypnotic in the television set.

The commonest form of the identification mentioned in the last section, is with the hero or the heroine of a story, and is a kind of wish-fulfilment. It reaches its apotheosis in the star system, which had its roots in the cinema, but now stretches beyond it into television, radio, popular songs. Although it is a modern manifestation, the naïve emotional attitudes and beliefs on which it is based have their roots in remote prehistory. In *The Golden Bough*, Frazer distinguishes between magical and rational views of the universe. Primitive magic implied various attitudes, but only one of them need concern us here: that is, an attitude which entailed much closer identification of art and reality than an intelligent modern audience would accept. In primitive art the magic image was just as real as its physical counterpart. When the primitive artist made a statuette of his enemy and stuck pins in it, he was wounding his enemy. When the Egyptian made a model of a cook with his ingredients and utensils to go into a Pharaoh's tomb it was to fulfil the role of a real cook and do real cooking in another world. Then, when, at different times in different parts of the world, a critical, scientific outlook developed – more sceptical, questioning, discriminating – one result was that art and reality were relegated to different categories. However, old beliefs survived alongside the new. Instead of magic there was religion, and although modern religion has been intellectualized and re-fined, popular religion in the Middle Ages retained many magical, superstitious elements. There can be no doubt that these popular, irrational elements – saints' relics, accounts of miracles, wonders and marvels, conjuring tricks such as sacred portraits that wept real tears, animals that answered holy questions, and so on – served a human need, whether as di-version or as escape. There was an element of the fairground even in the church. Most of these aspects of religion were dis-approved of by reformers and, at any rate in Protestant coun-tries, done away with during the Reformation. But the devil driven out will return again in another guise. Human nature needs both diversion and escape. So, even after the Reforma-tion, the frivolous aspects of medieval religion returned in secu-lar form, and found their legitimate descendants in the music hall, and some of the theatre, cinema and television of today.

Despite differences in attitude and motive, it is not too much to say, then, that the cinema has replaced these popular aspects of religion, that film stars are analogous to the saints of popular legend and to the gods of earlier cults, and that film-fans are their modern devotees. As Edgar Morin says in *The Stars*:

. . . the star is ideally beautiful . . . the star is pure . . . the star is pro-foundly good . . . beauty and spirituality combine to form a mythic super-personality . . . worshipped as heroes, divinized, the stars are more than objects of admiration. A religion in embryo has formed round them . . . the star is like a patron saint to whom the faithful dedicate themselves. . . .

Compared with the great religious figures of history, the stars of the cinema may seem paltry enough; but they are no worse than many of the cruel and trivial local divinities which men have worshipped. And, as Morin also says,

Behind the star system there is not only the 'stupidity' of fanatics, the lack of invention of screen writers, the commercial chicanery of producers. There is the world's heart and there is love, another kind of nonsense, another profound humanity . . .

It is easy to condemn the star system, and the reponse of a mass audience is sometimes immature and unintelligent. However, this is because – for reasons which cannot be attributed solely to the films themselves – the cinema audience has been traditionally a young audience naturally immature, and an uneducated audience, naturally other than intellectual. Even at its worst, there is no evidence that bad films do any more positive harm than bad art in other spheres, while there is evidence that they do provide an emotional outlet and an innocuous pastime. Frequently what is most to be regretted is that the audience is not looking at, or doing, something better.

SUBJECTIVITY OF VALUES IN ART

The foregoing analysis of the artist's and the viewer's contribution to the film illusion enables us to attempt an answer to the questions: 'How are we to judge a work of art? What is good? What is bad? How are we to tell?' We have said that, because every spectator himself contributes to the total artistic impression, the same film may be viewed differently by different people. The world of art is different from that of mathematics and science in which, once the basic postulates are accepted, the conclusions follow by an impersonal logic, demonstrably and universally the same for everybody. The scientist can prove everything. The artist on the contrary can prove nothing; he can only offer his experience which the individual viewer may or may not recognize and accept, as corresponding to something he esteems. Nor can the critic prove anything. For the value of a work of art can be assessed only by reference to a subjective judgement.

Scientific rules or laws, are far more particular, exact, rigid,

and universal than those of art. Unless they are based on falla-
cious reasoning or faulty observation, they are permanently
valid although they may be 'absorbed' into a wider concept
as Newtonian physics have been absorbed into Einsteinian
physics. In art we have stressed the provisional nature of rules.
This applies whether we are considering the artist's technique
(rules of procedure) or what the finished product should be
like (critical dictates). It is perhaps better to regard rules in art
as a matter of style and having the same sanction as style.
Within a style certain conventions must be accepted though
even here there is room for development and personal variation. But in a different style the conventions may be completely
different.

At the same time, the artist needs to have rules in the sense of
procedures. E. H. Gombrich shows clearly that a graphic artist
cannot paint or draw without following a formula (a *schema*)
and even the greatest artists have 'played the sedulous ape' by
imitating previous artists. The formulae or rules will be more
important for the learner, and the mature artist may modify or
disregard them more and more as his work develops. Also the
artist may be able to deal intuitively with very complex situations which it would be impossible to cover by formulated
rules. This is exactly what we found when discussing the complex combinations of sound and images in a film. In this case,
presumably, we must assume that, either as a result of long experience or as a result of insight, some kind of guiding rules
have come to exist in the artist's subconscious. The film-maker
has not got the graphic artist's problem of imitating reality, as
the camera provides him with ready-made fragments. But the
case of the film-maker is still generally similar, and study of
previous models, or rules (of cutting, of framing, of camera
movement) is necessary to learn the art. It is not the function
of this book to discuss them in detail but they are taught in
film schools, are current in professional circles, are formulated
in such books as Karel Reisz's *The Technique of Film Editing*

which represented the views of a committee of leading British film-makers at the time it was written.

The particular difficulty of film lies in the mobility, the number and the complexity of the elements which compose it. This complexity can be reduced by 'neutralizing' or omitting one or other of the factors, e.g. in the silent film or the black-and-white film. But it can also be reduced by rules or conventions (whether of method or finished form) accepted by the artist and the audience. The complexity of the film medium both increases the difficulty of formulating rules (which may have to remain intuitive) and enhances the value of rules as a means of simplifying the situation. Thus the classification and clarification which can be obtained by rules is desirable in the interests of communication, but it must still be recognized that the rules have no other sanction than that of the best current practice and as such can be upset by the different practice of new artists of sufficient stature.

It seems to follow that different interpretations and even different evaluations of the same work of art are valid, and this might be thought at first sight to lead to a state of chaos in which qualitative judgements were meaningless. But, just as the value of the execution will depend on the quality of the artist, so the value of the interpretation or evaluation will depend on the quality of the spectator. Evaluation is a function of the critic, ideally a superior, trained spectator who sees more clearly and more deeply.

There is also the criterion of numbers – in a free atmosphere a consensus of opinion will be formed, which generally will constitute some guide to quality. Popular taste in the cinema is often criticized for being juvenile and debased. But the juvenility is natural enough, for, at any rate in the past, the mass cinema audience has *been* juvenile; the debasement has perhaps been due more to commercial, assembly-line methods than to real popular demand. Commercial interests sometimes try to justify low standards in the entertainment they offer by claiming they are 'giving the public what it wants', but in fact their methods of deciding what the public wants may be open to criticism.[1] No doubt there are certain difficult artists whose appreciation demands more hard work or more erudition than a popular audience will stand for. But, despite this reservation, one has only to mention Shakespeare, ballads, folk-songs, folk art, and, in the cinema, Charlie Chaplin, John Ford and René Clair to realize that popular taste can be as good as any.

More than current popularity, more than any single critic, the judgement of posterity will carry the greatest weight, because it consists of layer upon layer both of popular and of the 'best' individual judgements, and this must be recognized as our best criterion of quality in a work of art. Even in this case, to set against the gain in determinacy there are disadvantages; for as works of art recede they become part of a social tradition and valued unquestioningly for other than artistic reasons. They become sacrosanct and, by growing beyond criticism, grow more remote and formidable. Secondly, the canon by which they were created becomes archaic so that it is impossible for any but an antiquary to enter fully into the spirit of their creation. Contemporary appreciation, although it may be more debatable, can be both more spontaneous and more complete.

It may be a sign of richness in a work of art both that it attracts a conflict of critical judgements and also that it appeals strongly from several different aspects. To take the first point, many of the artists and works of art which are ultimately most highly valued have difficulty in gaining acceptance in the first place. This is perhaps because most important artists have an originality which in one way or another fails to accord with current artistic fashions; they break 'the rules' and it may take them a lifetime or longer to convince anybody that their method of expression is equally valid. *Greed* is one film masterpiece that almost failed to reach the screen. *L'Année dernière à*

1. See the Pilkington Report, H.M.S.O., 1962.

Marienbad is a recent film which aroused the most violent critical controversy.

As for the second point, different aspects (or levels) do exist in most art, but only the occasional work has the resources and balance to appeal with equal force from them all. In Shakespeare's plays we have the beauty of the poetry, the excitement of the plot, the interest of the characters, the morality of their actions, the intellectual impact of their conversation. A film like *Kameradschaft* exists as a very exciting story of a mine disaster, of heroism and endurance, but also as a passionate plea against national enmity, and also again as a beautiful mobile composition in black-and-white.[1] Renoir's *La Règle du jeu* is in one aspect a knock-about bedroom farce, in another a study of tragic personal relationships, in yet another a serious criticism of the society of the period. *Jour de fête* is, on the surface, merely a gay comedy full of Tati's inimitable slapstick. But, underneath, it is a criticism of the senseless pace of modern life and of modern bureaucracy and from this aspect it has as much depth as many more pretentious works. Towards the end of the film, the postman's cap is donned by a little boy who delivers the letters while the postman takes off his coat and gets on with a useful job – harvesting. Different aspects may be appreciated by different audiences and they may be given different values. Thus the same film may be several different things to different people and, for the audience concerned, one aspect or level is just as real and important as another.

NATURE OF FILM: CONCLUSION

Because the film gives such a feeling of reality this does not mean that it can only be used, or ought only to be used, naturalistically. Like any form of art the cinema is capable of an infinite range of styles and can take in its stride fantasy, formalism, symbolism, surrealism, and abstract compositions. The very

1. Plate 48.

realistic quality of photography can be used to give a special force to fantastic elements.[1] It is significant that the most effective ghosts in the cinema are the most realistic. The young African boxer in *Un Coeur gros comme ça*, who is a fan of Michèle Morgan, sees her in plain medium-shot on the balcony of the house opposite, until, by means of a dissolve, she turns into another woman. In Pier Pasolini's *The Gospel according to St Matthew*, both the angel who announces the birth of Christ and the devil who tempts Jesus during his forty days of fasting are treated like any other character in the film and in both cases are wholly convincing. These scenes are far more effective than they would have been with double-exposure or misty soft-focus. The force of the effect arises from the contrast between the absolute realism of the image and the knowledge that it is after all a ghost. The same is true of the closing sequences of *Ugetsu Monogatari*, when the husband comes back and talks to his wife who has been dead for weeks;[2] of the mad scene in Buñuel's *El;* of the ghosts of memory in Bergman's *Wild Strawberries;* and of a dozen other figures of imagination or dream.

High among the reasons for the realistic impact of the film we have put the technical photographic process which gives greater guarantees of invariability and conformity to reality than any handwork. But the conformity is to a great extent an illusion for, from the start, it is the film-maker who determines the final result; by choice; by manipulating the natural differences between film and reality; by deliberate faking. *Battleship Potemkin* is the story of oppressed sailors who revolt against their wicked officers; Bela Balazs reports an attempt, by merely changing the position in the film of one of the sequences, to turn it into a story of wicked sailors who revolt without cause against the just authority of their officers. Films have continually been used for propaganda and counter-propaganda but, carried too far, persuasion, even in this medium, defeats

1. Plate 53.   2. Plate 54.

itself, and audiences finally become suspicious of the realism of the cinema as they do of the authority of the printed word. In the end the tags about 'seeing is believing' and 'the camera cannot lie' will wear thin. The illusion of the cinema has definite limits and if the audience is not mentally prepared to accept it, a propaganda film will fail however plausible it may seem.

The spectator does not expect – or only partially expects – a physical illusion from the cinema. The audience seek to believe not what they see so much as what they conceive, and (as already said) it is not the fidelity of the image to reality which counts, but the ease with which it can be accepted as a reality in its own right. The impression it makes on us is not perceptual so much as psychological, emotional, and aesthetic. The representative quality of a picture, says Dr Oldfield,[1] cannot be defined in a formal way as any exact relation of likeness between the image and the object, but derives rather from the psychological reactions aroused by the perception. Also the subjective reality will be the stronger the more actively the viewer, worked on by the film-maker's art, participates in its creation.

Consequently it is not a question of reproducing real objects on the screen but of creating filmic objects which exist in their own right and belong to an autonomous category of reality that borrows only its appearance from that of nature. Further, the transformation from the one to the other cannot be realized technically – the methods of art must always be used.

To move us a work of art must possess both authenticity and credibility; but the authenticity and credibility which we demand of a work of art are not those which we require of natural objects. In our eyes the two worlds are different and we do not adopt the same physical reactions or attitude of mind towards them. The real world appeals to our senses more than our imagination, while the world of art is designed to work the other way round.

1. Op. cit. p. 227.

The world of the imagination has its own premises, laws, and conventions, but they are not the same as those of the physical world. The artist knows them, the physicist does not. At the same time the world of imagination is just as real and important as the world of the senses. There is nothing unreasonable or perverse about it except in the case of lunatics and eccentrics. When it is creative, as with the thinker, the philosopher, the artist, or the inventor, it functions in just as 'real' terms as the physical world. In fact, it is the mind that we know directly *cogito ergo sum*) while the physical world comes to us at secondhand through the partial and distorted report of the senses. Certainly in art the imagination is the final arbiter of the real.

Throughout the artistic process, from the real experience fermenting in the artist's imagination and being embodied in an idea, a script, a finished film, it is the artist who matters, using both the realistic endowment of the cinema, and also its differences from reality, to a common end – the expression of artistic truth. The process is completed by the spectator's appreciation of the emotionally charged work of art and by the re-creation in his mind of an experience matching that of the artist.

We have variously described the cinema as a profound form of communication, as a means of catharsis or of wish-fulfilment, as a ground for social experiment, as a revelation of the physical world, as a way of demonstrating universal truths and of illustrating human nature. It is all these and more. Its functions and forms have been as various and will continue to be as various as the descriptions of art given in the first chapter. It would be as much a lost endeavour to try and imprison its infinite resources within a rigid formula as to imprison life itself – for the cinema like all art is an expression, and a form of life.

Appendix: A Note on Technical Terms

THE central feature of the cinema is that it presents a stream of different views, in movement, on a screen of limited size. The view on the screen may be changed in three ways:

(a) by movement of the subject, which need not be further discussed here;

(b) by *cutting*, *editing*, or *montage* which changes the picture all at once from one view to another;

(c) by *camera movement* which alters the picture continuously and presents a gradually changing view.

The second type of change is effected by filming (*shooting*) different views with a movie-camera, selecting the *shots* desired and assembling them (the French word is *monter*, 'to mount') into coherent *sequences* which when run through the projector will form the scenes and episodes of the complete film. On the Continent this process is called *montage*; in England it is called *cutting* or *editing*. The meaning of the words is similar but they stress different aspects of the process: *montage* stresses the assembly, the total effect of the shots in combination; *cutting* and *editing* refer more to the process itself in the *cutting-room*. In this book either word is used as seems more appropriate in the context.

If different views are being obtained by this method of changing from one shot to another (*shot-change*) the transition may be performed in various ways, giving the following effects on the screen: *cut* (one image replaces another instantly); *fade-out-fade-in* (one image fades into darkness and the next image comes out of darkness); *mix* or *dissolve* (as the old image disappears, the new image appears and, for a short time, the two images are superimposed on the screen); *wipe* (a line passes across the screen wiping out the old image and replacing it with the new); *iris-out-and-iris-in* (the old image fades from the edges of the screen to the centre, then the new image grows in a widening circle from the centre of the screen); *turn-over* (the whole screen seems to turn over and continue on the other side).

The third method of giving a changing view is by continuous movement of the camera while shooting instead of by switching from one shot to another. If the whole camera is moved bodily, this is known as *tracking* and the type of shot will be a *forward, backward- vertical- lateral-* or *diagonal*-tracking-shot, according to the direction in which the camera moves. If the camera is kept in the same place but turned on its axis this is known as *panning* (from the word *panorama*). In England the word 'panning' is used for a horizontal turn and *tilting* for a vertical turn; but the Continental practice of calling the movements *vertical, horizontal* or *diagonal* panning (a diagonal pan is the movement needed to follow a man up or down a flight of stairs) is simpler and more complete, and is followed here. Panning and tracking can be at various speeds. A very fast turn is called a *zip-pan*. A movement (which may be very fast) similar to tracking can be achieved by turning a special lens called a *zoom-lens*.

The extent of the view shown on the screen and its *scale* depends on the distance of the camera from the objects being photographed and the lens used. There are infinite possibilities ranging from a *long-shot* (a wide view on a small scale) through *medium-shots* (views of medium extent on a medium scale) to a *close-up* (a restricted view on a large scale). The extent of the view will vary in inverse ratio to the scale on which it is shown. The limits for our purpose would be on the one hand a view of a distant horizon with (say) ships as big as tiny dots and on the other hand, a big close-up of an eye or lip or nose filling the whole screen. Extremes outside this range such as telescopic views of the stars or microscopic views of atoms are of scientific rather than artistic interest, but, for instance, in *Woman of the Dunes* the director, Hiroshi Teshigahara, uses shots of sand grains, and of the human face and hands many times enlarged. The exact choice of what is to be shown on the screen in each shot depends on the *framing* of the picture. The frame is rectangular and the most common ratios of width to height (called *aspect ratios*) are four to three (normal) or five to two (cinemascope) although other ratios also exist. The frame may be made tall and narrow, or circular, or any shape, by *masking* – i.e. covering over part of the picture in developing the film, so that it will appear black on the screen.

The camera may look at the scene being filmed from different *shooting-angles*. There are an infinite number of possible angles from vertically downwards (downward angles) through the horizontal to vertically upwards (upwards shooting-angles). Although the projector throws its picture on a flat screen the photographic image has the property of giving a very vivid impression of the third dimension, that is, an impression of *relief* and also of *depth* (or *depth of field*). The depth of field of a photo is the distance between the *foreground* and the *background* and the distance which is sharply focused is known as the depth of field of the lens. With a pinhole camera, sharply-focused depth of field is theoretically unlimited. Depth of field will differ with the *aperture* (the smaller the aperture the greater the depth) the kind of lens used (a *long-focus* lens gives less depth than a *short-focus* lens) and the distance from the camera, (beyond a certain distance everything can be focused sharply). Part of the picture may be deliberately left blurred or *out-of-focus*, an effect known as *soft-focus*. Instead of only a part, the whole picture may be kept in *soft-focus* either by leaving the lens out of focus over the whole depth of field, or by covering the lens with gauze. Sometimes lenses have been smeared with grease and the scene has even been shot through a sheet of ice.

Mechanically, the illusion of movement in the cinema is obtained by showing very rapidly on the screen a series of still photographs: in the case of silent films, sixteen photographs a second and, in the case of sound films, twenty-four per second. Each photograph is called a *frame* (a rather different meaning from the *framing* of a shot referred to above though related to it) and the speed of projection is referred to as so many frames per second (or f.p.s.). For the movement on the screen to be at normal speed, the camera and the projector must be running at the same rate. If the camera takes pictures faster than the projector shows them, then the movement on the screen will be slowed down and a *slow-motion* effect given. If the camera takes pictures slower than they are projected, then the screen will show *accelerated motion*.

This book is mainly about normally photographed films. *Cartoons* or *animated films* are a different artistic medium, but it may be necessary to refer to them. The accepted definition of an animated film is, not that it is drawn by hand, but that it is created frame-by-frame – i.e. one picture is taken by the camera at a time instead of twenty-four pictures per second.

As regards general terms. The word *film* is used both as a noun and an adjective, but where a weightier adjective seems called for, the word *cinematographic* is used. The word *cinema* is used synonymously with *film* in certain of its connotations, but also to indicate areas of meaning not covered by the word *film*. The *director* is regarded as the author or artist chiefly responsible for creating a film, although the word *film-maker* is sometimes used. In other cases the role of the particular person intended (script-writer, camera man, art-director) is given. *Scene* and *sequence* are two words whose meanings are difficult to differentiate. A distinction given by Marcel Martin is that a *scene* is determined by unity of time and place, and a *sequence* by unity of action.

There are a great many other technical terms, but in some cases it is more convenient to explain them when they occur, and in others (as this is not a technical book) they are not relevant to our purpose.

Bibliography

THE following list contains suggestions for further reading. References to books quoted from, but not necessarily recommended for reading, are given as footnotes.

GENERAL AESTHETICS

Dewey, John: *Art as Experience*, Allen & Unwin, 1934.

Gombrich, E. H.: *Art and Illusion*, Phaidon Press, 1962.

Read, Herbert: *The Meaning of Art*, Faber & Faber, 4th edn. 1956; Penguin Books, 1949.

Richards, I. A.: *Principles of Literary Criticism*, Routledge, 2nd edn. 1926.

FILM AESTHETICS

Arnheim, Rudolph: *Film as Art*, Faber & Faber, 1958.

Balazs, Bela: *Theory of the Film*, Dennis Dobson, 1952.

Bazin, André: *Qu'est-ce que le Cinéma?* (four volumes), Éditions du Cerf, Paris, 1958, 1959, 1961, 1962.

Bluestone, George: *Novels into Film*, University of California, 1961.

Debrix, Jean: *Les Fondements de l'art cinématographique*, Éditions du Cerf, Paris, 1961.

Eisenstein, S. M.: *The Film Sense*, Faber & Faber, 1948.

Kracauer, Siegfried: *The Nature of Film*, Dennis Dobson, 1961.

Lindgren, Ernest: *The Art of the Film*, Allen & Unwin, revised edition 1963.

Martin, Marcel: *Le Langage cinématographique*, Éditions du Cerf, Paris, 1962.

Pudovkin, V. I.: *Film Technique and Film Acting*, translated Ivor Montague, Vision/Mayflower, 1958.

HISTORY AND SPECIAL ASPECTS OF FILM

Houston, Penelope: *The Contemporary Cinema*, Penguin Books, 1963.

BIBLIOGRAPHY

Leprohon, Pierre: *Histoire du cinema*, Éditions du Cerf, Paris, 1961.
Morin, Edgar: *The Stars*, John Calder, 1960.
Reisz, Karel: *The Technique of Film Editing*, Focal Press, 1952.
Sadoul, Georges: *Histoire du cinema*, Flammarion, Paris, 1962.
Tyler, Parker: *The Liveliest Art*, Mentor Books, New York, 1959.

Index of Directors and Films

THIS index is based on film examples quoted in the text and these are also given in the general index with page references. However, to make this list more |comprehensive some outstanding directors and films not mentioned in the text have been added. s indicates short film. A.T. indicates American title.

ALDRICH, ROBERT (U.S.A.): *What Ever Happened to Baby Jane?*, 1963; *Hush, Hush, Sweet Charlotte*, 1964; *Flight of the Phoenix*, 1965; *The Dirty Dozen*, 1966.

ALEXANDROV, GRIGORI (U.S.S.R.): *October* (with EISENSTEIN), 1928; *Volga Volga*, 1938.

ALLEGRET, YVES (Fr.): *Germinal*, 1962; *Les Orgueilleux*, 1953.

ALVENTOSA, RICARDO (Arg,): *The Inheritance*, 1963.

ANDERSON, LINDSAY (U.K.): *This Sporting Life*, 1963.

ANDERSON, MICHAEL (U.K.): *The Dam Busters*, 1954; *Around the World in 80 Days*, 1956.

ANNAKIN, KEN (U.K.): *Quartet*, 1948; *Three Men in a Boat*, 1956.

ANSTEY, EDGAR (U.K.): *Granton Trawler*, 1935 (s).

ANTONIO, EMILE DE (U.S.A.): *Point of Order*, 1963.

ANTONIONI, MICHELANGELO (It.): *Cronaca di un amore*, (*Love Story*) 1950; *I vinti* (*These our Children*), 1952; *Le amiche* (*The Girl Friends*), 1955; *Il grido* (*The Cry*), 1958; *L'avventura* (*The Adventure*), 1960; *La notte* (*The Night*), 1961; *L'eclisse* (*The Eclipse*), 1962; *Il deserto rosso* (*The Red Desert*), 1964; *The Blow-up*, 1966.

ASQUITH, ANTHONY (U.K.): *Pygmalion*, 1938; *The Way to the Stars*, 1945; *The Browning Version*, 1951; *The Importance of Being Earnest*, 1952; *The Young Lovers*, 1955; *Orders to Kill*, 1958; *The Yellow Rolls Royce*, 1964.

ASTRUC, ALEXANDRE (Fr.): *Le Rideau cramoisi* (*The Crimson Curtain*), 1953 (s); *La Longue Marche*, 1966.

AUTANT-LARA, CLAUDE (Fr.): *Faits divers* (*News in Brief*), 1923; *Douce* (*Sweetheart*), 1943; *Le Diable au corps* (*Devil in the Flesh*), 1946; *L'Auberge rouge* (*The Red Inn*), 1951; *La Traversée de Paris* (*Pig across Paris*), 1954; *Tu ne tueras pas* (*Thou Shalt not Kill*), 1961; *Le Magot de Josefa* (*Josefa's Nest-Egg*), 1963.

BAKY, JOSEF VON (Germ.): *Münchhausen*, 1943.

BARATIER, JACQUES (Fr.): *Goha*, 1957; *Dragées au poivre* (*Sweet and Sour*), 1963; *L'Or du duc*, 1965.

BARDEM, JUAN ANTONIO (Sp.): *Death of a Cyclist*, 1955.

BARNET, BORIS (U.S.S.R.): *Okraina* (*Suburbs*), 1933; *A Wonderful Summer*, 1950.

BARRY, MAURICE (Fr.): *Les Gisants* (*Tomb Statues*) (s), 1949.

BAYLIS, PETER (U.S.A.): *The Finest Hours*, 1964.

BECKER, JACQUES (Fr.): *Goupi mains rouges* (*It Happened at the Inn* A.T.), 1943; *Casque d'or* (*Golden Marie*; *Golden Helmet* A.T.), 1952; *Le Trou* (*The Hole*), 1960.

Visiteurs du soir (*The Evening Visitors*), 1942; *Les Enfants du paradis* (*Children of Paradise*), 1943–5; *Les Portes de la nuit* (*Doors of the Night*), 1946; *La Marie du port* ('Dockside Mary'), 1951; *Thérèse Raquin*, 1953; *Du Mouron pour les petits oiseaux* (*Bait for Suckers*), 1963.

CASSAVETES, JOHN (U.S.A.): *Shadows*, 1959; *A child is Waiting*, 1963.

CAVALCANTI, ALBERTO (U.K. and Germ.): *Rien que les heures* (*Nothing but the Hours*), 1926; *Coalface* (s), 1935.

CAYATTE, ANDRÉ (Fr.): *Les Amants de Verone* (*Lovers of Verona*), 1948; *Nous sommes tous des assassins* (*We are All Murderers*), 1952; *Le Passage du Rhin*, 1960; *La Vie conjugale* (*Married Life*), 1963.

CHABROL, CLAUDE (Fr.): *Le Beau Serge* (*Handsome Serge*), *Les Cousins*, 1958; *Les Bonnes Femmes* (*The Women*), 1960; *Landru*, 1962; *Le Tigre Aime la Chair Fraiche*, 1964; *Le Tigre se Parfume à la Dynamite*, 1965.

CHAPLIN, CHARLES (U.S.A.): Many short films including: *The Immigrant*, *The Pawnshop*, 1917; *Pay Day*, 1922; *The Pilgrim*, 1923, Long films: *The Kid*, 1921; *A Woman of Paris*, 1923; *The Gold Rush*, 1925; *The Circus*, 1928; *City Lights*, 1931; *Modern Times*, 1936; *The Great Dictator*, 1940; *Monsieur Verdoux*, 1947; *Limelight*, 1952; *A King in New York*, 1957; *Countess from Hong Kong*, 1966.

CHÔMETTE, HENRI (Fr.): *A quoi rêvent les jeunes filles* (*Daydreams*), 1925.

CHOUX, JEAN (Fr.): *Jean de la Lune*, 1931.

CHRISTENSEN, BENJAMIN (Denmark): *Witchcraft through the Ages*, 1921.

CHRISTIAN-JAQUE (Fr.): *Boule de Suif* (*Madame Fifi*), 1945; *Fanfan-la-tulipe*, 1951; *Les Bonnes Causes* (*Don't Tempt the Devil*), 1963.

CHUKRAI, GRIGORI (U.S.S.R.): *Ballad of a Soldier*, 1959; *There was an Old Man and an Old Woman*, 1965.

CLAIR, RENÉ (Fr.): *Entr'acte* (s), 1924; *Un Chapeau de paille d'Italie* (*The Italian Straw Hat*), 1927; *Sous les toits de Paris* ('Under Paris Rooftops'), 1930; *Le Million* (*The Million*), 1931; *À nous la liberté* ('Liberty is Ours'), 1932; *The Ghost Goes West*, 1938; *Village dans Paris* (*Village in Paris*) (s), 1939; *Les Belles de nuit* (*Night Beauties; Beauties of the Night*, A.T.), 1952; *Les Grandes Manoeuvres* (*Grand Manoeuvres*), 1955; *La Porte des Lilas* ('Gate of Lilacs'), *Tout l'Or du monde* (*All the Gold in the World*), 1961; *Fêtes Galantes*, 1965.

CLAYTON, JACK (U.K.): *Room at the Top*, 1958; *The Innocents*, 1961; *The Pumpkin Eater*, 1964; *Our Mother's House*, 1967.

CLÉMENT, RENÉ (Fr.): *La Bataille du rail* (*Battle of the Railway*), 1946; *Le Château de verre* (*The Glass Castle*), 1950; *Jeux Interdits*, 1951; *Knave of Hearts*, 1954; *Gervaise*, 1955; *Plein Soleil* (*Blazing Sun*), 1959; *Les Felins* (*The Love Cage*), 1964; *Is Paris Burning?*, 1966.

CLOUZOT, HENRI-GEORGES (Fr.): *Le Corbeau* (*The Crow*), 1943; *Le Salaire de la peur* (*The Wages of Fear*), 1952; *Les Diaboliques* (*The Fiends*), 1954; *Le Mystère Picasso* (*The Picasso Mystery*), 1956.

COCTEAU, JEAN (Fr.): *Le Sang d'un poète* (*Blood of a Poet*), 1930; *La Belle et la Bête* (*Beauty and the Beast*), 1945; *Les Parents terribles* (*Intimate Relations*), 1948; *Orphée* (*Orpheus*), 1950; *Le Testament d'Orphée* (*The Will of Orpheus*), 1959.

COLPI, HENRI (Fr.): *Une Aussi Longue Absence* (*A Long Absence*), 1961; *Codine*, 1963.

EAMES, RAY and CHARLES (U.S.A.): *Parade* (s), 1952; *House* (s), 1955; *Toccata for Toy Trains* (s), 1957.

EDWARDS, BLAKE (U.S.A.): *Breakfast at Tiffany's*, 1961; *Days of Wine and Roses*, 1962; *The Pink Panther*, 1963.

EISENSTEIN, SERGEI (U.S.S.R.): *Strike*, 1924; *Battleship Potemkin*, 1925; *October* (A.T. *Ten Days That Shook the World*) 1928; *The General Line* (A.T. *Old and New*) 1929; *Que Viva Mexico*, 1932; *Alexander Nevsky*, 1937; *Ivan the Terrible*, 1943–6.

EKK, NICOLAS (U.S.S.R.): *The Road to Life*, 1931.

EMMER, LUCIANO (It.): *Il drammo di Cristo* (*The Drama of Christ*) (s), 1947; *Hieronymus Bosch* (s), 1948; *Paradiso terrestre* (*Earthly Paradise*) (s), 1947 (all with Enrico Gras); *Woman in the Window* (*La ragazza in vetrina*), 1961.

ENGEL, MORRIS (U.S.A.); *The Little Fugitive*, 1953; *Lovers and Lollipops*, 1955; *Weddings and Babies*, 1958.

ENRICO, ROBERT (Fr.): *Au coeur de la vie* (*In the Midst of Life*), 1962 incl. *Incident at Owl Creek* (*La Rivière du hibou*), (s) 1961.

EPSTEIN, JEAN (Fr.): *Finis Terrae* (*World's End*), 1928; *Morvan*, 1930; *Le Tempestaire* ('The Tempest Calmer'), 1947.

ÉTAIX, PIERRE (Fr.): *Le Soupirant* (*The Suitor*), 1962; *Yoyo*, 1964.

FABRI, ZOLTAN (Hungary): *Professor Hannibal*, 1956; *Twenty Hours*.

FAIRBANKS, DOUGLAS: *The Black Pirate* (with Albert Parker), 1926.

FEJOS, PAUL (Hungary, Fr., and U.S.A.): *The Last Moment*, 1927.

FELLINI, FEDERICO (It.): *Lo sceicco bianco* (*The White Sheik*), 1952; *I vitelloni* (*The Spivs*), 1953; *La strada* (*The Road*), 1954; *Il bidone* (*The Swindlers*), 1955; *Le notti di Cabiria* (*Nights of Cabiria*), 1957; *La dolce vita* (*The Sweet Life*), 1959; *8½*, 1963; *Giulietta degli spiriti* (*Julia of the Angels*), 1965.

FEYDER, JACQUES (Fr.): *Les Nouveaux Messieurs* ('The New Set'), 1928; *Pension Mimosas*, 1935; *La Kermesse héroïque* (*Carnival in Flanders*), 1936.

FLAHERTY, ROBERT (U.S.A.): *Nanook of the North*, 1922; *Moana*, 1926; *Man of Aran*, 1934; *Louisiana Story*, 1948.

FLEMING, VICTOR (U.S.A.): *The Wizard of Oz, Gone with the Wind*, 1939.

FOLDES, JOAN AND PETER (U.K.): *A Short Vision* (s), 1956.

FORBES, BRYAN (U.K.): *Whistle Down the Wind*, 1961; *The L-Shaped Room*, 1962; *Seance on a Wet Afternoon*, 1964; *King Rat*, 1965.

FORD, ALEKSANDER (Poland): *Five Boys from Barska Street*, 1953; *Knights of the Teutonic Order*, 1960; *The First Day of Freedom*, 1964.

FORD, JOHN (U.S.A.): *The Informer*, 1935; *Drums Along the Mohawk, Stagecoach*, 1939; *The Grapes of Wrath, The Long Voyage Home*, 1940; *My Darling Clementine*, 1947; *Two Rode Together*, 1961; *Cheyenne Autumn*, 1964; *Seven Women*, 1966.

FOREMAN, CARL (U.S.A.): *The Victors*, 1962.

FORMAN, MILOS (Czech.): *Peter and Pavla*, 1964; *A Blonde in Love*, 1965.

FOSCO, PIERO (or Giovanni Pastrone) (It.): *Cabiria*, 1914.

FRANJU, GEORGES (Fr.): *Le Sang desbêtes* ('The Slaughterhouse') (s), 1949; *Hôtel des Invalides* (s), 1951; *Le Grand Méliès* (*The Great Méliès*) (s), 1952; *La Tête contre les murs* (*The Keepers*), 1958; *Les Yeux sans visage* (*Eyes Without a*

Rebecca, 1939; *Spellbound*, 1945; *Notorious*, 1946; *Rope*, 1948; *Strangers on a Train*, 1951; *Dial M for Murder*, 1952; *Rear Window*, 1953; *The Trouble with Harry*, 1956; *Vertigo*, 1958; *Psycho*, 1960; *The Birds*, 1963; *Marnie*, 1964; *Torn Curtain*, 1966.

HOLMSEN, EGIL (Sweden): *The Time of Desire*, 1961.

HORST, HERMAN VAN DER (Holland): *Praise the Sea* (s), 1958; *Symphony of the Tropics*, 1961.

HUSTON, JOHN (U.S.A.): *The Maltese Falcon*, 1941; *The Treasure of the Sierra Madre*, 1947; *The Asphalt Jungle*, 1950; *The Red Badge of Courage*, *The African Queen*, 1951; *Moulin Rouge*, 1952; *Moby Dick*, 1955; *The Misfits*, 1960; *The Night of the Iguana*, *The Bible*, 1964-5.

ICHIKAWA, KON (Jap.): *The Burmese Harp*, 1955, *The Key* (or *Odd Obsessions*), 1959; *Fires on the Plain*, 1960; *Alone on the Pacific* (*My Enemy the Sea*, A.T.), 1963; *Tokyo Olympiad*, 1965; *Hey! Buddy*, 1966.

INAGAKI, HIROSHI (Jap.): *The Rickshaw Man*, 1958.

IVENS, JORIS (Holland): *Rain* (s), 1929; *Borinage* (s) (with HENRY STORCK), 1935; *; La Seine a rencontré Paris*, 1957; *A Valparaiso* (s), 1963.

IVORY, JAMES (India): *Shakespeare Wallah*, 1965.

JENNINGS, HUMPHREY (U.K.): *Listen to Britain* (s), 1941; *Fires were Started*, 1943; *A Diary for Timothy* (s), 1945.

JANCSO, MIKLOS (Hungary): *The Round-up*, 1965.

KANIN, GARSON (U.S.A.): *My Favorite Wife*, 1940.

KÄUTNER, HELMUT (Germ.): *Romanze in Moll*, 1943; *The Last Bridge*, 1954; *The Devil's General*, 1955.

KAWALEROWICZ, JERZY (Poland): *Mother Joan of the Angels*, 1961; *The Pharaoh*, 1965.

KAZAN, ELIA (U.S.A.): *Panic in the Streets*; *A Streetcar Named Desire*, 1950; *Viva Zapata!*, 1952; *On the Waterfront*, 1954; *Baby Doll*, *A Face in the Crowd*, 1956; *America* (or *The Anatolian Smile*), 1963.

KAZMIERCAK, WACLAW: see BOSSAK, JERZY

KEATON, BUSTER (U.S.A.): *Day Dreams*, 1922; *The Balloonatic*, *The Love Nest*, 1923; *The Navigator*, 1924; *The General*, 1926; *The Cameraman*, 1928.

KELLY, GENE (U.S.A.): see DONEN, STANLEY

KINOSHITA, KEISUKE (Jap.): *The Legend of Narayama*, 1928.

KINUGASA, TEINOSUKE (Jap.): *Gate of Hell*, 1953; *A Woman of Osaka*, 1958.

KIRSANOFF, DIMITRI (Fr.): *Brumes d'automne* (*Autumn Mists*), 1926.

KOENIG, WOLF (Canada): *Lonely Boy* (with ROMAN KROITER) (s), 1962.

KOZINTSEV, GRIGORI (U.S.S.R.): *Don Quixote*, 1957; *Hamlet*, 1964.

KRAMER, STANLEY (U.S.A.): *The Pride and the Passion*, 1957; *The Defiant Ones*, 1958; *Judgment at Nuremberg*, 1961; *Ship of Fools*, 1964.

KROITOR, ROMAN (Canada): see KOENIG, WOLF

KUBRICK, STANLEY (U.S.A.): *The Killing*, 1956; *Paths of Glory*, 1958; *Spartacus*, 1960; *Lolita*, 1962; *Dr Strangelove* or *How I Learned to Stop Worrying and Love the Bomb*, 1963; *2,000; A Space Odyssey*, 1966.

Factory) (s), *Arrivée d'un train en gare (de La Ciotat) (Train Coming into a Station)* (s), *Le Déjeuner de bébé (Baby's Breakfast)* (s), *L'Arroseur arrosé (The Waterer Watered)* (s): 1895–8,

MACHATY, GUSTAV (Czech,): *Erotikon*, 1929; *Extase (Ecstasy)*, 1933.

MACKENDRICK, ALEXANDER (U.K. and U.S.A.): *The Man in the White Suit*, 1951; *The Maggie*, 1953; *The Ladykillers*, 1955; *Sweet Smell of Success*, 1957; *Sammy Going South*, 1962; *High Wind in Jamaica*, 1964; *Don't Make Waves*, 1966.

MCLEOD, NORMAN Z. (U.S.A.): *The Paleface*, 1948.

MALLE, LOUIS (Fr.): *Ascenseur pour l'échafaud (Lift to the Scaffold)*, 1957; *Les Amants (The Lovers)*, 1958; *Zazie dans le métro (Zazie)*, 1960; *Le Feu follet (Will o' the Wisp* or *A Time to Live and a Time to Die)*, 1963; *Viva Maria*, 1965; *Le Voleur*, 1966.

MAMOULIAN, ROUBEN (U.S.A.): *Love Me Tonight*, 1932; *Queen Christina*, 1933; *Becky Sharp*, 1935.

MANKIEWICZ, JOSEPH L. (U.S.A.): *A Letter to Three Wives*, 1948; *Julius Caesar*, 1953; *The Quiet American*, 1958; *Suddenly Last Summer*, 1959; *Cleopatra*, 1961–3; *The Honeypot*, 1966–7.

MANN, ANTHONY (U.S.A.): *El Cid*, 1961; *The Fall of the Roman Empire*, 1963.

MANN, DELBERT (U.S.A.): *Marty*, 1955; *Bachelor Party*, 1957; *Quick Before it Melts*, 1964.

MARKER, CHRIS (Fr.): *Une Lettre de Sibérie (Letter from Siberia)*, 1958; *Cuba Si!*, 1961; *La Jetée ('The Jetty')* (s), 1963; *Le Joli Mai (The Lovely Month of May)*, 1963; *Le Mystère Koumiko*, 1965; *If I had Four Dromedaries*, 1966.

MASSINGHAM, RICHARD (U.K.): Many short films including: *Tell Me if it Hurts*, 1934; *And So to Work*, 1936; *The Five-Inch Bather, We Speak to India*, 1942; *The Cure*, 1950; *The Blakes Slept Here*, 1953.

MAZZETTI, LORENZA (U.K.): *Together* (with DENIS HORNE), 1955.

MÉLIÈS, GEORGES (Fr.): *L'Homme à la tête de caoutchouc (The India-rubber Head)*, 1901; *Le Voyage dans la lune (Trip to the Moon)*, 1902; *Le Dédoublement cabalistique (The Magic Double)*, 1904; *Les Quatre Cents Farces du Diable (400 Tricks of the Devil)*, 1906; *À la Conquête du Pôle (Conquest of the Pole)*, 1912; (All s.)

MEKAS, ADOLFAS (U.S.A.): *Hallelujah the Hills*, 1963; *The Brig*, 1964.

MELVILLE, JEAN-PIERRE (Fr.): *Le Silence de la mer (Silence of the Sea)*, 1948; *Les Enfants terribles (The Strange Ones)*, 1949; *Bob, le flambeur ('Bob, the Gambler')*, 1956; *Léon Morin, prêtre (Léon Morin, Priest)*, 1961; *L'Aîné des Ferchaux (Magnet of Doom)*, 1963; *Le Deuxieme Souffle*, 1966.

MENOTTI, GIAN-CARLO (It., U.S.A.): *The Medium*, 1951.

METZNER, ERNO (Germ.): *Überfall (Hold-up)*, 1929.

MEYER, JEAN (Fr.): *Bourgeois Gentilhomme (The Bourgeois Gentleman)*, 1958.

MILESTONE, LEWIS (U.S.A.): *All Quiet on the Western Front*, 1930; *A Walk in the Sun*, 1945; *Mutiny on the Bounty*, 1962.

MINNELLI, VINCENTE (U.S.A.): *Cabin in the Sky*, 1942; *Meet Me in St Louis*, 1944; *The Pirate*, 1948: *An American in Paris*, 1950; *Lust for Life*, 1956; *Gigi*, 1958; *Goodbye Charlie*, 1964.

RAY, MAN (U.S.A. and Fr.): *Starfish (Etoile de mer)* (s), 1928; *Les Mystères du Château de Dé*, 1929.

RAY, NICHOLAS (U.S.A.): *55 Days at Peking*, 1962.

RAY, SATYAJIT (India): *Pather Panchali (Ballad of the Road)*, 1955; *Aparajito (The Unvanquished)*, 1956; *The Philosopher's Stone*, 1957; *The Music Room, The World of Apu*, 1958; *Devi (The Goddess)*, 1959–60; *Two Daughters*, 1961; *Mahanager (The Big City), Kanchen-junga*, 1963; *Charulata (The Story of Charu)*, 1964; *Nayak*, 1966.

REED, SIR CAROL (U.K.): *Bank Holiday*, 1938; *The Stars Look Down*, 1939; *Odd Man Out*, 1947; *The Fallen Idol*, 1948; *The Third Man*, 1949; *Our Man in Havana*, 1959; *The Agony and the Ecstasy*, 1965.

REICHENBACH, FRANÇOIS (Fr.): *Les Marines (The Marines)*, 1957; *L'Amérique insolite (America Through a Keyhole, America the Unexpected, A.T.)*, 1960; *Un Coeur gros comme ça* ('Boxer's Heart'), 1962.

REISZ, KAREL (U.K.): *We Are the Lambeth Boys*, 1959; *Saturday Night and Sunday Morning*, 1960; *Morgan, A Suitable Case of Treatment*, 1966.

RENOIR, JEAN (Fr.): *Nana*, 1926; *Tire au flanc (The Sad Sack)*, 1928; *La Chienne (The Bitch)*, 1931; *Toni, Le Crime de Monsieur Lange (The Crime of M. Lange)*, 1935; *Une Partie de campagne (Country Excursion)*, 1935; *La Grande Illusion (The Great Illusion), La Marseillaise*, 1937; *La Bête humaine (Judas Was a Woman)*, 1938; *La Règle du jeu (The Rules of the Game)*, 1939; *The River*, 1950; *Le Carrosse d'or (The Golden Coach)*, 1952; *Le Déjeuner sur l'herbe (Lunch on the Grass)*, 1959; *Le Caporal épinglé (The Vanishing Corporal)*, 1961.

RESNAIS, ALAIN (Fr.): *Van Gogh* (with Diehl and Hessens) (s), 1948; *Guernica* (s), 1950; *Nuit et Brouillard (Night and Fog)*, 1955; *Toute la mémoire du monde (A World of Memory)* (s), 1956; *Hiroshima mon amour (Hiroshima, My Love)*, 1959; *L'Année dernière à Marienbad (Last Year at Marienbad), Muriel ou le temps d'un retour (Muriel)*, 1963; *La Guerne set Fini*, 1966.

RICHARDSON, TONY (U.K.): *Look Back in Anger*, 1958; *The Entertainer*, 1960; *A Taste of Honey, The Loneliness of the Long Distance Runner*, 1962; *Tom Jones*, 1963; *The Loved Ones*, 1964; *Mademoiselle*, 1966; *The Sailor from Gib*, 1966.

RIEFENSTAHL, LENI (Germ,): *The Blue Light*, 1932; *The Triumph of the Will*, 1936; *Olympic Games*, 1936–8.

RITT, MARTIN (U.S.A.): *Hud*, 1962; *The Outrage*, 1964; *Hombre*, 1966.

RIVETTE, JACQUES (Fr.): *Paris nous appartient (Paris Belongs to Us)*, 1960; *La Religieuse*.

ROBBINS, JEROME: see WISE

ROOM, ABRAM (U.S.S.R.): *Bed and Sofa*, 1927; *The Ghost that Never Returns*, 1929.

ROSEWICZ, STANISLAS (Poland): *Birth Certificate*, 1961.

ROSI, FRANCESCO (It.): *Salvatore Giuliano*, 1962; *Le mani sulla città (Hands Over the City)*, 1963; *Il momento della verita (A Moment of Truth)*, 1964.

ROSSELLINI, ROBERTO (It.): *Roma, città aperta (Rome, Open City)*, 1945; *Paisà (Landscapes)*, 1946; *Francesco Guillare di Dio (Flowers of St Francis)*, 1950; *Voyage in Italy*, 1953; *I generale della Rovere (The General of Rovere)*, 1959; *Vanina Vanini (The Betrayer)*, 1961; *The Rise of Louis XIV*, 1966.

ROSSEN, ROBERT (U.S.A.): *All the King's Men*, 1949; *The Hustler*, 1961; *Lilith*, 1965.

TASHLIN, FRANK (U.S.A.): *Artists and Models*, 1955; *Bachelor Flat*, 1961; *Who's Minding the Store*, 1963.

TATI, JACQUES (Fr.): *Jour de fête (The Big Day* A.T.), 1947; *Les Vacances de Monsieur Hulot (Monsieur Hulot's Holiday)*, 1953; *Mon oncle (My Uncle)*, 1958; *Playtime*, 1965.

TESHIGAHARA, HIROSHI (Jap.): *Woman of the Dunes*, 1963; *The Face of Another*, 1966.

THORNDIKE, ANNELIE and ANDREW (E. Germ.): *Holiday on Sylt* (s), 1958.

TORRE NILSSON, LEOPOLDO (Arg.): *The House of the Angel*, 1957; *The Hand in the Trap*, *Summer Skin*, 1961; *Homage at Siesta Time (Four Women for One Hero* A.T.), 1962; *The Eavesdropper*, 1964.

TURIN, VICTOR (U.S.S.R.): *Turksib*, 1929.

TRUFFAUT, FRANÇOIS (Fr.): *Les Mistons (The Mischiefmakers)* (s), 1958; *Les Quatre Cents Coups (The 400 Blows)*, 1959; *Tirez sur le pianiste (Shoot the Pianist)*, 1960; *Jules et Jim*, 1962; *La Peau douce (Silken Skin)*, 1964; *Fahrenheit 451*, 1966.

TRNKA, JIRI (Czech.); *A Midsummer Night's Dream*, 1959.

USTINOV, PETER (U.K.): *Billy Budd*, 1962.

VADIM, ROGER (Fr.): *Et Dieu créa la femme (And God Created Woman)*, 1956; *Les Bijoutiers du clair de lune (Heaven Fell that Night)*, 1957; *Le Repos du guerrier (Warrior's Rest)*, 1963.

VARDA, AGNES (Fr.): *La Pointe courte* ('The Short Point'), 1955; *Cléo de 5 à 7 (Cleo from 5 to 7)*, 1961; *Le Bonheur*, 1964–5; *Les Créatures*, 1966.

VASILIEV, SERGEI and GEORGI (U.S.S.R.): *Chapayev*, 1934.

VÉDRÈS, NICOLE (Fr.): *Paris*, 1900; *Life Begins Tomorrow*, 1949.

VERTOV, DZIGA (U.S.S.R.): *Man with a Movie Camera*, 1929.

VIDOR, CHARLES (U.S.A.): *The Spy*, 1932; *Cover Girl*, 1944.

VIDOR, KING (U.S.A.): *The Big Parade*, 1925; *The Crowd*, 1928; *Hallelujah*, 1929; *The Citadel*, 1938; *War and Peace*, 1955.

VIGO, JEAN (Fr.): *A propos de Nice (About Nice)* (s), 1930; *Zéro de conduite (Nought for Behaviour)*, 1933; *L'Atalante*, 1934.

VISCONTI, LUCHINO (It.): *Ossessione (Obsession)*, 1942; *La terra trema (The Earth Trembles)*, 1948; *Bellissima*, 1951; *Senso (The Wanton Countess)*, 1954; *Rocco e i suoi fratelli (Rocco and His Brothers)*, 1960; *Il Gattopardo (The Leopard)*, 1963; *Vaghe stelle dell' orsa (Of a Thousand Delights)*, 1965.

VULCHANOV, RANGHEL (Bulg.): *Sun and Shadow*, 1962.

WAJDA, ANDRZEJ (Poland): *A Generation*, 1955; *Kanal* ('Sewer'), 1956; *Ashes and Diamonds*, 1958; *A Siberian Lady Macbeth*, 1961; *Ashes*, 1964–5.

WALTERS, CHARLES (U.S.A.): *Easter Parade*, 1948: *The Tender Trap*, 1955; *Billy Rose's Jumbo*, 1962.

WATT, HARRY (U.K.): *Night Mail* (with BASIL WRIGHT) (s), 1935; *The Overlanders*, 1946.

WEISS, JIRI (Czech.): *Romeo, Juliet and Darkness*, 1960.

WELLES, ORSON (U.S.A.): *Citizen Kane*, 1940; *The Magnificent Ambersons*, 1942;

General Index

THIS index gives page (or plate) references to the main subjects discussed and the names of films, directors, writers, etc., mentioned in the text. It does not contain the additional films and directors included in the Index of Directors and Films.

259

*Some other books published by Penguins
are described in the following
pages.*

THE CONTEMPORARY CINEMA

Penelope Houston

Of the total history of the cinema one quarter belongs to the years since the war. *The Contemporary Cinema* thus ranges from neo-realism to the new wave, from *On the Town* to five years of *South Pacific*, from the Gainsborough Lady to *This Sporting Life;* and the directors include not only Antonioni, Truffaut, and Anderson, but also Renoir, Buñuel, and de Sica; not only Ford, Hitchcock, and Hawks, but also Kubrick, Ray, and Cassavetes.

In a sustained, imaginative survey of the whole post-war scene, Penelope Houston, the Editor of *Sight and Sound*, shows how the cinema has adjusted itself to meet a new audience which approaches films more critically than before, but in doing so encourages new talent. At the same time she makes clear the industrial problems (in particular, the fight to co-exist with TV) which are inseparable from the business of film-making. The book is illustrated with over 30 plates, and a check-list of films provides a guide to more than one hundred directors.

'It does extremely well what it is meant to do, provide a quick glimpse of what has happened globally to film since the last, or Second, World War . . . I cannot think of a better short survey of world cinema at present' – Andrew Sinclair in the *Spectator*

'An extremely readable and much-needed assessment of films and their makers since the war' – Eric Shorter in the *Daily Telegraph*

DISCRIMINATION AND POPULAR CULTURE

Edited by Denys Thompson

This new Pelican is a guide to the saccharine world – the world of newspapers, films, radio, television, pulp magazines, commercial design, and 'pop' songs, with their attendant advertising. The editor and his contributors make a youthful, critical, and at the same time constructive approach to the whole array of modern mass-produced media. Must a dead-safe competence be the necessary result, they ask, of the search for big audiences? And is a squalid mediocrity the highest common factor of popular culture, the best we can expect?

Contending that the public is being denied the quality of service to which it has a right they point to the possibilities for enjoyment and enlightenment which are inherent in the mass media. While the most promising overall remedy for this situation is obviously education, each of the contributors proposes reasonable improvements in the field he is discussing.

This is no dry, sociological investigation. The problems are clearly outlined, the evidence is up to date, and the solutions practical. Moreover the authors suggest ways in which the consumer can turn the mass media to good account and not merely accept their offerings passively as drugs.